JavaScript for .NET Developers

Unlock the potential of evergreen browsers and increase the efficiency of your ASP.NET applications by learning how to write JavaScript

Ovais Mehboob Ahmed Khan

BIRMINGHAM - MUMBAI

JavaScript for .NET Developers

First published: July 2016

Production reference: 1260716

Published by Packt Publishing Ltd.
Livery Place
35 Livery Street
Birmingham B3 2PB, UK.

ISBN 978-1-78588-646-1

www.packtpub.com

Credits

Author

Ovais Mehboob Ahmed Khan

Reviewer

Nicholas Suter

Commissioning Editor

Edward Gordon

Acquisition Editor

Nitin Dasan

Content Development Editor

Deepti Thore

Technical Editors

Pranil Pathare

Deepti Tuscano

Copy Editor

Vibha Shukla

Project Coordinator

Shweta H Birwatkar

Proofreader

Safis Editing

Indexer

Mariammal Chettiyar

Graphics

Disha Haria

Production Coordinator

Nilesh Mohite

Cover Work

Nilesh Mohite

About the Author

Ovais Mehboob Ahmed Khan is a seasoned programmer and solution architect with more than 13 years of software development experience. He has worked in different organizations across Pakistan, the USA, and the Middle East. Currently, he is working for a government entity based in Dubai, and also provides consultancy services to a Microsoft gold partner firm based in New Jersey.

He is a Microsoft MVP in Visual Studio and Development Technologies and specializes mainly in Microsoft .NET and web development. He has authored numerous technical articles on different websites such as MSDN, TechNet, DZone, and personal blog at `http://ovaismehboob.wordpress.com`.

He is an active speaker and group leader of Microsoft Developers UAE Meetup, Microsoft Technology Practices, and Developers and Enterprise Practices user groups, and has presented various technical sessions in different events and conferences.

In short, Ovais is a passionate developer who is always interested in learning new technologies. He can be reached at `ovaismehboob@hotmail.com` and on Twitter, `@ovaismehboob`.

I would like to thank my family for supporting. Especially my mother, wife, and brother, who have always encouraged me in every goal of my life. My father, may he rest in peace, would have been proud of my achievements.

About the Reviewer

Nicholas Suter is a .NET software craftsman, focused on patterns, practices, and quality development in a Microsoft environment. He has been nominated for Microsoft .NET MVP since 2014.

He works for Cellenza, a French agile consulting company based in Paris, where he leads, trains, and audits teams more on technical matters than team practices.

He wrote a book in 2013 on web development called *Visual Studio 2013, Concevoir et développer des projets Web, les gérer avec TFS 2013*, (French) for *ENI Editions*, and reviewed *Entity Framework Tutorial, Second Edition*, for *Packt Publishing* in 2015.

www.PacktPub.com

eBooks, discount offers, and more

Did you know that Packt offers eBook versions of every book published, with PDF and ePub files available? You can upgrade to the eBook version at www.PacktPub.com and as a print book customer, you are entitled to a discount on the eBook copy. Get in touch with us at customercare@packtpub.com for more details.

At www.PacktPub.com, you can also read a collection of free technical articles, sign up for a range of free newsletters and receive exclusive discounts and offers on Packt books and eBooks.

https://www2.packtpub.com/books/subscription/packtlib

Do you need instant solutions to your IT questions? PacktLib is Packt's online digital book library. Here, you can search, access, and read Packt's entire library of books.

Why subscribe?

- Fully searchable across every book published by Packt
- Copy and paste, print, and bookmark content
- On demand and accessible via a web browser

Table of Contents

Preface

This is a book about the JavaScript programming language, and is targeted at .NET developers who want to develop responsive web applications using popular client-side JavaScript-based frameworks and create a rich user experience. It is also intended for programmers who have a basic knowledge of the JavaScript programming language and wanted to learn some core and advanced concepts followed by some industry-wide best practices and patterns to structure and design web applications.

This book starts with the basics of JavaScript and helps the reader to gain knowledge about the core concepts and then proceeds towards some advanced topics. There is a chapter that primarily focuses on the jQuery library, which is widely used throughout web application development, followed by a chapter on Ajax techniques that help developers to understand how asynchronous requests can be made. This is followed by the options to make requests either through the plain vanilla JavaScript XHR object or through the jQuery library. There is also a chapter that develops a complete application using Angular 2 and ASP.NET Core, and introduces TypeScript, a superset of JavaScript that supports the latest and evolving features of ECMAScript 2015. We will also explore the Windows JavaScript (WinJS) library to develop Windows applications using JavaScript and HTML and use this library to bring Windows behavior, look, and feel to ASP.NET web applications. There is a complete chapter on Node.js that helps developers to learn how powerful the JavaScript language is on the server side, followed by a chapter on using JavaScript in a large-scale project. Finally, this book will end with a chapter about testing and debugging and discuss what testing suites and debugging techniques are there to troubleshoot and make an application robust.

This book has some very dense topics that require full concentration, hence is ideal for someone having some prior knowledge. All the chapters are related to JavaScript and work around JavaScript frameworks and libraries to build rich web applications. With this book, the reader will get the end-to-end knowledge about the JavaScript language and its frameworks and libraries built on top of it, followed by the techniques to test and troubleshoot the JavaScript code.

What this book covers

Chapter 1, JavaScript for Modern Web Applications, focuses on the basic concepts of JavaScript that involve declaration of variables, datatypes, implementing arrays, expressions, operators, and functions. We will write simple programs in JavaScript using Visual Studio 2015, and see what this IDE offers for writing JavaScript programs. We will also study how JavaScript code can be written and compare the .NET runtime with the JavaScript runtime to clarify the execution cycle of code-compilation process.

Chapter 2, Advanced JavaScript Concepts, covers the advanced concepts of JavaScript and gives developers an insight into the JavaScript language. It will show the extent to which the JavaScript language can be used as far as features are concerned. We will discuss variables hoisting and their scope, property descriptors, object-oriented programming, closures, typed arrays, and exception handling.

Chapter 3, Using jQuery in ASP.NET, discusses jQuery and how to use it in web applications developed in ASP.NET Core. We will discuss the options jQuery provides and the advantages it has when comparing it with the plain vanilla JavaScript for manipulating DOM elements, attaching events, and performing complex operations.

Chapter 4, Ajax Techniques, discusses the techniques of making asynchronous requests known as Ajax requests. We will explore the core concepts of using the XMLHttpRequest (XHR) object and study the basic architecture of how Ajax request is processed and the events and methods it provides. On the other hand, we will also explore what the jQuery library provides in comparison with the plain XHR object.

Chapter 5, Developing an ASP.NET Application Using Angular 2 and Web API, teaches the basic concepts of TypeScript and uses it with Angular 2. We will develop a simple application in ASP.NET Core using Angular 2 as a frontend client-side framework, Web API for backend services, and Entity Framework Core for database persistence. At the time of writing, Angular 2 was in a beta version, and we have used the beta version in this chapter. With the future releases of Angular 2, there are chances of having some changes in the framework, but the basic concepts will almost be the same. For future updates, you can refer to http://angular.io/.

Chapter 6, Exploring the WinJS Library, explores the Microsoft developed WinJS library, which is a JavaScript library to not only develop Windows applications using JavaScript and HTML, but also use it with ASP.NET and other web frameworks. We will discuss the core concepts of defining classes, namespaces, deriving classes, mixins, and promises. We will also look into the data-binding techniques and how to use Windows controls or specific attributes in HTML elements to change the behaviour, look, and feel of the control. Moreover, we will end up using the WinRT API to access a device's camera in our web application and discuss the concepts of a Hosted app through which any web application can be transformed into a Windows application using a Universal Window template in Visual Studio 2015.

Chapter 7, JavaScript Design Patterns, shows that design patterns provide efficient solutions to software design. We will discuss some of the industry-wide best design patterns spread into creational, structural, and behavioral categories. Each category will be covering four types of design patterns that can be used and implemented using JavaScript to solve a particular design problem.

Chapter 8, Node.js for ASP.NET Developers, focuses on the basics of Node.js and how to use it to develop server-side applications using JavaScript. In this chapter, we will discuss view engines such as EJS and Jade and the use of controllers and services to implement the MVC pattern. Moreover, we will end this chapter by performing some examples of accessing a Microsoft SQL Server database to perform, create, and retrieve operations on a database.

Chapter 9, Using JavaScript for Large-Scale Projects, provides best practices of using JavaScript for large-scale applications. We will discuss how to structure our JavaScript-based projects by splitting them into modules to increase the scalability and maintainability. We will see how effectively we can use the Mediator pattern to provide communication between modules and the documentation frameworks that increase the maintainability of your JavaScript code. Finally, we will discuss how the application can be optimized by compressing and merging JavaScript files into a minified version and increase performance.

Chapter 10, Testing and Debugging JavaScript, focuses on the testing and debugging JavaScript applications. We will discuss one of the most popular testing suites of JavaScript code known as Jasmine, and use it with Karma to run the test cases. For debugging, we will discuss some tips and techniques to debug JavaScript with Visual Studio and what Microsoft Edge offers to make debugging easy. In the end, we will study the basic concepts of how Microsoft Edge enables debugging for TypeScript files and the configuration needed to achieve it.

What you need for this book

Throughout the book, we will be using Visual Studio 2015 to practice examples. For the server-side technology, we have used ASP.NET Core for web application development, and used JavaScript on top of it. In *Chapter 8, Node.js for ASP.NET Developers*, we used Node.js to show how JavaScript can be used on the server side. For Node.js, we will require some extensions for Visual Studio 2015 to be installed, and the details are specified in the chapter.

Who this book is for

This book is targeted at .NET developers who have solid programming experience in ASP.NET Core. Throughout this book, we have used ASP.NET Core for web development and assumed that developers have thorough knowledge or working experience in .NET Core and ASP.NET Core.

Conventions

In this book, you will find a number of text styles that distinguish between different kinds of information. Here are some examples of these styles and an explanation of their meaning.

Code words in text, database table names, folder names, filenames, file extensions, pathnames, dummy URLs, user input, and Twitter handles are shown as follows: "JavaScript can be placed in the <head> or <body> sections of your HTML page."

A block of code is set as follows:

```
<html>
  <head>
    <script>
      alert("This is a simple text");
    </script>
  </head>
</html>
```

Any command-line input or output is written as follows:

```
dotnet ef database update -verbose
```

New terms and **important words** are shown in bold. Words that you see on the screen, for example, in menus or dialog boxes, appear in the text like this: "When the page loads, it will show the pop-up message and a text as **This is a simple text**."

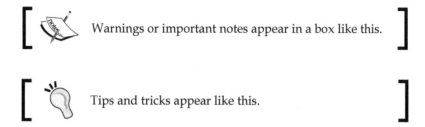

Warnings or important notes appear in a box like this.

Tips and tricks appear like this.

Reader feedback

Feedback from our readers is always welcome. Let us know what you think about this book—what you liked or disliked. Reader feedback is important for us as it helps us develop titles that you will really get the most out of.

To send us general feedback, simply e-mail feedback@packtpub.com, and mention the book's title in the subject of your message.

If there is a topic that you have expertise in and you are interested in either writing or contributing to a book, see our author guide at www.packtpub.com/authors.

Customer support

Now that you are the proud owner of a Packt book, we have a number of things to help you to get the most from your purchase.

Downloading the example code

You can download the example code files for this book from your account at http://www.packtpub.com. If you purchased this book elsewhere, you can visit http://www.packtpub.com/support and register to have the files e-mailed directly to you.

You can download the code files by following these steps:

1. Log in or register to our website using your e-mail address and password.
2. Hover the mouse pointer on the **SUPPORT** tab at the top.
3. Click on **Code Downloads & Errata**.
4. Enter the name of the book in the **Search** box.
5. Select the book for which you're looking to download the code files.
6. Choose from the drop-down menu where you purchased this book from.
7. Click on **Code Download**.

You can also download the code files by clicking on the **Code Files** button on the book's webpage at the Packt Publishing website. This page can be accessed by entering the book's name in the **Search** box. Please note that you need to be logged in to your Packt account.

Once the file is downloaded, please make sure that you unzip or extract the folder using the latest version of:

- WinRAR / 7-Zip for Windows
- Zipeg / iZip / UnRarX for Mac
- 7-Zip / PeaZip for Linux

The code bundle for the book is also hosted on GitHub at `https://github.com/ PacktPublishing/JavaScript-For-.NET-Developers`. We also have other code bundles from our rich catalog of books and videos available at `https://github. com/PacktPublishing/`. Check them out!

Downloading the color images of this book

We also provide you with a PDF file that has color images of the screenshots/ diagrams used in this book. The color images will help you better understand the changes in the output. You can download this file from `https://www.packtpub. com/sites/default/files/downloads/JavaScriptForNETDevelopers_ ColorImages.pdf`.

Errata

Although we have taken every care to ensure the accuracy of our content, mistakes do happen. If you find a mistake in one of our books—maybe a mistake in the text or the code—we would be grateful if you could report this to us. By doing so, you can save other readers from frustration and help us improve subsequent versions of this book. If you find any errata, please report them by visiting `http://www.packtpub.com/submit-errata`, selecting your book, clicking on the **Errata Submission Form** link, and entering the details of your errata. Once your errata are verified, your submission will be accepted and the errata will be uploaded to our website or added to any list of existing errata under the Errata section of that title.

To view the previously submitted errata, go to `https://www.packtpub.com/books/content/support` and enter the name of the book in the search field. The required information will appear under the **Errata** section.

Piracy

Piracy of copyrighted material on the Internet is an ongoing problem across all media. At Packt, we take the protection of our copyright and licenses very seriously. If you come across any illegal copies of our works in any form on the Internet, please provide us with the location address or website name immediately so that we can pursue a remedy.

Please contact us at `copyright@packtpub.com` with a link to the suspected pirated material.

We appreciate your help in protecting our authors and our ability to bring you valuable content.

Questions

If you have a problem with any aspect of this book, you can contact us at `questions@packtpub.com`, and we will do our best to address the problem.

1
JavaScript for Modern Web Applications

The growth in web development evolved with a rapid pace in recent years. Most of the business applications that developed on a desktop platform are now shifted to the web platform, and the reason is the ease of access and continuous addition of rich capabilities on the web platform. Typically, any web application that provides the characteristics of the desktop applications is considered as rich web application. Thus, it involves extensive use of JavaScript and its frameworks and libraries.

JavaScript plays an important role in developing rich applications and allows developers to do less server-side post-backs and call server-side functions through ajaxified requests. Not only this, but now many companies and communities are developing good frameworks such as Angular, Knockout, ReactJS, and so on to bring state-of-the-art and groundbreaking capabilities. Microsoft has also released the **WinJS** library to access mobile native device features such as camera, storage, and so on from a web application running on mobile browsers. **myNFC** is also a great JavaScript library that allows developers to create applications for smartphones.

Importance of JavaScript

All the client-side frameworks are based on JavaScript. Being an ASP.NET developer, we should have solid concepts of JavaScript before using or integrating them in our applications. JavaScript is the client-side scripting language and one of the most popular programming languages of all times that run on top of a browser. When working on a web development project, this language serves you in many better ways to make **user interface** (**UI**) responsive. With JavaScript, you can manipulate HTML page **Document Object Model** (**DOM**) elements, call server-side code through ajaxified requests and bring new rich experience to your customers. There are many innovations being done at the core JavaScript library, and different frameworks and various libraries have been developed.

What is JavaScript?

JavaScript is a programming language created in 1995 by Brenden Eich. Initially, it was only supported by Netscape Browser, but later they decided to release a standard known as ECMA specification to let other browsers implement and provide engines to execute JavaScript on their browsers. The reason for providing the standard is to have the complete specification details for the party to follow and provide consistent behavior.

Earlier it was only targeted to execute on browsers and perform client-side operations that work with HTML pages and provide features such as manipulating DOM elements and defining event handlers and other functionalities. Later, and in recent years, it has become a powerful language and not only bounded to the client-side operations. With Node.js, we can use JavaScript on server side and there are various modules and plugins provided by Node to perform I/O operations, server-side events, and more.

Comparing runtimes

As this book is targeted for .NET developers, let's compare the JavaScript runtime with .NET runtime. There are a few things in common, but the basic runtime is different.

In .NET, **Common Language Runtime** (**CLR**) does the **just-in-time** (**JIT**) compilation on the code that is running and provides memory management. JIT compilation is done on the **Intermediate Language** (**IL**) code that is generated once you build your project.

In the JavaScript world, browser engine is the runtime for the JavaScript language. Every browser interprets JavaScript in its own way, but follows the ECMA scripting standards. Different browsers have different implementations, for example, Microsoft Edge uses Chakra engine, Chrome uses V8, and Firefox has Monkey engines. Initially, JavaScript was implemented as an interpreted language, but few modern browsers now perform JIT compilation. Every engine provides a set of services such as memory management, compilation, and processing.

The following diagram shows the comparison between both the architectures:

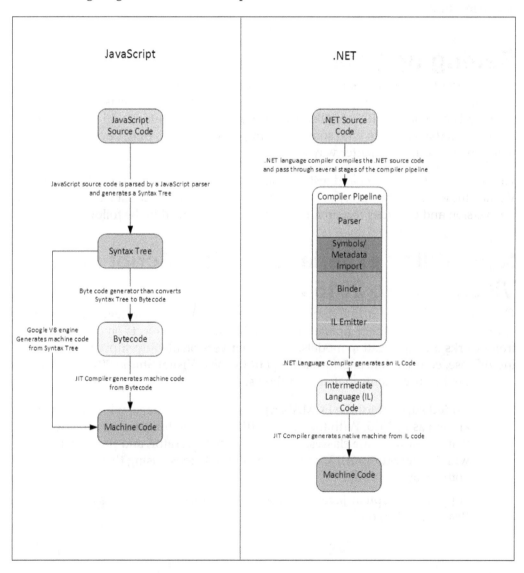

The JavaScript parser parses and tokenizes the JavaScript code into a syntax tree. All the browsers, except Google V8, parse the syntax tree and generate a bytecode that finally converts into a machine code through JIT compilation. On the other hand, Google V8 engine parses the syntax tree and instead of generating a bytecode first, it directly generates the machine code.

The .NET source code is compiled by its own language compiler, such as C# or VB.NET compiler and passes through the several stages of the compiler pipeline to generate an IL code. This IL code is then read by the JIT compiler that generates the native machine code.

Setting up your environment

Before going through this book, let's set up your environment. There are many renowned editors available in the market to create JavaScript projects such as Sublime Text, Komodo IDE, NetBeans, Eclipse, and more, but we will use Visual Studio 2015 that came up with some good improvements, helping developers to work on JavaScript in a better way than before.

To proceed, let's download and install Visual Studio 2015. You can download the Visual Studio 2015 community edition from `https://www.visualstudio.com/`, it's a free version and provides certain improvements as described in the following section.

New editing experience of JavaScript in Visual Studio 2015 IDE

The new Visual Studio 2015 IDE provides many rich features for developing web applications and various templates are available to create projects on different frameworks and application models. The earlier version already supported IntelliSense, colorization, and formatting but the new Visual Studio 2015 IDE has some more improvements that are as follows:

- Added support for the ECMAScript 6 scripting language, which is formally known as ES2015. With the new ES2015, many features have been added, you can now define classes, lambdas, spread operator, and proxy objects. So, with Visual Studio 2015, you can get all IntelliSense using these features in your JavaScript code.

- Support for popular JavaScript client-side frameworks such as Angular, ReactJS, and so on.

- Documentation comments that help you add comments to your JavaScript methods and show the description when you use them:

```
<head>
    <script type="text/javascript">
        /**
        * This method returns the list of products based on filter criteria
        * @param {string}[name] name of the product
        * @param {string}[desc] description of the product
        * @param {number}[price] price of the product
        * @return {Array} The filtered products
        */
        function FilterProduct(name, desc, price)...

        FilterProduct("Product1", )
            Array FilterProduct([String name], [String desc], [Number price])
    </scr This method returns the list of products based on filter criteria
</head>     desc: description of the product
```

- IntelliSense for new JavaScript APIs such as touch event and Web Audio API.

- You can use tokens such as //TODO, //HACK, and //UNDONE, and it gives you a listing in the **Task List** window that helps to trace the to-do items:

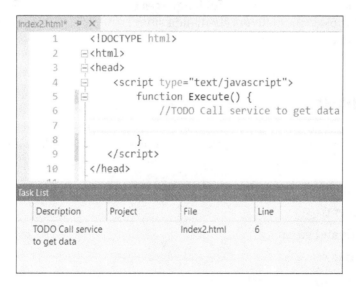

- With JavaScript files, Visual Studio 2015 provides the same navigation bar we used to see when writing classes in any .NET language. Selecting and navigating to different methods of JavaScript is far easier with this feature:

```
<global>                                              ▼  ◎ SaveProduct(name, desc, price)     ▼
    1  ⊟      /**                                        ◎ FilterProduct(name, desc, price)
    2          * This method returns the list of products based o ◎ SaveProduct(name, desc, price)
    3          * @param {string}[name] name of the product
    4          * @param {string}[desc] description of the product
    5          * @param {number}[price] price of the product
    6          * @return {Array} The filtered products
    7          */
    8  ⊟      function FilterProduct(name, desc, price) {
    9              //TODO Call service to Save product
   10          }
   11
   12  ⊟      function SaveProduct(name, desc, price) {
   13              //TODO call service to save product
   14          }
```

Programming in JavaScript

JavaScript is one of the most powerful languages that plays a vital role in any web development project and delivers client-side support and rich functionality. In this section, we will discuss the core concepts of writing programs in JavaScript and use them in web applications.

Core fundamentals of JavaScript

Like any other programming language, JavaScript also has statements, expressions, operators, and specific syntax to write and run programs. We will go through the following topics in this section:

- Adding JavaScript to an HTML page
- Statements
- Literals and variables
- Data types
- Expressions and operators

Adding JavaScript to an HTML page

Every modern browser has a JavaScript engine that compiles your JavaScript defined on the page. JavaScript can be placed in the `<head>` or `<body>` sections of your HTML page. Any statement that is defined under `<script></script>` tags will be considered a JavaScript statement and will be processed and understood by the browser's engine.

The following code snippet shows a simple HTML page containing the `<script></script>` tags defined within the `<head></head>` section:

```
<html>
  <head>
    <script>
      alert("This is a simple text");
    </script>
  </head>
</html>
```

When the page loads, it will show the pop-up message and a text as **This is a simple text**. The browser's JavaScript engine executes any script that is defined under the `<script>` tag and runs the statements defined within this block. Any statement that is defined directly under the scripting tag is executed every time the page is loaded.

Similarly, we can also define the JavaScript within the `<body>` section of the HTML page:

```
<html>
  <body>
    <script>
      alert("hello world");
    </script>
  </body>
</html>
```

 It is a good idea to place scripts at the bottom of the page because the compilation can slow down the page loading.

Normally, in every project, irrespective of the project size, separating the `<script>` section from HTML makes the code look cleaner and easy to maintain. JavaScript file extensions are named .js and you can also create these files separately in some scripts folder and reference them in our HTML page.

In Visual Studio, you can easily create a JavaScript file using the **Add | JavaScript File** option as shown in the following:

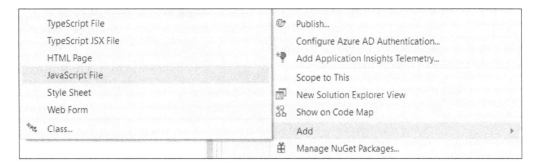

Once the file is created, we can directly write the JavaScript syntax without any `<script></script>` tags. JavaScript files can be referenced in your HTML page using the `src` attribute of `<script></script>` tags. Here we referenced `test.js` in the HTML page:

```
<script src="~/test.js">
</script>
```

Placing the `<script>` tag either in the `<head>` or in the `<body>` section depends on the page. If your page referencing some large JavaScript files takes a long time to load, it is better to define them at the end of the `<body>` section. This is a better approach, so when the browser starts parsing your page, it is not stuck downloading your scripts and delaying the rendering. On the other hand, we can define JavaScript files in the `<head>` section only if they do not impact the performance or page life cycle. Scripts defined at the bottom get parsed when the whole page loads. There are also a few attributes such as `async` and `defer` that we can use within the `<script>` tag and most of the browsers support this.

The following is an example showing the use of `async` in the `<script>` tag:

```
<script src="~/test1.js" async></script>
<script src="~/test2.js" async></script>
```

Scripts defined with `async` are executed asynchronously without blocking the browser to load the page. However, if multiple scripts are there, then each script will be executed asynchronously and at the same time. This may lead to the possibility of completing the second script before the first one gets completed and might throw some errors if one is dependent on the other. For example, when working with some client-side frameworks, such as Angular framework, JavaScript code that is using Angular components is dependent on AngularJS library, and in this case, if our custom JS files are loaded before the AngularJS library on which they are dependent, they will throw an exception.

To overcome this scenario, we can use `defer` to execute scripts in a sequence. We can use `defer` as follows:

```
<script src="~/test1.js" defer></script>
<script src="~/test2.js" defer></script>
```

The basic difference between `async` and `defer` is that `async` downloads the file during HTML parsing and pauses the HTML parser to execute it until it is completely downloaded, whereas `defer` downloads the file during the HTML parsing and executes it after the HTML parser is completed.

Statements in JavaScript

Statements are the collection of words, expressions, and operators to perform a specific task. Like other programming languages, statements in JavaScript could also be assigning a value to the variable, performing arithmetic operations, implementing conditional logic, iterating through collection, and so on.

For example:

```
var a; //variable declaration
a = 5; //value assignment
a = 5 * b; //value assignment
a++; // equivalent to a= a+1
a--; // equivalent to a= a-1
var method = function () { … } // declare function
alert("Hello World") // calling built-in function
if(…) {…} else {…}
for (…) {…}
while(…) {…}
```

However, you can use semicolons with the `do while` loop:

```
do {…} while (…);
function statement
function (arg) { //to do }
```

 If multiple statements are defined in the same line, they should be separated by a semicolon, otherwise they will be treated as a single statement. On different lines, a semicolon is not mandatory but a good practice to use.

Literals and variables

There are two types of values in JavaScript: literals or fixed values and variables.

Literals could be number, string, or date objects.

For example:

```
Numbers
22.30
26
Strings
"John"
"10/Jan/2015"
```

Variables are used to store values. In JavaScript, we can define variables using the `var` keyword. JavaScript is not a type-safe language and the type is identified when the value is assigned.

For example:

```
var x=6;
var x="Sample value";
```

Data types

Every programming language has certain data types available to hold specific data. For example, in C#, we can use `String` to hold string values, `int` to hold 32-bit integer value, `DateTime` to hold value in the date and time format, and so on. JavaScript does not provide strong data types such as C# and other programming languages, and it's a loosely typed language. As per the latest ECMA 6 standard, JavaScript provides six primitive data types and an object. All primitive data types are immutable, this means that assigning a new value will be allocated into a separate memory. Object is mutable and its values can be changed.

The primitive types are as follows:

- **Boolean**: This holds the logical value `true` or `false`.
- **Null**: This holds the `null` value.
- **Undefined**: This is a variable that does not assign a value and has value as undefined.
- **Number**: This holds numeric values. The size of the `number` type is double-precision 64 bit in which the number (fraction) is stored from 0 to 51 bits, the exponent in 11 bits from 52 to 62, and sign in 1 bit 63.
- **String**: This holds any kind of textual value.

Complex types are termed as **object**. In JavaScript, the object is formulated in a JSON format.

Array in JavaScript

Array is used to store collections of data. You can simply define an array in JavaScript as shown in the following:

```
var browsers = ["Microsoft Edge", "Google Chrome", "Mozilla
    Firefox", "Safari"];
```

You can access them through the array index. The index starts from 0 till the number of items in the array.

We can access the array items as follows:

```
var a= browsers[0]; //returns Microsoft Edge
var b= browsers[1]; //returns Google Chrome
var c= browsers[3]; //returns Safari
```

In order to get the total number of items in an array, you can use the `length` property:

```
var totalItems = browsers.length;
```

The following is a list of some of the most commonly used methods:

Method	Description
indexOf()	This returns the first index of an element available within the array equal to the specific value, returns -1 if not found.
lastIndexOf()	This returns the last index of an element available within an array equal to the specified value, returns -1 if not found.
pop()	This deletes the last element from an array and returns that element.
push()	This adds one element to an array and returns the length of an array.
reverse()	This reverses the order of elements in an array. The first element becomes the last and last one becomes the first.
shift()	This deletes the first element and returns that element.
splice()	This is used to add or remove elements from an array.
toString()	This returns all the elements in a string representation.
unshift()	This adds elements to the front of an array and returns the new length.

What is JSON?

JavaScript Object Notation (JSON) is a lightweight, interchangeable format for defining objects in JavaScript. Any kind of object can be defined through JSON and it is used to build universal data structures. Whether it's a simple object, arrays, nested arrays, or complex object, each can handle in the JSON format.

Simple objects in JSON

The following code snippet shows the `person` object that has three properties, namely `name`, `email`, and `phone`:

```
var person = {
   "name" : "John Martin",
   "email": johnmartin@email.com,
   "phone": "201892882"
}
```

We can access these object properties as follows:

```
person.name;
person.email;
person.phone;
```

Declaring arrays in JSON

The following code snippet shows the way of declaring arrays in JSON:

```
var persons =
[{
   "name":"John",
   "email": "john@email.com",
   "phone":"201832882"
},
{
   "name":"Steve",
```

```
    "email": "steve@email.com",
    "phone":"201832882"
},
{
"name":"Smith",
"email": "smith@email.com",
"phone":"201832882"
}]
```

According to the preceding declaration of an array, it can be accessed as follows:

```
//returns name of the first item in the collection i.e. John
Persons[0].name
//returns email of the first item in the collection i.e.
    john@email.com
Persons[0].email
//returns name of the second item in the collection i.e. Steve
Persons[1].name
```

Nesting data in JSON

The JSON format easily handles nested arrays. Let's look at the complex objects containing an employee object that contains the Experiences array with the nested array to hold projects, and each project has a nested array to hold technologies used in each project:

```
var employee=
{
  "ID":"00333",
  "Name":"Scott",
  "DateOfJoining":"01/Jan/2010",
  "Experiences":[
    {
      "companyName":"ABC",
      "from":"Nov 2008",
      "to":"Oct 2009",
      "projects" :[
        {
        "title":"Sharepoint Migration",
        "noOfTeamMembers":5,
        "technologyUsed":[{"name":"SharePoint Server"},
          {"name":"C#"}, {"name":"SQL Server"}]
        },
        {
        "title":"Messaging Gateway",
        "noOfTeamMembers":5,
```

```
            "technologyUsed":[{"name":"ASP.NET"}, {"name":"C#"},
                {"name":"SQL Server"}]
            }
        ]
    },
    {
        "companyName":"XYZ",
        "from":"Nov 2009",
        "to":"Oct 2015",
        "projects" :[
            {
            "title":"ERP System",
            "noOfTeamMembers":5,
            "technologyUsed":[{"name":"ASP.NET"}, {"name":"C#"},
                {"name":"SQL Server"}]
            },
            {
            "title":"Healthcare System",
            "noOfTeamMembers":4,
            "technologyUsed":[{"name":"ASP.NET"}, {"name":"C#"},
                {"name":"SQL Server"}]
            }
        ]
    }
    ]
}
```

In the preceding script, the array has an employee object containing some properties such as ID, name, and date of joining, and then one experiences property that holds an array of experiences and each experience holds the projects that the employee did in a particular workplace.

Conversions in data types

As the data types in JavaScript are dynamic in nature and data type is determined based on the value assignment, JavaScript does not throw any exception on type conversion and deals in several ways as follows.

For example, the following is the JavaScript code snippet showing the assignment of different expressions.

First assign the string to the res variable:

```
var res="Hello World";
```

Then assign numeric to the same `res` variable:

```
res= 2;
```

Finally, concatenate string 3 to the `res` variable that holds the following numeric, but due to the higher precedence of numerical value, the resultant value becomes 5:

```
var result = res + "3"
```

So, no matter what was the type of the variable first assigned to it, it will change its type based on the assignment and dynamically handle the conversions.

Elements of JavaScript

Here are some of the important elements of JavaScript that are essential to learn before we start programming in JavaScript.

Constants in JavaScript

Constants in JavaScript can be defined with a `const` keyword. Constants are the immutable values that are known at compile time, and values do not change throughout the life cycle of the program.

The following is the JavaScript code showing the assignment of a constant variable. When using `const`, `var` is not required and you can declare constant values with only the `const` keyword:

```
const pi= 3.42
```

Comments

Comments can be added with `//` and `/* */`. To comment a single line, you can use `//`, otherwise `/* */` for a block of code.

The following is the JavaScript code showing the way of commenting a single line or block of code:

```
<script type="text/javascript">

function showInformation() {

  //var spObj = window.document.getElementById("spInfo");
  spObj.innerHTML =
    "Available Height: " + screen.availHeight + "<br>" +
    /*"Available Width: " + screen.availWidth + "<br>" +
    "Height: " + screen.height + "<br>" +*/
```

```
        "Width: " + screen.width + "<br>"
}

</script>
```

Case sensitivity

JavaScript is a case-sensitive language and it follows the Pascal naming convention to define variables and methods.

For example, if the method name is doWork(), it can only be accessed by calling it with the exact case, and calling either DoWork() or Dowork() will not work and throw exception.

Character set

JavaScript is based on a Unicode character set and follows the Unicode Standard.

What is the Unicode Standard?

It is a worldwide coding standard that most languages use. C# and VB.NET follow the same Unicode Standard. It provides a unique number for every character, for example, A = 41, a = 61, and so on.

The current version of the Unicode Standard is Unicode 8.0.0 and the documentation can be located at http://www.unicode.org/versions/Unicode8.0.0/.

Expressions

Expression can be recognized as the statement of code that assigns some value to the variable. Expressions are categorized into two types.

The first type of expression can be termed as simple expressions that assigns a value to the variable:

```
var x = 2;
```

The preceding example denotes the simple expression of assigning numeric value 2 to an x variable.

The second type of expression can be termed as any arithmetic or string operation to the values on the right and assigning them to any variable. These type of expressions perform the operation first before assigning value to the variable:

```
var x = 2+3
var x = "Hello" + "World";
```

This is an example of the second type of expression that adds two numbers and assigns the resultant value to the x variable. Same goes for the second statement that performs the string concatenation operation and assigns the `Hello World` value to the x variable.

The this keyword

Just like C# and other object-oriented languages, JavaScript has objects and there are certain ways to define classes, functions, and so on that we will study later in this chapter. Just like C#, in JavaScript, we can access the object and its properties through the `this` keyword. Let's take a look at some examples showing the scope of the `this` keyword in JavaScript.

The following is a `customer` object that contains a few properties and the utilization of the `this` keyword:

```
var customer =
  {
    name: "John Marting",
    email: "john@xyz.com",
    mobile: "109293988844",
    show: function () {
      alert("Name: "+this.name + " Email: " + this.email + "
        Mobile: " + this.mobile);
    }
  }
```

In the preceding example, we have defined a JavaScript object that contains three properties and a function. To access these properties, we can use the `this` keyword just like C#. However, we can also access the properties using the `customer` variable, as shown in the following:

```
var customer =
  {
    name: "John Marting",
    email: "john@xyz.com",
    mobile: "109293988844",
    show: function () {
```

```
        alert("Name: "+ customer.name + " Email: " + customer.email
          + " Mobile: " + customer.mobile);
      }
    }
```

The scope of the `this` keyword is limited within the boundary of an object. Whereas, the `customer` variable in the preceding example could be defined somewhere else on the page and may lead to an incorrect behavior. It is a better approach to use the `this` keyword wherever possible and avoid using object variables directly.

All variables and functions defined directly under the `<script>` tag are termed as global variables and functions. We can also access them through the `this` keyword. In this case, `this` will be referred as the global window object and not the child, that is, the `customer` object we have used in the previous example:

```
<script type="text/javascript">
  var name = "";

  function ShowMessage() {
    alert(this.name);
  }
</script>
```

Unlike `this`, you can also refer the variables and functions through the `window` keyword. The following code snippet will show the name of the window in the dialog box:

```
alert(window.name);
```

Let's take a look at the complete example, where we have global variables defined, as well as child objects, and the scope of `this` will be determined based on the context of its call:

```
<script type="text/javascript">
  var name = "Scott Watson";

  var customer =
    {
      name: "John Marting",
      email: "john@xyz.com",
      mobile: "109293988844",
      show: function () {
        alert("Name: " + this.name + " Email: " + this.email + "
          Mobile: " + this.mobile);
      }
    }
```

```
function ShowMessage() {
  alert("Global name is " + this.name);
  alert("Customer info is " + customer.show());
}
</script>
```

In this preceding example, we will get two JavaScript alert messages. The first alert will display **Scott Watson**, which is defined globally, and the second popup shows the customer name, e-mail address, and mobile number. Hence, we can use this in two places, but the scope is determined based on the context from where it is calling from.

Sequence of code execution in JavaScript

When programming in JavaScript, we have to keep the sequence of defining things before they get called. Considering the preceding example, if we define the customer object after the ShowMessage() method, it will not be recognized and nothing will be displayed.

Using the this keyword on a calling method

Let's take a look at the sample HTML page that has a JavaScript function named Multiply and takes two parameters: obj and val. This method will be called when the user enters any input into the textbox and it will pass the reference of the textbox control at the first parameter. This can be passed through the this keyword:

```
<html>
<head>
  <script type="text/javascript">
    function Multiply(obj, val) {
      alert(obj.value * val);
    }
  </script>
</head>
<body>
  <input type="text" onchange ="Multiply(this, 2);" />
</body>
</html>
```

The function statement and expression

The function statements are a way of defining methods in JavaScript. Each function has a signature, containing the name and parameters passed in. Functions can be declared in many ways in JavaScript. For example, the following is the sample `GetPerson(id)` function that returns the `person` object based on the ID passed as a parameter. This is the normal way of declaring function in JavaScript:

```
<script>

  function GetPerson(id) {
     return service.GetPerson(id);
  }


</script>
```

The `function` return type is computed at runtime and not part of the function signature. Returning values is not mandatory and you can keep functions without returning any values.

On the other hand, anonymous functions do not have any name and they can either be passed as an argument to other functions or defined without a function name. The following are the examples of anonymous functions:

```
var showMessage = function(message){
   console.log(message);
}
showMessage("Hello World");
```

Another example of defining anonymous function and passing it as a parameter is as follows:

```
function messageLogger(message ,logMessage) {
   logMessage();
}

function consoleMessage() {
   alert("Hello World");
}
messageLogger(consoleMessage());
```

The function expression is equivalent to function, but the only difference is that it should not start with the function name.

Class statement and expression

With ECMAScript 6, we can create classes in JavaScript. Just like other programming languages, we can create a class using the `class` keyword. With this, we can write cleaner code than developing functions that were represented as classes in the earlier version of ECMAScript.

Let's take a look at the `Rectangle` class that calculates an area:

```
<script>
  class Rectangle {
    constructor(height, width) {
      this.height=height;
      this.width=width;
    }
    get Area() {
      return this.calcArea();
    }
    calcArea(){
      alert("Area is "+ this.height * this.width);
    }
  }
</script>
```

Each class should have one constructor and give an error if multiple constructors are specified. Class expression is another way of defining classes. Just like anonymous functions, we can define classes in a similar way.

Let's take a look at the example of the same class defined earlier:

```
<script>
  var Rectangle = class{
    constructor(height, width) {
      this.height=height;
      this.width=width;
    }
    get Area() {
      return this.calcArea();
    }
    calcArea(){
      alert("Area is "+ this.height * this.width);
    }
  }
</script>
```

The next chapter will cover more details about classes and the attributes and keywords available to structure them.

Grouping operator

For any arithmetic expression, JavaScript uses the **BODMAS** rule. The precedence will be given to brackets then multiplication, division, addition, and subtraction. The grouping operator is used to give higher precedence to the expression if any of the member in the expression have higher precedence by default.

For example:

```
var a = 1;
var b = 2;
var c = 3;
var x = a + b * c;
```

The resultant x will be 7 as multiplication gets the higher precedence. However, what if we need to perform addition first?

We can use grouping operator as follows that gives the result 9:

```
var x = (a + b) * c;
```

new

In the same way as C#, the new keyword is used to instantiate any object in JavaScript. In order to create an instance of any user-defined or predefined type, use the new keyword:

```
var obj=new objectType();
```

super

The super keyword is used to call methods of the parent object. In C#, we use the base keyword to call the base class method or properties. In JavaScript, we can use it as follows:

```
super.functionOnParent();
```

Operators

Operators are the object used to manipulate values of an operand. For example, 1 + 2 results in 3, where 1 and 2 are operands and + is an operator. In JavaScript, we can use almost all the operators to concatenate strings, do arithmetic operations, and so on. In this section, let's see what type of operators we can use when writing programs in JavaScript language.

We will discuss the following operators in this section:

- Assignment operators
- Arithmetic operators
- Unary operators
- Comparison operators
- Logical operators
- Bitwise operators
- Bitwise shift operators
- The typeof operator
- The void operator
- The delete operator
- Miscellaneous operators

Assignment operators

Assignment operator is represented as (=) and the assignment is done from right to left.

For example, x=y means that the value of y is assigned to x.

Arithmetic operators

The following is a list of arithmetic operators you can use to perform addition, subtraction, division, and multiplication and use them with the assignment statements:

Name	Operator	Meaning
Addition	x + y	The value of x is added to y
Subtraction	x - y	The value of y is subtracted from x
Division	x / y	The value of x is divided by y
Multiplication	x * y	The value of x is multiplied to y
Remainder	x % y	The value of x is divided by y and the remainder is returned
Addition assignment	x += y	x = x + y that is, the value of x and y will be added and assigned to x

Name	Operator	Meaning
Subtraction assignment	x -= y	x= x - y that is, the value of x and y will be subtracted and assigned to x
Multiplication assignment	x *= y	x = x * y that is, the value of x and y will be multiplied and assigned to x
Division assignment	x /= y	x = x / y that is, the value of x will be divided by y and assigned to x
Remainder assignment	x %= y	x = x % y that is, the value of x will be divided by y and the remainder will be assigned to x
Exponentiation assignment	x **= y	x = x ** y that is, the value of x will be exponentially multiplied twice to y and assigned to x

Unary operators

Unary operator works with only one operand. It can be used for increment, decrement, inversion, and so on:

Name	Operator	Meaning
Increment operator	x++	The value of x will be incremented by 1
Decrement operator	x--	The value of x will be decremented by 1
Logical complement operator	!(x)	This inverts the value of x

Comparison operators

Comparison operator is used to compare operands that returns a Boolean `true` value if the comparison is `true`. Operands can be of any data type, have an associativity from left to right, and perform dynamic conversion if they are of different types.

For example, if the value of x is 2 and y is "2". Here, y denotes that it's a string, but in comparison, it will return `true`:

```
x==y //returns true
```

Similar to C# or any programming language, JavaScript supports all these operators, such as equal (==), not equal (!=), greater than (>), and less than(<), but due to the dynamic type binding, it also provides two operators such as strict equal (===) and strict not equal (!===) to confirm if the type is also the same if the value is same and vice versa.

We will now have a look at strict operators. There are the following two types of strict operators:

- Strict equal operator
- Strict not equal operator

Strict equal operator

In the previous section, we discussed that JavaScript provides dynamic binding and if the value of two different data types, suppose number and string, are the same, it will return `true` on comparison. For example, if x is 1 and y is "1", it will return `true`. Now, what if we have to do the comparison work only if the type is also the same? Here comes the strict equal operator that does not only check the value, but also match the types of both the operands.

The strict equal operator can be represented as `===`.

For example, if x = 1 and y = "1" and the comparison is done like (x===y), it will return `false` as x represents number and y represents string.

Strict not equal operator

Contrary to the strict equal operator, if we want to compare the values of two operands of same type, we can use the strict not equal operator.

The strict not equal operator can be represented as `!===`.

If x = 1 and y = 2 and the comparison is done like (x!==y), it will return `true`. This is because the types are the same and the values are different.

Logical operators

Just like C#, JavaScript uses the same types of logical operators to handle logical conditions. Logical operators are used to handle multiple conditions in a logical statement.

Logical AND

Logical AND is represented as `&&` and is used in two or more operands or conditions in statements.

For example, the following is the code snippet that shows the method that takes three parameters and the logic is defined that checks whether `number1` is equal to `number2` and the summation of `number1` and `number2` is equal to `number3` to return `true`:

```
<script>
  function CheckNumbers(number1, number2, number3) {
    if ((number1 == number2) && ((number1 + number2) == number3)) {
      return true;
    }
  }
<script>
```

Logical OR

Logical OR is represented as || and is used with two or more operands or logical conditions.

For example, the following is the code snippet that shows the method that takes three parameters, and if any of the numbers is equal to the value `10`, it will return `true`:

```
<script>
  function AnyNumber10(number1, number2, number3) {
    if ((number1 ==10 || number2 == 10 || number3 ==10) {
      return true;
    }
  }
</script>
```

Logical NOT

Logical NOT is represented as `!` and used with conditions that return a Boolean value. For example, if any logical condition returns `true`, this operator will make it `false`. It can be used as follows. In the code snippet, if `number1`, `number2`, and `number3` are equal to `10`, the method will return `false`. If they are different, the return value will be `true`:

```
<script>
  function AnyNumber10(number1, number2, number3) {
    return !(number1 ==10 && number2 == 10 && number3==10) {
    }
  }
</script>
```

Bitwise operators

Bitwise operators consider each number or operand as binary (a combination of 0 and 1). Every number has specific binary corresponding to it. For example, number 1 binary is represented as 0001 and 5 represented as 0101.

Bitwise operators work on 32-bit numbers and any numeric operand is first converted into a 32-bit number and then converted back to JavaScript number.

Bitwise operators perform their operations in binary and return the result as numbers.

For example, x is 1 and y is 9.

1 represented as 0001.

9 represented as 1001.

Bitwise AND

Bitwise AND is represented as & and the following is the comparison of each bit of operand 1 and 9. If both value on each bit is 1, the result will be 1, otherwise 0:

Number = 1	Number = 9	Result
0	1	0
0	0	0
0	0	0
1	1	1

In the JavaScript code, we can use it as follows:

```
<script>
  var a = "1";
  var b = "9";
  var c = a & b;
</script>
```

Finally, the resultant value will be 0001, which is equal to 1.

Bitwise OR

Bitwise OR is represented as | and the following is how the bit OR will be operated:

Number = 1	Number = 9	Result
0	1	1
0	0	0
0	0	0
1	1	1

The following code snippet shows the usage in JavaScript:

```
<script>
  var a = "1";
  var b = "9";
  var c = a | b;
</script>
```

Finally, the resultant value will be 1001, which is equal to 9.

Bitwise NOT

Bitwise NOT is represented as ~ and it works on a single operand and inverse each bit of the binary.

For example, if the number 9 is represented as 1001, it will be converted to a 32-bit number and then bitwise NOT will make it 11111111111111111111111111110110, which is equal to -10.

The following is the code snippet:

```
<script>
  var a = ~9;
</script>
```

Bitwise XOR

Bitwise XOR is represented as ^ and it works with two or more operands.

The following table shows how the bitwise XOR is operated:

Number = 1	Number = 9	Result
0	1	1
0	0	0
0	0	0
1	1	0

The following code snippet shows the usage in JavaScript:

```
<script>
  var a = "1";
  var b = "9";
  var c = a ^ b;
</script>
```

Finally, the resultant value will be 1000, which is equal to 8.

Bitwise shift operators

There are three kinds of bitwise shift operators, as follows:

- Bitwise left shift operator
- Bitwise right shift operator

Bitwise left shift

It is represented as << and is used to shift a bit from the right side to the binary value of any number.

For example, number 9 is represented as 01001, and if we use bitwise left, the resultant value will be 10010, which shifted one bit from the right.

The following code snippet shows the usage in JavaScript:

```
<script>
  var a = 9;
  var result = a << 1;
</script>
```

Finally, the resultant value will be 10010, which is equal to 18.

Bitwise right shift

It is represented as `>>` and is used to shift a bit from the left side to the binary value of any number.

For example, number `9` is represented as `1001`, using bitwise right will give the resultant value as `0100`.

The following code snippet shows the usage in JavaScript:

```
<script>
  var a = "9";
  var result = a >> 1;
</script>
```

Finally, the resultant value will be `0100`, which is equal to `4`.

The typeof operator

This is used to check whether the type of the variable is an object, undefined, number, and so on. In JavaScript, we can use this as follows:

```
<script>
  if (typeof a=="number") {
    alert("this is a number");
  }
</script>
```

Here is the list of possible values returned by the `typeof` operator:

Value returned	Description
`"number"`	If operand is a number
`"string"`	If operand is a string
`"boolean"`	If operand is a Boolean
`"object"`	If operand is an object
`null`	If operand is null
`"undefined"`	If operand is not defined

The void operator

The `void` operator prevents an expression to return any value. It is essential in conditions where you need to evaluate the expression but don't need the return value in the program.

You can write any expression or statement inside the `void` method.

For example, the following code snippet shows the simple example of using a `void` operator to display alert message when the link is clicked. Here, the `alert` expression is evaluated once the user clicks on the link:

```
<html>
<head></head>
<body>
  <a href="javascript:void(alert('You have clicked!'));">
  </a>
</body>
</html>
```

When the page runs and the user clicks on the link, it will display an alert message box as shown in the following:

Moreover, passing `0` as an expression within the `void` method will do nothing:

```
<html>
<head></head>
<body>
  <a href="javascript:void(0);">
  Do Nothing
  </a>
</body>
</html>
```

Another example here is using `void` to add two numbers and returning `undefined` for the assigned operand:

```
<script>
  var n1 = 6;
  var n2 = 7;
  var n3;
  var result = void (n3 = n1 + n2);
  alert ("result=" + result + "and n3 =" + n3);
</script>
```

The delete operator

A `delete` operator is used to delete objects and its properties, but not the local variables. The following example shows the way you can use the `delete` operator in JavaScript:

```
var country = { id: 1, name: "USA" };

delete country.id;

alert(country.id);
```

Calling `country.id` will return `undefined`, as this was already deleted in the preceding statement. On the other hand, if we delete the `country` object, it would not delete and display the country ID as 1:

```
var country = { id: 1, name: "USA" };

delete country;

alert(country.id);
```

Miscellaneous operators

Here are few other operators that are available in JavaScript.

Conditional operators

Conditional operator is represented as (`?:`):

```
expression1 ? expression2: expression3
```

It works as cross-selector to evaluate expressions. If the first expression is `true`, the second expression will be executed, otherwise the third will be executed.

The following is the code snippet for using conditional operator to evaluate expression. There is a `compareValues()` function that takes two parameters, and an alert will be displayed stating whether both the parameters are equal or not equal:

```
<script>
  function compareValues(n1, n2)
    (n1 == n2) ? alert("Both values are equal") : alert("Passed
      values are not equal");
</script>
```

Spread operator

The spread operator is represented as (...). It is used where you expect multiple arguments to be passed in for a function call.

For example, if your function is taking five parameters, you can either pass those values one by one as the parameter value when calling that method or keep them in an array and pass that array through the spread operator.

The following code snippet shows the actual example of using this in JavaScript:

```
function multipleArgs(a, b, c, d, e){
}
var args = [1,2,3,4,5]
multipleArgs(...args);
```

Built-in display methods in JavaScript

The following are the display methods available in JavaScript to provide notifications and messages to users in different forms.

Displaying messages

There are the following three types of pop-up dialog boxes:

- Alert message box
- Confirmation message box
- Prompt message box

Alert box

Using `window.alert()`, we can pop up an alert dialog box:

```
<!DOCTYPE html>
<html>
<body>

  <h1>My First Web Page</h1>
  <p>My first paragraph.</p>

<script>
  window.alert(5 + 6);
</script>

</body>
</html>
```

Confirm box

Using `window.confirm()`, we can pop up a confirm dialog box that returns the event result the user has taken. When a confirm dialog box pops up, it provides two action events: **OK** and **Cancel**. If a user click on **OK**, `true` will be returned, otherwise `false`. The following code shows the usage of the confirm dialog box on your HTML page.

The following is the code snippet for using a confirm dialog box to confirm with the user before saving a record:

```
<!DOCTYPE html>
<html>
<body>

<script>
  var r = window.confirm("are you sure to save record");
  if(r==true){
    alert("Record saved successfully");
  }
  else {
    alert("Record couldn't be saved");
  }
</script>

</body>
</html>
```

Prompt box

Prompt dialog box is used in cases when you want the user to supply the value. It can be used in conditions where you require user input.

The following code snippet shows the way of using a prompt message box in the JavaScript program:

```
<!DOCTYPE html>
<html>
<body>

<script>
  var name = window.prompt("Enter your name","N/A");
  if(name !=null){
    alert("hello "+ name "+, how are you today!");
  }
</script>

</body>
</html>
```

Writing on a page

We can use the `document.write()` method to write anything on the screen.

The following code snippet shows the way of writing any text on a web page in JavaScript:

```
<!DOCTYPE html>
<html>
<body>
  <script>
  document.write("Hello World");
  </script>
</body>
</html>
```

Writing into the browser's console window

Using `console.log()`, we can write any text into the browser's console window.

The following code snippet shows the way of writing text into the browser console window for tracing or debugging purposes in JavaScript:

```
<!DOCTYPE html>
<html>
<body>
  <h1>My First Web Page</h1>
  <p>My first paragraph.</p>
  <script>
  console.log("Entered into script execution context");
  </script>
</body>
</html>
```

Browser Object Models in JavaScript

JavaScript provides some predefined global objects that you can use to manipulate the DOM, close browsers, and so on. The following are the browser objects we can use to perform different operations:

- Window
- Navigator
- Screen
- History
- Location

Window

Window object refers to the open window in a browser. If in the HTML markup, some iframes are defined, a separate window object will created. Through the window object, we can access the following objects:

- All global variables
- All global functions
- The DOM

The following shows an example of accessing the DOM from the window object and accessing the textbox control.

Document

`window.document` returns the document object and we can use its properties and methods for a specific reason:

```html
<html>
<body>
  <input type="text" name="txtName" />
  <script>
  var textbox = Window.document.getElementById("txtName");
  textbox.value="Hello World";
  </script>
</body>
</html>
```

The `window` object itself contains many methods and few of them are as follows:

Event	Description	Syntax
Close	To close current window	`window.close();`
Open	To open new window	`window.open();`
Move	To move window to the specified position	`window.moveTo();`
Resize	To resize window to specified width and height	`window.resizeTo();`

Navigator

This object provides the information about the browser. It is beneficial when you need to run specific scripts based on the browser version or do something specific to the browser. Let's look into the methods it exposes.

Properties

The properties are described as follows:

- `appCodeName`: This returns the code name of the browser
- `appName`: This returns the name of the browser
- `appVersion`: This returns the version of the browser
- `cookieEnabled`: This determines whether cookies are enabled in the browser
- `geoLocation`: This gets the location of the user accessing the page
- `language`: This returns the language of the browser

- online: This determines whether the browser is online
- platform: This returns the platform that the browser has compiled
- product: This returns the engine name of the browser
- userAgent: This returns the user agent header sent by the browser to the server

The example code is as follows:

```
<!DOCTYPE html>
<html>
<head>
  <script type="text/javascript">
    function showInformation() {
      var spObj = window.document.getElementById("spInfo");
      spObj.innerHTML =
      "Browser Code Name: " + navigator.appCodeName + "<br>" +
      "Application Name: " + navigator.appName + "<br>" +
      "Application Version: " + navigator.appVersion + "<br>" +
      "Cookie Enabled? " + navigator.cookieEnabled + "<br>" +
      "Language: " + navigator.language + "<br>" +
      "Online: " + navigator.onLine + "<br>" +
      "Platform: " + navigator.platform + "<br>" +
      "Product: " + navigator.product + "<br>" +
      "User Agent: " + navigator.userAgent;
      navigator.geolocation.getCurrentPosition(showPosition);
    }
    function showPosition(position) {
      var spObj = window.document.getElementById("spInfo");
      spObj.innerHTML =  spObj.innerHTML + "<br> Latitude: " +
        position.coords.latitude +
      "<br>Longitude: " + position.coords.longitude;
    }
  </script>
</head>
<body onload="showInformation();">
  <span id="spInfo"></span>
</body>
</html>
```

The output is shown as follows:

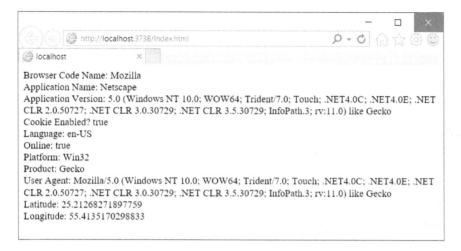

Screen

Through the screen object, you can get information about the user's screen. This is helpful to know from which screen the user is viewing the content. If it's a mobile browser or standard desktop screen, you can get the size and other information and modify the content as required.

Properties

The properties are described as follows:

- `availHeight` : This returns the height of the screen
- `availWidth`: This returns the width of the screen
- `colorDepth`: This returns the bit depth of the color palette for displaying images
- `height`: This returns the total height of the screen
- `pixelDepth`: This returns the color resolution (in bits per pixel) of the screen
- `width`: This returns the total width of the screen

The example code is as follows:

```
<!DOCTYPE html>
<html>
<head>
  <script type="text/javascript">
```

```
        function showInformation() {
          var spObj = window.document.getElementById("spInfo");
          spObj.innerHTML =
          "Available Height: " + screen.availHeight + "<br>" +
          "Available Width: " + screen.availWidth + "<br>" +
          "Height: " + screen.height + "<br>" +
          "Width: " + screen.width + "<br>"
        }
    </script>
  </head>
  <body onload="showInformation();">
    <span id="spInfo"></span>
  </body>
</html>
```

The output is shown as follows:

History

This contains the URLs that the user visited. You can access it through the `window.history` object.

You can use this object to navigate to the recently visited links.

Methods

The methods are described as follows:

- `Window.history.back()`: This loads the previous URL
- `Window.history.forward()`: This loads the recent URL in the history list
- `Window.history.go()`: This loads a specific URL available in the history list

Location

The location object gives you information about the current URL. Just like history, it can also be accessed through `window.location`. There are a few methods and properties you can use to perform specific operations.

Properties

The properties are described as follows:

- `window.location.host`: This returns the hostname and port number of the URL
- `window.location.hostname`: This returns only the hostname of the URL
- `window.location.href`: This provides the complete URL
- `window.location.origin`: This returns the hostname, port number, and protocol of the URL
- `window.location.pathname`: This returns the pathname of the URL
- `window.location.port`: This returns only the port number of the URL
- `window.location.protocol`: This returns the protocol of the URL, for example, HTTP or HTTPS
- `window.location.search`: This returns the query string of the URL

Methods

The methods are described as follows:

- `window.location.assign()`: This loads a new document.
- `window.location.reload()`: This reloads the current URL.
- `window.location.replace()`: This can be used to replace the current URL with the new one. Replace does not refresh the page, it can only change the URL.

Summary

In this chapter, we discussed the basic concepts of JavaScript and how to use it in our web applications. We discussed the core fundamentals of declaring variables and implementing arrays, functions, and data types to start writing programs in JavaScript. In the next chapter, we will discuss some advanced concepts about object-oriented programming and working with closures, scopes, and prototype functions with practical implementation.

2
Advanced JavaScript Concepts

JavaScript, when initially designed, was not expected to become the core programming language for Web development. It was normally used to perform some basic client-side operations that require some manipulation of the **Document Object Model (DOM)** elements. Later on, with the recent pace in Web development, things have pretty much changed. Now, many applications are purely using JavaScript and HTML to handle complex situations. From time to time, with different versions, different features were added and, as per the specification of ECMAScript 6, you can now have classes, you can do inheritance as you do with any other programming language, such as C# or Java. Closures, prototype functions, property descriptors, and many more that we will discuss in this chapter make it more powerful and robust.

In the previous chapter, we learned the core concepts and some basic fundamentals of writing programs in JavaScript and what features as a language it provides. In this chapter, we will be focusing more on the advanced topics, which help us to use these concepts in large and complex applications.

We will also focus on scoping and hoisting variables, object-oriented programming, prototype functions, property descriptors, closures, exception handling, and so on. Some topics, such as promises, asynchronous patterns and **Asynchronous JavaScript and XML (Ajax)** techniques, are broader topics and are covered in other chapters.

Variables – scope and hoisting

We already know how variables are declared in JavaScript using the var keyword. Any variable that is declared using the var keyword is termed a hoisted variable, and the term *hoisting* is the JavaScript default behavior of moving declarations to the top. When JavaScript is compiled by the JavaScript engine, all the variables that are declared using the var keyword are placed at the top within its scope. This means that if the variable is declared within a function block, it will be placed at the top of the function; otherwise, if it's declared outside any function and at the root of the script, it will become globally available. Let's have a look at this example to clarify our understanding.

Let's suppose the following code is the simple program that returns the GMT of the country name passed in the function's parameter:

```
function getCountryGMT(countryName) {
  if (countryName == "Pakistan") {
    var gmt = "+5.00";
  }
  else if (country == "Dubai") {
    var gmt = "+4.00";
  } else {
    return null;
  }
}
```

When the JavaScript engine compiles the script, the var gmt variable will be placed at the top:

```
function getCountryGMT(countryName) {
  var gmt;
  if (countryName == "Pakistan") {
    gmt = "+5.00";
  }
  else if (country == "Dubai") {
    gmt = "+4.00";
  } else {
    return null;
  }
}
```

This is called hoisting, where the var variables are placed at the top within its scope. Moreover, if you try to access the variable value in the last else condition, it will give an undefined value and could be accessible in every condition block.

This code shows another example of declaring the gmt variable globally and declaring it in the bottom of the code:

```
function getCountryGMT(countryName) {
  if (countryName == "Pakistan") {
    gmt = "+5.00";
  }
  else if (country == "Dubai") {
    gmt = "+4.00";
  } else {
    return null;
  }
}


var gmt;
```

When the script compiles, it will put the declaration of gmt at the top of the code:

```
var gmt;

function getCountryGMT(countryName) {
  if (countryName == "Pakistan") {
    gmt = "+5.00";
  }
  else if (country == "Dubai") {
    gmt = "+4.00";
  } else {
    return null;
  }
}
```

To overcome this behavior in ECMAScript 6, there is a new let keyword introduced to declare variables and the scope remains where it is defined. These variables are inaccessible outside its scope.

 Note that ECMAScript 6 is not supported by older browser versions but Microsoft Edge, Google Chrome 11, and Mozilla Firefox support it.

Declaring let

As with `var`, you can use `let` to declare variables in the same way. You can use this keyword in your programs but it will be accessible within the scope where it is defined. So, for example, if some variable is defined within the condition block, it will not be accessible outside its scope.

Let's have a look at the following example, where a variable is declared inside a condition block and the final output after compilations remains as it is. This is beneficial in conditions where you want to declare variables within a scope for a particular logic or scenario. In the `else` condition, `gmt` will not be accessible, as it is defined within the `if` condition:

```
function getCountryGMT(countryName) {
  if (countryName == "Pakistan") {
    let gmt = "+5.00";
  }
  else {
    return null;
  }
}
```

Once the `let` variable is declared within the scope of the function or script, it cannot be redeclared. Also, if the variables are declared using the `var` keyword, they cannot be redeclared using `let`.

This code will not throw an exception as the scope is different. However, within the same block, it cannot be redeclared:

```
function getCountryGMT(countryName) {
  var gmt;
  if (countryName == "Pakistan") {
    let gmt = "+5.00";
  }
  else {
    return null;
  }
}
```

Conditions where let is efficient to use

Here are the conditions where let is used.

Functions in loops

If we use the var variables in functions inside loop, these variables generate issues. Consider the following example, where there is an array of values and, through looping, we are inserting a function at each index of any array. This will make an error and pass the i variable as a reference. So, if you traverse each index and call function, the same value, that is, 10, will be printed:

```
var values = [];
for(var i=0;i<10;i++)
  {
    values.push(function () { console.log("value is " + i) });
  }
  values.forEach(function(valuesfunc) {
    valuesfunc();
  })
```

Whereas with let, each value will be passed by value and does not change when the variable value is updated inside the loop.

The code snippet of using let is as follows:

```
var values = [];
  for(let i=0;i<10;i++)
  {
    values.push(function () { console.log("value is " + i) });
  }
  values.forEach(function(valuesfunc) {
    valuesfunc();
  })
```

Events in JavaScript

Events play an important role in any business application where you want to save a record on a button-click event, or show some message, or change some element's background color. Any of these events can be defined from the control level itself or register directly through the script.

Let's have a look at this example, which changes the inner `html` code of the `div` control when the mouse is entered:

```
<html>
  <body>
    <div id="contentPane" style="width:200px; height:200px;">
    </div>
    <script>
      var divPane = document.getElementById("contentPane");
      divPane.onmouseenter = function () {
        divPane.innerHTML = "You are inside the div";
      };
      divPane.onmouseleave = function () {
        divPane.innerHTML = "You are outside the div";
      };
    </script>
  </body>
</html>
```

The preceding example registered two events on the script side for an HTML `div` control. It changes text, if the mouse has entered the function or has left the boundary of `div`. Alternatively, we can also register events on the control itself, and this example shows the way you can display a message on a button-click event. If you have noticed the scripting block is defined after the `div` pane, the reason is that when the page loads, it will try to execute the script and throw an error because the `contentPane` element was not created at that time:

```
<html>
  <body>
    <script>
      function displayMessage() {
        alert("you have clicked button");
      }
    </script>
    <input type="button" onclick="displayMessage();" />
  </body>
</html>
```

In this example, the scripting block is defined at the top of the page. In this scenario, it can be defined anywhere in the page because it will only be executed when the user clicks on a button.

Function arguments

We already know that the JavaScript functions can have parameters. However, the type of the parameters cannot be specified when creating a function. JavaScript neither performs any type checking on the parameter values passed nor validates the number of parameters when the function is called. So, for example, if a JavaScript function is taking two parameters, as shown in this code, we can even call it without passing any parameter value or by passing any type of the values or more values than the expected number of the parameters defined:

```
function execute(a, b) {
  //do something
}

//calling without parameter values
execute();

//passing numeric values
execute(1, 2);

//passing string values
execute("hello","world");

//passing more parameters
execute(1,2,3,4,5);
```

The missing parameters are set as undefined, whereas if more parameters are passed, these parameters can be accessed through the arguments object. The arguments object is a built-in object in JavaScript that contains an array of the arguments used when the function is invoked. We can use it as shown in this code:

```
function execute(a, b) {
  //do something
  alert(arguments[0]);
  alert(arguments[1]);
  alert(arguments[2]);
  alert(arguments[3]);
  alert(arguments[4]);
}

  //passing more parameters
  execute(1, 2, 3, 4, 5);
}
```

Arguments are passed by value; this means if the values are changed inside the function, it will not change the parameter's original value.

Object-oriented programming in JavaScript

All the objects in JavaScript are inherited from an object. JavaScript provides different patterns to adhere to the **object-oriented programming (OOP)** principles when building applications. There are different patterns, such as constructor patterns, prototype patterns, and object literal representation, and, with ECMAScript 6, a completely new way of representing objects through classes and inheriting a base class using the extends keyword.

In this section, we will see how we can implement the OOP principles with different methodologies.

Creating objects

A class represents the structure of an object and every class has certain methods and properties used by the object, whereas an object is an instance of a class and is known as a class instance.

JavaScript is a prototype-based language and based on objects. In a class-based language such as C# and Java, we have to first define the class that contains some methods and properties and then use its constructor to create objects. In JavaScript, any object can be used as a template to create new objects and use the properties or methods defined within it. New objects can also define their own properties or methods and can be associated as a prototype for another object. ECMAScript 6, however, introduces classes in JavaScript, which is syntactical sugar over existing paradigms and makes it easy for developers to write simpler and cleaner code to create objects. In the next section, we will see different ways of creating objects in JavaScript.

Defining objects using object literal notation

Object literals are comma-separated lists of name value pairs wrapped in curly braces.

Object literals are defined using the following syntax rules:

- A colon separates a property name from a value
- A value can be any data type, including array literals, functions, and nested object literals
- Each name value pair is separated by a comma from the next name value pair defined
- The last name value pair should not contain any comma after it

Here is the basic representation of a `person` object in object literal notation:

```
var person = {id: "001", name: "Scott", isActive: true,
   Age: 35 };
```

Here is another representation of a `personModel` object with a `savePerson()` method in object literal notation:

```
var personModel = {id: "001", name: "Scott", isActive: true,
   Age: 35, function: savePerson(){ //code to save person record } };
```

Defining objects using a constructor pattern

Classes can be defined using functions in JavaScript. This code shows the simple way of defining a customer class in JavaScript:

```
var person = new function(){};
```

The preceding code just defined an empty class with a default constructor and no properties and methods. Objects can be initialized using a new keyword, as shown in this code:

```
var p1 = new person();
```

The same function can be defined in a regular function declaration style:

```
function person(){};
```

With the regular function declaration, the JavaScript engine knows to fetch the function when it is needed. For example, if you call it before the function declaration in your script, it will call this function, whereas the variable defining approach needs the variable to be declared first before calling it.

Using the class keyword

ECMAScript 6 provides a new way of defining classes and introduced a class keyword, which can be used just like in other programming languages. This code is the representation of defining a customer object. The default constructor is `constructor()` that takes no parameters and can be overridden with more parameters, depending on the requirements. Each class allows you to define only one constructor, and if the constructor is overridden, the default constructor will not be used to instantiate objects:

```
class Person {
   constructor() { }
}
```

Properties

Properties are used to store and return values. We can define properties when initializing functions and these properties will be available each time the object is created.

Defining properties using object literal notation

Properties can be defined in objects as literal strings. For example, in this code, there is the customer object containing two properties and a method. The drawback with this approach is that there is no constructor and we cannot restrict users to supply property values when initializing an object. Either it can be set as hardcoded, as shown here, or after initializing an object:

```
var person = {
   id: "001",
   name:"Person 1",
   savePerson: function(){
   }

}
```

Defining properties using a constructor pattern

A constructor function pattern allows you to define parameters that restrict users to pass property values when instantiating objects. Consider this example; it contains a customer object with two properties, namely `id` and `name`:

```
var person = function(id, name){
   this._id = id;
   this._name = name;
}
```

The `this` keyword refers to the current object and properties can be accessed using `this` when calling inside the class, or through the instance variable, as shown in the following code:

```
var p1 = new person("001","Person 1");
console.log("Person ID: "+ p1.PersonID);
console.log("Person Name: "+ p1.name);
```

Property values can also be set after initializing an object, as shown in the following code:

```
var person = function(){
}
var p1 = new person();
```

```
p1.id="001";
p1.name="Person 1";
```

This snippet also represents the same approach of defining a person object that takes two parameters. We will see the limitations of using this approach in the next section when dealing with prototypes:

```
function person(id, name){
  this.id = id;
  this.name = name;
  this.logToConsole: function(){
    console.log("Person ID is "+ this.id  +",Name: "+
      this.name);
  };
}
```

Defining properties using setters/getters in ECMAScript 6

In ECMAScript 6, there is a new way of defining properties and it follows the standard way like other programming languages:

```
class Person {
  constructor(id, name) {
    this.id = id;
    this.name = name;
  }
}
var p1 = new person("001", "Person 1");
console.log ("Person ID: " + p1.id);
```

Unlike this approach, we can also define setters and getters using the set and get keywords. Constructors are optional in JavaScript when defining classes; if no constructor is defined, the default constructor, constructor(), will be invoked on object initialization. Let's have a look at this example containing a personName property for both setter and getter:

```
class Person {
  set Name(name) {
    this.personName = name;
  }
  get Name() {
    return this.personName;
  }
}
var p1 = new Person();
p1.Name = "Person 1";
console.log("personName " + p1.Name);
```

JavaScript property descriptors

Every property has the property descriptor, which is used to configure, and has the following meaning:

- **Writable**: This attribute is used to make the code read-only or writable. The `false` keyword makes it read-only and the value cannot be modified.

- **Enumerable**: This attribute is used to hide/unhide the property to be accessible or serializable. Setting this attribute to `false` will not show up the property when you iterate through an object's members and also could not be serialized when using `JSON.stringify`.

- **Configurable**: This attribute is used for the `on` and `off` configuration changes. For example, setting this attribute to `false` will prevent a property to be modified or deleted.

All these attributes are `true` by default but can be overridden, as shown in the following example. This example has a `car` object containing two properties, namely `name` and `color`:

```
var car = {
  name: "BMW",
  color: "black"
};
```

Display property descriptors

You can display the existing properties using the following statement:

```
display(Object.getOwnPropertyDescriptor(car, 'name'));
```

Managing property descriptors

The property descriptors of any object's property can be managed as shown in the following code:

```
Object.defineProperty(car, 'color',{enumerable: false});
Object.defineProperty(car, 'color',{configurable: false});
Object.defineProperty(car, 'color',{writable: false});
```

Using getters and setters

Through `Object.defineProperty`, we can also add setters and getters for properties. This example adds the full name of the car by concatenating `make` and `name`, and then splitting `name` to get the model and name through two different properties:

```
var car = { name: { make: "honda",  brand: "accord"} };
Object.defineProperty(car, 'fullname',
```

```
{
  get: function(){
    return this.name.make + ' ' + this.name.brand
  },
  set: function (value) {
    var names= value.split(' ');
    this.name.make = names[0];
    this.name.brand = names[1];
  }
});
car.fullname = "Honda Accord";
display(car.fullname);
```

Methods

Methods are the actions that can be performed on objects. In JavaScript, it can be represented as a property containing a function definition. Let's have a look at a different approach to defining the methods of the JavaScript objects.

Defining methods through object literal notation approach

An example showing the `logToConsole()` method defined in the object literal notation approach is shown here:

```
var person = {
  id: "001",
  name:"Person 1",
  logToConsole: function()
  {
    console.log("Person ID is "+ this.id  +", Customer Name:
      "+ this.name);
  }
}
```

Defining objects using the constructor function approach

The `constructor` function approach to defining methods is shown in the following code:

```
var person = function (id, name) {
  this._id = id;
  this._name = name;
  this.LogToConsole= function(){
    console.log("Person Name is "+ this._name);
  }
```

```
  }
var p1 = new person("001", "Person 1");
p1.LogToConsole();
```

Another way is to declare the `constructor` function approach is as follows:

```
function person(id, name) {
   this._id = id;
   this._name = name;
   this.LogToConsole= function(){
     console.log("Name is "+ this._name);
   }
}
var p1 = new person("001","Person 1");
p1.LogToConsole();
```

In ECMAScript 6, there is a better syntax for defining methods. The code snippet with the same example is as follows:

```
class Person {

   constructor() {

   }

   set Name(name) {
      this._name = name;
   }

   get Name() {
      return this._name;
   }

   logToConsole() {
      console.log("Person Name is " + Name);
   }
}

var p1 = new Person();
p1.Name = "Person 1";
p1.logToConsole();
```

The method return type is not needed when defining a method and it is realized based on the method body.

Extending properties and methods

Every JavaScript object has an object known as a prototype. A prototype is a pointer to another object. This prototype can be used to extend the object properties and methods. For example, if you are trying to access some property of an object that is not defined, it will look into the prototype object and proceed through the prototype chain until it is found or returns undefined. Therefore, whether an object is created using a literal syntax approach or a constructor function approach, it inherits all the methods and properties from a prototype known as `Object.prototype`.

For example, an object created using `new Date()` inherits from `Date.prototype`, and so on. However, the base object itself does not have any prototype.

We can easily add properties and functions to objects, as shown here:

```
var Person = function (name) {
    this.name = name;
}
var p1 = new Person("Person 1");
p1.phoneNo = "0021002010";
alert(p1.name);
```

Extending existing functions without initializing an object is done using a prototype object. Let's have a look at this example, where we add one method, `logToConsole()`, and a `phoneNo` property on a `Person` function:

```
var Person = function (name) {
    this.name = name;
}
Person.prototype.phoneNo = "";
Person.prototype.logToConsole = function () {
    alert("Person Name is " + this.name +" and phone No is "+
        this.phoneNo)
};
var p1 = new person("Person 1");
p1.phoneNo = "XXX"
p1.logToConsole();
```

Private and public members

In JavaScript, there are no access modifiers like we have in C#. All the members that are defined as `this` or with prototypes are accessible from the instance, whereas other members, which are defined in some other way, are non-accessible.

Let's have a look at this example, which enables only the y and y1() methods to be accessible outside the function:

```
function a() {
  var x = 1;
  this.y = 2;
  x1 = function () {
    console.log("this is privately accessible");
  }
  this.y1 = function () {
    console.log("this is publicly accessible");
  }
}
```

Inheritance

Inheritance is a core principle of OOP. In JavaScript, if you are working with an older version that does not comply with the ES6 standard, it is done using prototype-based programming.

Prototype-based programming is an OOP model that does not use classes but extends objects or inheritance using the prototype chain. This means that every object has an internal prototype property, which points to a particular object or null if not used. This property is not accessible through the program and is private to the JavaScript engine. So, for example, if you are calling some property, such as customer.getName, it will first check the getName property locally on the object itself, otherwise go through the chaining process and try to find it by linking objects through the prototype property until it is found. If no property is defined, it will return undefined.

Consider the following **entity–relationship model (ERD)** that has a base person object with some generic properties and two child objects, namely **Vendor** and **Employee**, with specific properties:

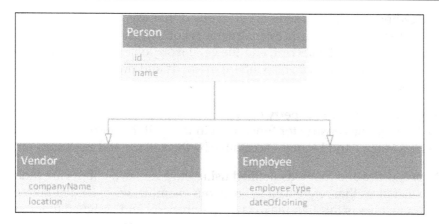

In order to articulate the same inheritance using the JavaScript constructor function approach, we can use the prototype property of both Vendor and Employee to the person object, as shown in this code:

```
var Person = function (id, name) {
  this.id = id;
  this.name = name;
}

var Vendor = function (companyName, location) {
  this.companyName = companyName;
  this.location = location;
}

var Employee = function (employeeType, dateOfJoining) {
  this.employeeType = employeeType;
  this.dateOfJoining = dateOfJoining;
}

Vendor.prototype = new Person("001", "John");
Employee.prototype = new Person("002", "Steve");

var vendorObj = new Vendor("ABC", "US");
alert(vendorObj.id);
```

In the preceding example, `vendorObj` is an object that was created from the `Vendor` constructor function. The `Vendor` constructor is both an object and a function because functions are objects in JavaScript, and the `vendorObj` object can have its own properties and methods. It can also inherit methods and properties from the `Vendor` object.

By setting the `prototype` property of the `Vendor` and `Employee` objects to the `Person` instance through the constructor function, it inherits all the properties and methods of the `Person` object and becomes accessible by the `Vendor` and `Employee` objects.

Object's properties and methods defined using the `prototype` object are inherited by all the instances that referenced it. So, in our example, we extended the `Vendor` and `Employee` objects through the `prototype` property and assigned them to the `Person` instance. This way, whenever any instance of the `Vendor` or `Employee` object is created, it can access all the properties or methods of an object of `Person`.

Properties and methods can also be added through the object; for example, we can add a property to the `Vendor` object, as shown in the following code, but this will become the static property and not accessible by the `Vendor` instance:

```
Vendor.id="001";
```

On the other hand, we can also add properties and methods to the `Vendor` instance as well but this will be accessible by that particular instance only:

```
var vendorObj = new Vendor("ABC", "US");
vendorObj.id="001";
```

Another technique of achieving inheritance is by assigning the parent's prototype to the child's prototype object, as shown here:

```
Vendor.prototype = Person.prototype;
```

With this technique, any methods or properties added in the `Person` prototype will be accessible by the `Vendor` object:

```
var Person = function (id, name) {
  this.id = id;
  this.name = name;
}

//Adding method to the Person's prototype to show message
Person.prototype.showMessage = function (message) {
  alert(message);
}

var Vendor = function (companyName, location) {
  this.companyName = companyName;
```

```
        this.location = location;
    }

    //Assigning the parent's prototype to child's prototype
    Vendor.prototype = Person.prototype;
    var vendorObj = new Vendor("XYZ", "Dubai");
    vendorObj.showMessage(vendorObj instanceof Person);
```

After running this script, it will show `true` in an alert message. This is because the `Vendor` object becomes an instance of the `Person` object and any method or property added in any of the objects will be accessible by both.

If we modify the preceding example and add another method through a `Vendor` prototype property after the assignment of the `Person` prototype to the `Vendor` prototype, it will be accessible by the `Person` object. This is because, in JavaScript, when the child's object prototype is set to the parent's object prototype, any methods or properties added in either object after the assignment will be accessible by both.

Let's add a `showConsoleMessage()` method in the `Vendor` object through a `prototype` property and access it through the `Person` instance, as shown in this code:

```
var Person = function (id, name) {
    this.id = id;
    this.name = name;
}

//Adding method to the Person's prototype to show message
Person.prototype.showMessage = function (message) {
    alert(message);
}

var Vendor = function (companyName, location) {
    this.companyName = companyName;
    this.location = location;
}

//Assigning the parent's prototype to child's prototype
Vendor.prototype = Person.prototype;

//Adding method to the Vendor's prototype to show at console
Vendor.prototype.showConsoleMessage = function (message) {
    console.log(message);
}

var personObj = new Person("001", "John");
//Person object access the child's object method
personObj.showConsoleMessage("Console");
```

Chaining constructors in JavaScript

In the example in the previous section, we have seen how to inherit objects. However, if some base object has some overloaded constructor, accepting properties will require some extra effort. Every function in JavaScript has a `call` method, which is used to chain constructors for an object. We can use the `call` method to chain constructors and call base constructors. As the `Person` object takes two parameters, we will modify the `Vendor` function and two properties, `id` and `number`, which can be passed while creating a `Vendor` object. So, whenever the `Vendor` object is created, the `Person` object will be created and the values will be populated:

```javascript
var Person = function (id, name) {
   this.id = id;
   this.name = name;
}

var Vendor = function (companyName, location, id, name) {
   this.companyName = companyName;
   this.location = location;
   Person.call(this, id, name);
}

var employee = function (employeeType, dateOfJoining, id, name) {
   this.employeeType = employeeType;
   this.dateOfJoining = dateOfJoining;
   Person.call(this, id, name);
}

Vendor.prototype = Person.prototype;
Employee.prototype = Person.prototype;

var vendorObj = new Vendor("ABC", "US", "V-01","Vendor 1");
alert(vendorObj.name);
```

Inheritance using Object.create()

With ECMAScript 5, you can easily inherit your base object through the `Object.create()` method. This method takes two parameters, the object to use as a prototype and an object containing properties and methods for the new object to create. The `Object.create()` method improves constructor-based inheritance. It's a good choice for creating an object without going through its constructor. Let's see the example of `Vendor` and `Employee` inheriting the `Person` object using the `Object.create()` approach:

```javascript
var Person = function (id, name) {
   this.id = id;
   this.name = name;
```

```
}

var Vendor = function (companyName, location, id, name) {
  this.companyName = companyName;
  this.location = location;
  Person.call(this, id, name);
}

var Employee = function (employeeType, dateOfJoining, id, name) {
  this.employeeType = employeeType;
  this.dateOfJoining = dateOfJoining;
  Person.call(this, id, name);
}

Vendor.prototype = Object.create(Person.prototype);
Employee.prototype = Object.create(Person.prototype);

var vendorObj = new Vendor("ABC", "US", "V-01", "Vendor 1");
alert(vendorObj.name);
```

In the preceding example, we used `Object.create()` to inherit the `Person` object to the `Vendor` and `Employee` objects. Whenever the `Vendor` or `Employee` instances are created, they can access the properties of the `Person` object. The `Object.create()` method automatically instantiates an instance of an object defined as the parameter in its `call` method.

Predefined properties of Object.create()

An `Object.create()` method does not execute the `Person` function; instead, it will just set the `Person` function as a prototype of the customer function. Another representation of the customer object, containing property as `CustomerCode`, is shown in the following code:

```
var customerObj = Object.create(Object.prototype, {
  customerCode: {
    value: "001",
    enumerable: true,
    writable: true,
    configurable: true
  }
});
alert("" + customerObj.customerCode);
```

Here, value is the actual value representing the customer code, whereas `enumerable`, `writable`, and `configurable` are predefined attributes.

Defining inheritance using class

In the example in the previous section, we have already seen how to define
classes using ECMAScript 6. Just like Java, we can inherit a parent class using the
extends keyword.

An example of using extends is shown here:

```
class Person {

  constructor(id, name) {
    this._id = id;
    this._name = name;
  }

  get GetID() {return this._id;}
  get GetName() {return this._name;}
}

class Vendor extends Person {
  constructor(phoneNo, location, id, name){
    super(id, name);
    this._phoneNo = phoneNo;
    this._location = location;

  }
  logToConsole() {
    alert("Person ID is " + this.GetID);
  }
}

var vendorObj = new Vendor("XXX", "US", "V-01", "Vendor 1");
vendorObj.logToConsole();
```

With ECMAScript 6, you can get the true essence of declaring static variables and
methods in the class. Let's have a look at the following example, which contains
one static method, logToConsole(), and calls it from the customer class without
initializing its object after inheriting it from the Person class:

```
class Person {
  static logToConsole() {
    console.log("Hello developers!");
  }
}
```

```
class Vendor extends Person {
}

Vendor.logToConsole();
```

Encapsulation

In the example in the previous section, the `Vendor` object doesn't need to know the implementation of the `logToConsole()` method in the `Person` class and can use that method. The `Vendor` class doesn't need to define this method unless overriding for a specific reason. This is called encapsulation, in which the `Vendor` object doesn't need to know the actual implementation of the `logToConsole()` method and each `Vendor` object can use this method to log to console. This is how the encapsulation is done, through which every class is encapsulated into a single unit.

Abstraction

Abstraction is used to hide all the information except the data, which is relevant about an object, to reduce complexity and increase efficiency. This is one of the core principles of OOP.

In JavaScript, there is no built-in support for abstraction and it does not provide any type such as an interface or abstract to create interfaces or abstract classes to achieve abstraction. However, there are certain patterns through which you can implement abstraction but still it does not restrict and ensures that all the abstract methods are completely implemented by the concrete class or function.

Let's have a look at the following example, where we have a `person` controller that takes a concrete object as a parameter, and then calls its specific implementation:

```
var person = function (id, name) {
  this._id = id;
  this._name = name;
  this.showMessage = function () { };
}
var vendor = function (companyName, location, id, name) {
  this._companyName = companyName;
  this._location = location;
  person.call(this, id, name);
  this.showMessage = function () {
    alert("this is Vendor");
  }
}
var employee = function (employeeType, dateOfJoining, id, name) {
  this._employeeType = employeeType;
```

```
    this._dateOfJoining = dateOfJoining;
    person.call(this, id, name);
    this.showMessage = function () {
      alert("this is Employee");
    }
  }
}
vendor.prototype = Object.create(person.prototype);
employee.prototype = Object.create(person.prototype);
var personController = function (person) {
  this.personObj = person;
  this.showMessage = function () {
    this.personObj.showMessage();
  }
}

var v1 = new vendor("ABC", "USA", "V-01", "Vendor 1");
var p1 = new personController(v1);
p1.showMessage();
```

Alternatively, with ECMAScript 6, we can implement the same scenario, as shown in the following code:

```
class person {
  constructor(id, name) {
    this._id = id;
    this._name = name;
  }
  showMessage() { };
}
class vendor extends person {
  constructor(companyName, location, id, name) {
    super(id, name);
    this._companyName = companyName;
    this._location = location;

  }
  showMessage() {
    alert("this is Vendor");
  }
}
class employee extends person {
  constructor(employeeType, dateOfJoining, id, name) {
    super(id, name);
    this._employeeType = employeeType;
    this._dateOfJoining = dateOfJoining;
```

```
  }
  showMessage() {
    alert("this is Employee");
  }
}
class personController {
  constructor(person) {
    this.personObj = person;
  }
  showMessage() {
    this.personObj.showMessage();
  }
}

var v1 = new vendor("ABC", "USA", "V-01", "Vendor 1");
var p1 = new personController(v1);
p1.showMessage();
```

new.target

The `new.target` property is used to detect whether the function or a class is called using the `new` keyword. It returns a reference to the function or a class if it is called, otherwise `null`. Considering the example in the previous section, we can restrict creating the `call` objects of `person` by using `new.target`:

```
class person {
  constructor(id, name) {
    if(new.target === person){
      throw new TypeError("Cannot create an instance of
        Person class as its abstract in nature");
    }
    this._id = id;
    this._name = name;
  }

  showMessage() { };
}
```

Namespace

ECMAScript 6 introduced modules through which you can define namespaces and use the `export` and `import` keywords but they are still in draft and no implementations are present so far.

However, with earlier versions, namespaces can be simulated using local objects. For example, here is the syntax to define a local object represented as a namespace and we can add functions and objects inside it:

```
var BusinessLayer = BusinessLayer || {};
```

We can then add functions, as shown in this code:

```
BusinessLayer.PersonManager = function(){
};
```

Moreover, more nested namespace hierarchy can also be defined, as shown in the following code:

```
var BusinessLayer = BusinessLayer || {};
var BusinessLayer.Managers = BusinessLayer.Managers || {};
```

Exception handling

JavaScript is becoming a powerful platform for developing large applications, and exception handling plays an important role in handling exceptions in programs and propagate them where needed. Just like C# or any other programming language, JavaScript provides the `try`, `catch`, and `finally` keywords to annotate code for handling errors. JavaScript provides the same way of using the nested `try catch` statements and conditions for handling different conditions in the `catch` block.

When an exception occurs, an object is created that represents the error thrown. Just like C#, we have different types of exception, such as `InvalidOperationException`, `ArgumentException`, `NullException`, and `Exception`. JavaScript provides six error types, which are as follows:

- `Error`
- `RangeError`
- `ReferenceError`
- `SyntaxError`
- `TypeError`
- `URIError`

Error

The `Error` object represents generic exceptions and is mostly used in returning user-defined exceptions. An `Error` object contains two properties, namely name and message. Name returns the type of error and message returns the actual error message. We can throw error exceptions, as shown here:

```
try{ }catch{throw new Error("Some error occurred");}
```

RangeError

The `RangeError` exception is thrown if the range of any number is exceeded. For example, creating an array with a negative length will throw `RangeError`:

```
var arr= new Array(-1);
```

ReferenceError

The `ReferenceError` exception occurs when accessing an object or variable that does not exist; for example, the following code will throw a `ReferenceError` exception:

```
function doWork(){
   arr[0]=1;
}
```

SyntaxError

As the name states, `SyntaxError` is thrown if there is any syntax problem in the JavaScript code. So, if some closing bracket is missing, loops are not structured properly, and so on, this will come under the `SyntaxError` category.

TypeError

The `TypeError` exception occurs when a value is not of the excepted type. The following code throws a `TypeError` exception as the object is trying to call a method that does not exist:

```
var person ={};
person.saveRecord();
```

URIError

The `URIError` exception occurs with `encodeURI()` and `decodeURI()` when an invalid URI is specified. The following code throws this error:

```
encodeURIComponent("-");
```

Closures

Closures are one of the most powerful features of JavaScript. Closures provide a way to expose inner functions that are inside the body of other functions. A function can be termed a closure when one of the inner functions is made accessible outside the function in which it was contained and can be executed after the outer function is executed and use the same local variables, parameters, and function declarations when the outer function was called.

Let's have a look at the following example:

```
function Incrementor() {
  var x = 0;
  return function () {
    x++;
    console.log(x);
  }
}

var inc= Incrementor();
inc();
inc();
inc();
```

This is a simple closure example, in which `inc()` becomes the closure that references the inner function, which increments the x variable defined in the outer function. The x variable will be incremented on each call and the value will become 3 on the last call.

A closure is a special kind of object that combines the function and the environment in which that function was created. So, calling it multiple times will use the same environment and the values being updated in the previous call.

Let's have a look at another example, where we have a table generator function that takes a table number and returns the function, which can be used to get the result of any number multiplication with the table number supplied on the first call:

```
function tableGen(number) {
  var x = number;
  return function (multiplier) {
    var res = x * multiplier;
    console.log(x +" * "+ multiplier +" = "+ res);
  }
}
```

```
var twotable = tableGen(2);
var threetable = tableGen(3);

twotable(5);
threetable(6);
```

The resultant values after calling the `twotable()` and `threetable()` methods will be `10` and `18`. This is because the `twoTable()` function object was initialized by passing 2 as the parameter to the `tableGen()` function. This `tableGen()` function then stores the value passed as a parameter in the x variable and multiplies it with the variable passed in the second call when it is executed through the `twoTable()` and `threeTable()` method calls.

Hence, the output of the `twoTable(5)` function call will be `10`, as shown in the following screenshot:

```
2 * 5 = 10
```

The output of the second statement, `threeTable(6)`, will be `18`, as shown in the following screenshot:

```
3 * 6 = 18
```

Practical use

We have seen what closures are and how we can implement them. However, let's consider their practical implications. Closures let you associate some environment with a function that operates within that environment or data.

In JavaScript, functions mostly execute on any event or trigger on any action taken by the user. Let's have a look at the following example of the practical use of closures to log messages on a `console` and `dialog` window:

```
<body>
  <input type="text" id="txtMessage" />
  <button id="consoleLogger"> Log to Console </button>
  <button id="dialogLogger">Log to Dialog </button>
  <script>

    function getLogger(loggerType) {
      return function () {
        var message =
          document.getElementById("txtMessage").value;
```

```
            if (loggerType == "console")
            console.log(message);
            else if (loggerType == "dialog")
            alert(message);
        }
    }
    var consoleLogger = getLogger("console");
    var dialogLogger = getLogger("dialog");
    document.getElementById("consoleLogger").onclick =
        consoleLogger;
    document.getElementById("dialogLogger").onclick =
        dialogLogger;
    </script>
</body>
```

In the preceding example, we have two logger closures: one that logs to the console and the other one to a pop-up dialog window. We can initialize these closures and use them throughout our program to log messages.

JavaScript typed arrays

Client-side development in JavaScript has become a powerful platform and there are certain APIs and libraries available that allow you to work with media files, Web sockets, and so on, and handle data in binary. When working with binary data, it is required to save it in its own specific format. Here comes the role of typed arrays, which allow developers to manipulate data in a raw binary format.

Typed array architecture

Typed arrays keep the data in two portions, namely buffer and view. Buffer contains the actual data in binary but it cannot be accessible without view. View tells the actual metadata information and context about the buffer, such as data type, starting offset, and number of elements.

The array buffer

The array buffer is a data type that is used to represent binary data. Its content cannot be manipulated until it is assigned to a view, which represents the buffer in a specific format and performs manipulation on the data.

There are different types of type array views, which are as follows:

Type	Size in bytes	Description
Int8Array	1	This array is 8-bit signed integer.
UInt8Array	1	This array is 8-bit unsigned integer.
Int16Array	2	This array is 16-bit signed integer.
UInt16Array	2	This array is 16-bit unsigned integer.
Int32Array	4	This array is 32-bit signed integer.
UInt32Array	4	This array is 32-bit unsigned integer.
Float32Array	4	This array is 32-bit IEEE floating point number.
Float64Array	8	This array is 64-bit IEEE floating point number.
UInt8ClampedArray	1	This array is 8-bit unsigned integer (clamped).

Now, let's go through an example to see how we can store data in a buffer and manipulate it through a view.

Creating a buffer

First of all, we need to create a buffer, as shown in this code:

```
var buffer = new ArrayBuffer(32);
```

The preceding statement allocates the memory for 32 bytes. Now we can use any of the type array views to manipulate it:

```
var int32View= new Int32Array(buffer);
```

And finally, we can access the fields, as shown here:

```
for(var i=0;i< int32View.length; i++){
   int32View[i] = i;
}
```

This code will make eight entries into the view, from 0 to 7. The output will look as follows:

```
0 1 2 3 4 5 6 7
```

The same buffer can also be manipulated with the other view types. For example, if we wanted to read the populated buffer with a 16-bit array view, the result will be like this:

```
var Int16View =new Int16Array(buffer);
for(var i=0;i< int16View.length;i++){
  console.log(int16View[0]);
}
```

The output will look as follows:

```
0 0 1 0 2 0 3 0 4 0 5 0 6 0 7 0
```

This is how easily we can manipulate single buffer data with multiple views of different types and interact with the data objects containing multiple data types.

Maps, sets, weak maps, and weak sets

Maps, weak maps, sets, and weak sets are objects that represent collections. Maps are keyed collections that hold values in name value pairs, whereas sets store unique values of any type. We will discuss each of them in the next sections.

Maps and weak maps

A `Map` object provides a simple key/value map and iterates it based on the insertion. The first inserted value will be retrieved first. Weak maps are non-enumerable and hold object types only. No primitive types are allowed in weak maps and each key represents an object. Let's have a look at the following example of using a map for currencies:

```
var currencies = new Map();
currencies.set("US", "US Dollar");
currencies.set("UK", "British Pound");
currencies.set("CA", "Canadian Dollar");
currencies.set("PK", "Rupee");
currencies.set("UAE", "Dirham");
for (var currency of currencies) {
  console.log(currency[0] + " currency is " + currency[1]);
}
```

Some other properties and methods available on the `Map` object are shown in the following code:

```
currencies.get("UAE"); // returns dirham
currencies.size; // returns 5
currencies.has("PK") // returns true if found
currencies.delete("CA") // delete Canada from the list
```

Instead of simple primitive values, weak maps hold objects and their keys are represented as weak keys. This is because if there is no reference to the object stored in a weak map value and got collected in garbage, the key will become weak. It is normally used to store private data for an object or to hide implementation details.

We learned in the previous section that everything that is exposed on the instance level and prototype level is public. The practical example containing a function to authenticate a user from a Twitter account is shown in the following code. For **open authentication (OAuth)**, Twitter needs two keys: the consumer API key and a secret key. We don't wanted to expose and let the user to change this information. Therefore, we have kept this information using weak maps, and then retrieved it in the `prototype` function to authenticate the user:

```
var authenticatorsecrets = new WeakMap();

function TwitterAuthenticator() {
  const loginSecret = {
    apikey: 'testtwitterapikey',
    secretkey: 'testtwittersecretkey'
  };
  authenticatorsecrets.set(this, loginSecret);
}

TwitterAuthenticator.prototype.Authenticate = function () {
  const loginSecretVal = authenticatorsecrets(this);
  //to do authenticate with twitter
};
```

Sets and weak sets

Sets are the collections of values where each value should be unique. So, for example, if at any index you have a value, 1, already defined, you cannot insert it into the same set instance.

Sets are not typed and you can put any data, irrespective of any data type:

```
var set = new Set();
set.add(1);
set.add("Hello World");
set.add(3.4);
set.add(new Date());
```

On the other hand, weak sets are collections of unique objects and not the arbitrary values of any type. Just like weak maps, if there is no other reference to the object stored, it will be disposed and garbage collected. Similar to weak maps, they are not enumerable:

```
var no = { id: 1 };
var abc = { alphabets: ['a', 'b', 'c'] };

var x = new WeakSet();
x.add(no);
x.add(abc);
```

The strict mode

The `strict` mode is a literal expression introduced in ECMAScript 5. It is used to write a secure JavaScript and throws errors if there are any minor errors on your script and doesn't overlook them. Secondly, it runs faster than the normal JavaScript code because it sometimes fixes mistakes, which helps JavaScript engines to perform optimizations and make your code run faster.

We can invoke the `strict` mode on a global script level or a function level:

```
"use strict;"
```

For example, in the following code, it will throw an error as the x variable is not defined:

```
"use strict";
x=100;
function execute(){
    "use strict;"
    x=100;
}
```

For larger applications, it's a better choice to use the `strict` mode, which will throw an error if something is missing or not defined. The list of scenarios where using the `strict` mode will result in an error is shown in the following table:

Code	Reason for error
`x=100;`	In this code, variable is not declared.
`x= {id:1, name:'ABC'};`	In this code, object variable is not declared.
`function(x,x){}`	Duplicating the parameter name caused the error in this code.
`var x = 0001`	In this code, octal numeric literals are used.

Code	Reason for error
`var x=\0001`	Escape is not allowed, so the error occurred.

`var x = {get val() {return 'A'}};`
 	
`x.val = 'B'`
	Writing to a `get` value caused the error in this code.

`delete obj.prototype;`	Deleting object prototype is not allowed, so the error occurred.

`var x= 2;`
 	
`delete x;`
	Deleting a variable is not allowed, so the error occurred.

Moreover, there are certain reserved keywords, such as `arguments`, `eval`, `implements`, `interface`, `let`, `package`, `private`, `protected`, `public`, `static`, and `yield`, which are not allowed as well.

Summary

In this chapter, we learnt about some advanced concepts of JavaScript, such as hoisted variables and their scope, property descriptors, OOP, closures, typed arrays to store types of data, and exception handling. In the next chapter, we will learn about the most extensively used library, jQuery, to perform DOM traversal and manipulation, event handling, and more in a very simple and easy way.

3
Using jQuery in ASP.NET

We will start off this chapter with a short introduction to jQuery. jQuery is a JavaScript library developed to provide a better development experience and a faster coding experience by writing less code to do complex operations much faster compared to plain vanilla JavaScript. However, JavaScript is still there when writing custom scripts for specific reasons. So, jQuery helps you perform DOM manipulation, selecting elements based on class, element name, and so on, and provides a better event handling model to make it simpler for developers to use in their routine projects.

Compared to JavaScript, another advantage is the cross browser issues. It offers consistent behavior across browsers. JavaScript, on the other hand, is implemented differently by each browser. Also, in order to handle cross-browser issues in JavaScript, a developer tends to write some conditional logic to check what browser version JavaScript is running on and handle it accordingly; whereas jQuery handles all the heavy lifting of what the browser is and provides consistent behavior.

Some powerful features of jQuery that we will discuss in the current chapter are as follows:

- Working with selectors
- Manipulating the DOM elements
- Handling events

Getting started with jQuery

The jQuery library can be downloaded from `http://jquery.com`. The latest version of jQuery is 3.0.0 and you can use this library if you are targeting modern browsers; for example, IE 9 and Microsoft Edge support this version. For older versions—for example, IE 6-8—you can download jQuery 1.x.

Once jQuery is downloaded, you can add it to your project and reference it, as shown here:

```
<head>
  <script src="~/scripts/jquery.js"></script>
</head>
<body>
</body>
```

Using a content delivery network

Instead of loading jQuery from your server, we can also load it from some other server, such as the Microsoft server or Google server. These servers are called the **content delivery network (CDN)** and they can be referenced as shown here:

- Referencing the Microsoft CDN:

```
<script src="http://ajax.microsoft.com/ajax/jquery/
  jquery-2.0.js">
</script>
```

- Referencing the Google CDN:

```
<script
  src="http://ajax.googleapis.com/ajax/libs/jquery/2.0/
    jquery.min.js"></script>
```

The use of CDN

Actually, these CDNs are very common and most of the sites already use them. When running any application that references a CDN, there are chances that some other website might have also used the same CDN of Microsoft or Google, and the same file might be cached on the client side. This increases the page rendering performance. Also, downloading the jQuery library again from your local server uses the cached version of CDN. Moreover, Microsoft and Google have different servers available, based on different regions, and the user will get some speed benefits too when using it from a CDN.

However, there are certain cases when the CDN might be down, and in this case, you might have to refer to and download scripts from your own server. To handle this scenario, we can specify the fallback URL, which detects whether it has been downloaded from CDN; otherwise, it downloads from the local server. We can use the following script to specify the fallback:

```
<script
  src="//ajax.googleapis.com/ajax/libs/jquery/1.2.6/
    jquery.min.js"></script>
```

```
<script>if (!window.jQuery) { document.write('<script
   src="/path/to/your/jquery"><\/script>'); }
</script>
```

The `window.jQuery` instance tells us whether jQuery is loaded; otherwise, it writes the script on the DOM, which refers to the local server.

Alternatively, in ASP.NET Core, we can use the `asp-fallback-src` attribute to specify the fallback URL. ASP.NET Core 1.0 provides a wide range of tag helpers. Compared to the HTML helpers, these helpers can be used just by adding the HTML attributes to the page elements and they offer developers the same experience as writing the frontend code.

The same code can be written in a simple way to handle the fallback scenarios in ASP.NET:

```
<script src="https://ajax.aspnetcdn.com/ajax/jquery/
   jquery-2.1.4.min.js"
   asp-fallback-src="~/lib/jquery/dist/jquery.min.js"
   asp-fallback-test="window.jQuery">
</script>
```

In ASP.NET Core, there is one more tag helper, `<environment>`, which can be used to load scripts based on the current environment set in the `launchSettings.json` file:

```
"profiles": {
  "IIS Express": {
    "commandName": "IISExpress",
    "launchBrowser": true,
    "environmentVariables": {
      "Hosting:Environment": "Development"
    }
  },
  "web": {
    "commandName": "web",
    "environmentVariables": {
      "Hosting:Environment": "Development"
    }
  }
}
```

Based on the current environment set in the project's profile, we can load scripts to cater to debugging and production scenarios. For example, in a production environment, preferably, we used to specify the minified version of the JavaScript libraries as it removes all the white spaces and renames the variables to make it more compressed in size to load fast. However, for debugging purposes, the standard non-minified version is much better as far as the development experience is concerned. Therefore, we can use the environment tag helper, as shown in the following code, to load the minified version for production and standard when developing an application:

```
<environment names="Development">
  <script src="~/lib/jquery/dist/jquery.js"></script>
  <script src="~/lib/bootstrap/dist/js/bootstrap.js"></script>
  <script src="~/js/site.js" asp-append-version="true"></script>
</environment>
<environment names="Staging,Production">
  <script src="https://ajax.aspnetcdn.com/ajax/jquery/
    jquery-2.1.4.min.js"
    asp-fallback-src="~/lib/jquery/dist/jquery.min.js"
    asp-fallback-test="window.jQuery">
  </script>
  <script src="https://ajax.aspnetcdn.com/ajax/bootstrap/3.3.5/
    bootstrap.min.js"
    asp-fallback-src="~/lib/bootstrap/dist/js/
      bootstrap.min.js"
    asp-fallback-test="window.jQuery && window.jQuery.fn &&
      window.jQuery.fn.modal">
  </script>
  <script src="~/js/site.min.js"
    asp-append-version="true"></script>
</environment>
```

The document ready event

The jQuery library can be accessed through a $ sign or simply by writing jQuery. However, preferably, developers access it using a dollar sign. It also provides a way to catch an event when the DOM hierarchy is completely loaded. This means that once the DOM structure is loaded, you can catch this event to perform different operations, such as associating the CSS class with controls and manipulating control values. The DOM hierarchy is not dependent on the the images or CSS files when the page is loading and the document ready event is raised in parallel irrespective of whether the images or CSS files are downloaded or not.

We can use the document ready event, as shown in this code:

```html
<html>
  <head>
    <script src="http://ajax.aspnetcdn.com/ajax/jQuery/
      jquery-1.12.0.min.js"></script>
    <script>
      $(document).ready(function () {
        console.log("Document is loaded");
      });
    </script>
  </head>

</html>
```

As explained in the preceding code, $ is the way of accessing a jQuery object. It takes a document object, which is passed as a parameter, whereas ready checks whether the document object model hierarchy is loaded completely once. Finally, it takes an anonymous function in which we can write the operation that we need to perform. In the preceding example, we are just displaying a simple text message when the DOM hierarchy gets loaded.

The jQuery selectors

For DOM manipulation, the jQuery selectors play an important role and provide a better and easy one-line approach to select any element from DOM and manipulate its values and attributes, for example, searching a list of elements with a specific CSS class is easier with the jQuery selectors.

The jQuery selectors can be written with a dollar sign and parentheses. We can use the jQuery selectors to select elements based on the element's ID, tag name, class, attribute value, and input nodes. We will look into these elements one by one with a practical example in the next section.

Selecting the DOM elements using the ID

The following example shows you the way of selecting a div element with its ID:

```html
<!DOCTYPE html>
<html>
  <head>
    <script src="http://ajax.aspnetcdn.com/ajax/jQuery/
      jquery-1.12.0.min.js"></script>
    <script>
      $(document).ready(function () {
```

```
        $('#mainDiv').html("<h1>Hello World</h1>");

    });
  </script>
 </head>
 <body>
   <div id="mainDiv">

   </div>
 </body>
</html>
```

After selecting an element, we can call various methods to set values. In the given example, we called the `html()` method that takes the `html` string and sets `Hello World` as the first heading. On the other hand, the `html` content can be retrieved by calling this code:

```
<script>
  $(document).ready(function () {
    var htmlString= $('#mainDiv').html();

  });
</script>
```

Selecting the DOM elements using TagName

In JavaScript, we can retrieve the DOM elements by calling `document.getElementsByTagName()`. This element returns an array of elements matched with the tag name. In jQuery, this can be achieved in an easier way and the syntax is quite simple.

Consider the following example:

```
$('div') //returns all the div elements
```

Let's have a look at the following example to clarify our understanding:

```
<!DOCTYPE html>
<html>
 . <head>
    <script src="http://ajax.aspnetcdn.com/ajax/jQuery/
      jquery-1.12.0.min.js"></script>
    <script>
      $(document).ready(function () {
        $('div').css('text-align, 'left');
      });
```

```
      </script>
    </head>
    <body>
      <div id="headerDiv">
        <h1>Header</h1>
      </div>
      <div id="mainDiv">
        <p>Main</p>
      </div>
      <div id="footerDiv">
        <footer>Footer</footer>
      </div>
    </body>
  </html>
```

The preceding example sets all the `div` child controls alignment to the left. If you note here, we didn't have to loop through all the `div` controls to set the background color and the style has been set on `all`. However, there are certain cases in which you might need to set different values based on the index of each element residing, and this can be done using the `each()` function on `div`. For example, the following script shows you the way of assigning an `index` value as an `html` string on each `div` control using the `each` function:

```
<script>
  $(document).ready(function () {
    $('div').each(function (index, element) {
      $(element).html(index);
    });
  });
</script>
```

Each function takes a function with the index and elements as a parameter. We can access each element using a dollar sign, as shown in the preceding code, and set the index as the content by calling the `html` method. The output will be similar to the following screenshot:

Let's have a look at another example that displays the content of each div control in a console window. Here, the each() function takes no parameters and each item in the loop can be accessed through the this keyword:

```
<!DOCTYPE html>
<html>
  <head>
    <script src="http://ajax.aspnetcdn.com/ajax/jQuery/
      jquery-1.12.0.min.js"></script>
    <script>
      $(document).ready(function () {
        $('div').each(function () {
          alert($(this).html());
        });
      });
    </script>
  </head>
  <body>
    <div id="headerDiv">
      <h1>Demo </h1>
    </div>
    <div id="mainDiv">
      <p>This is a demo of using jQuery for selecting
        elements</p>
    </div>
    <div id="footerDiv">
      <footer> Copyright - JavaScript for .Net Developers
        </footer>
    </div>
  </body>
</html>
```

The output will be as follows:

There are various other methods available, which you can refer to in the jQuery documentation. Therefore, with selectors, we can search any element in a faster and more efficient way.

Another example is selecting multiple elements using the tag name, as follows.

```html
<html>
  <head>
    <script src="http://ajax.aspnetcdn.com/ajax/jQuery/
      jquery-1.12.0.min.js"></script>
    <script>
      $(document).ready(function () {
        $('div, h1, p, footer').each(function () {
          console.log($(this).html());
        });
      });
    </script>
  </head>
  <body>
    <div id="headerDiv">
      <h1>Demo </h1>
    </div>
    <div id="mainDiv">
      <p>This is a demo of using jQuery for selecting
        elements</p>
    </div>
    <div id="footerDiv">
      <footer> Copyright - JavaScript for .Net Developers
        </footer>
    </div>
  </body>
</html>
```

The result will be as follows. Each item's inner `html` code will be logged in the console:

```
Index.html

        <h1>Demo </h1>

Index.html (8,17)
Demo
Index.html (8,17)

        <p>This is a demo of using jQuery for selecting elements</p>

Index.html (8,17)
This is a demo of using jQuery for selecting elements
Index.html (8,17)

        <footer> Copyright - JavaScript for .Net Developers </footer>

Index.html (8,17)
Copyright - JavaScript for .Net Developers
Index.html (8,17)
```

Selecting nodes by the class name

The class name selector is quite similar to the ID selector; the only difference is that it uses a period character, ., before the class name. It facilitates traversing all the DOM elements and finding the elements that have the same class name specified in the selector. It can be used as follows:

```
$(.classname);
```

Let's have a look at the following example that shows you the way of selecting elements based on the class name selector. In the following code snippet, we use the `bootstrap` theme and apply different classes to the buttons. With the help of the class name selector, we can select controls and update the class name. The following example will return two elements based on the selection criteria specified:

```
<!DOCTYPE html>
<html>
  <head>
    <link rel="stylesheet" type="text/css"
      href="Content/bootstrap.css" />
    <script src="http://ajax.aspnetcdn.com/ajax/jQuery/
      jquery-1.12.0.min.js"></script>
    <script>
```

```
    $(document).ready(function () {
      var lst = $('.btn-primary');
      alert(lst.length);
    });
  </script>
</head>
<body>
  <div class="container">
    <p></p>
    <button type="button" class="btn btn-primary
      active">Edit </button>
    <button type="button" class="btn btn-primary
      disabled">Save</button>
    <button type="button" class="btn btn-danger"
      value="Cancel">Cancel</button>
  </div>
</body>
</html>
```

Unlike accessing class names, we can restrict the search by specifying the tag name before the period and class name. You can use `$('button.active')` to search for all the buttons that are active.

Selecting by the attribute value

In certain cases, you may have to select the elements based on the attribute or its value. The jQuery library provides a very concise way of searching elements based not only on the attribute, but its value as well.

The syntax of using this selector is specifying the element name followed by a square bracket containing the attribute name and value, which is optional:

```
$(elementName[attributeName=value])
```

For example, the following code selects all the elements that have `type` as an attribute:

```
<!DOCTYPE html>
<html>
  <head>
    <link rel="stylesheet" type="text/css"
      href="Content/bootstrap.css" />
    <script src="http://ajax.aspnetcdn.com/ajax/jQuery/
      jquery-1.12.0.min.js"></script>
    <script>
      $(document).ready(function () {
```

```
            var lst = $('input[type]');
            console.log(lst.length);
        });
    </script>
  </head>
  <body>

    <div class="container">
      <p></p>
      <input type="text" value="hello world" />
      <input type="text" value="this is a demo" />
      <input type="button" value="Save" />
    </div>
  </body>
</html>
```

In this example, we have three input controls that have a `type` attribute. So, the result will be 3. In the same way, if you want to search for the elements that have a value equal to `hello world`, we can use the following code:

```
<script>
  $(document).ready(function () {
    var lst = $('input[value="hello world"]');
    alert(lst.length);
  });
</script>
```

One thing to note is that the attribute value is case sensitive, and so, with this expression, you should consider the exact case as the attribute value. However, there are other ways as well, that is, using ^ to search a value that contains, starts, or ends with particular text.

Let's have a look at the following example, `alert`, which is based on searching a value that starts with an expression:

```
<!DOCTYPE html>
<html>
  <head>
    <link rel="stylesheet" type="text/css"
      href="Content/bootstrap.css" />
    <script src="http://ajax.aspnetcdn.com/ajax/jQuery/
      jquery-1.12.0.min.js"></script>
    <script>
      $(document).ready(function () {
        var lst = $('input[value^="Pr"]');
        alert(lst.length);
```

```
    });
  </script>
</head>
<body>

  <div class="container">
    <p></p>
    <input type="text" value="Product 1" />
    <input type="text" value="This is a description" />
    <input type="button" value="Process" />
  </div>
</body>
</html>
```

On the other hand, we can also search a value that ends with a text using the $ symbol. Here is the code to search the text that ends with 1:

```
<script>
  $(document).ready(function () {
    var lst = $('input[value$="1"]');
    alert(lst.length);
  });
</script>
```

Finally, searching for a text that contains some text can be achieved using * and here is the code to run this example:

```
<script>
  $(document).ready(function () {
    var lst = $('input[value*="ro"]');
    alert(lst.length);
  });
</script>
```

Selecting input elements

Input controls in HTML have a wide range of different controls. Controls such as textarea, button, input, select, image, and radio are input controls. These controls are normally used in form-based applications. Therefore, jQuery specifically provides the selecting option to select input controls based on different criteria.

This selector starts with a dollar and the input keyword followed by the attribute and value:

```
$(':input[attributeName=value]');
```

However, in the previous section, we have already seen how to search any element with the attribute name and value. So, if we want to search all the input controls with the type that equals to text, it is achievable.

This selector is less performance-efficient in particular scenarios and searches out all the controls that are a part of the input group and finds the attribute with its value; whereas, this selector will only search in the input controls. When writing programs, using this method is a better choice if something is specifically targeting the input control properties.

Let's have a look at the following example in ASP.NET Core MVC 6 that applies the CSS properties once the document is loaded completely:

```
@model WebApplication.ViewModels.Book.BookViewModel
@{
  ViewData["Title"] = "View";
}
<script src="http://ajax.aspnetcdn.com/ajax/jQuery/
  jquery-1.12.0.min.js"></script>
<script>
  $(document).ready(function () {
    $(':input').each(function () {
      $(this).css({ 'color': 'darkred', 'background-color':
        'ivory', 'font-weight': 'bold' });    });
  });
</script>
<form asp-action="View" class="container">
  <br />
  <div class="form-horizontal">
    <div class="form-group">
      <label asp-for="Name" class="col-md-2
        control-label"></label>
      <div class="col-md-10">
        <input asp-for="Name" class="form-control" />
        <span asp-validation-for="Name"
          class="text-danger" />
      </div>
    </div>
    <div asp-validation-summary="ValidationSummary.ModelOnly"
      class="text-danger"></div>
    <div class="form-group">
      <label asp-for="Description" class="col-md-2
        control-label"></label>
      <div class="col-md-10">
```

```
        <textarea asp-for="Description"
          class="form-control" ></textarea>
        <span asp-validation-for="Description"
          class="text-danger" />
      </div>
    </div>
    <div class="form-group">
      <div class="col-md-offset-2 col-md-10">
        <input type="submit" value="Save" class="btn
          btn-primary" />
      </div>
    </div>
  </div>
</form>

<div>
  <a asp-action="Index">Back to List</a>
</div>
```

The output of the preceding code snippet is as follows:

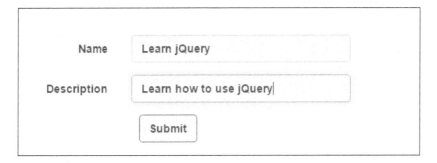

Selecting all the elements

The jQuery library provides you with a special selector that brings the collection of all the elements defined in a DOM. Instead of the standard controls, it also returns the elements, such as `<html>`, `<head>`, `<body>`, `<link>`, and `<script>`.

The syntax of getting all the elements is `$("*")` and the following example lists down all the elements of the DOM on the browser's console:

```
<!DOCTYPE html>
<html>
  <head>
    <link rel="stylesheet" type="text/css"
      href="Content/bootstrap.css" />
```

```
    <script src="http://ajax.aspnetcdn.com/ajax/jQuery/
      jquery-1.12.0.min.js"></script>
    <script>
      $(document).ready(function () {
        $("*").each(function () {
          console.log($(this).prop('nodeName'));
        });
      });
    </script>
  </head>
  <body>
    <form class="container">
      <div class="form-group">
        <label>Name</label>
        <input type="text" class="form-control"/>
      </div>
    </form>
  </body>
</html>
```

In the preceding code, we used the `prop` method that takes the property name to display element names. Here, in the `prop` method, we can use either `tagName` or `nodeName` to display name types. Finally, on the browser's console, a login page will be displayed, as follows:

```
Index.html
HTML
Index.html (9,17)
HEAD
Index.html (9,17)
LINK
Index.html (9,17)
SCRIPT
Index.html (9,17)
SCRIPT
Index.html (9,17)
BODY
Index.html (9,17)
FORM
Index.html (9,17)
DIV
Index.html (9,17)
LABEL
Index.html (9,17)
INPUT
Index.html (9,17)
```

Selecting the first and last child elements

The jQuery library provides special selectors to select all the first elements or last elements of their parent element.

The syntax of selecting the first child of all the parent elements is as follows:

```
$(elementName:first-child);
```

The syntax of selecting the last child of all the parent elements is as follows:

```
$(elementName:last-child);
```

The following example shows you the way of changing the font style of the first and last child of the select options:

```html
<!DOCTYPE html>
<html>
  <head>
    <link rel="stylesheet" type="text/css"
      href="Content/bootstrap.css" />
    <script src="http://ajax.aspnetcdn.com/ajax/jQuery/
      jquery-1.12.0.min.js"></script>
    <script>
      $(document).ready(function () {
        $('option:first-child').css('font-style',
          'italic');
        $('option:last-child').css('font-style',
          'italic');
        alert(lst.length);
      });
    </script>
  </head>
  <body>
    <select>
      <option>--select--</option>
      <option>USA</option>
      <option>UK</option>
      <option>Canada</option>
      <option>N/A</option>
    </select>
  </body>
</html>
```

The output will be as follows:

The contains selector in jQuery

The `contains` selector is used to find the text in the HTML container elements, such as `<div>` and `<p>`. This selector searches all the elements of a specific type and finds the text passed as a parameter to the `contains()` function. An example that displays the text of the `div` elements that contains the text is shown in the following code. This is case-sensitive, so make sure to supply the correct case when searching.

The following code will display an alert with the value, 2, as it finds two `div` elements containing the text, demo:

```
<!DOCTYPE html>
<html>
  <head>
    <link rel="stylesheet" type="text/css"
      href="Content/bootstrap.css" />
    <script src="http://ajax.aspnetcdn.com/ajax/jQuery/
      jquery-1.12.0.min.js"></script>
    <script>
      $(document).ready(function () {
        var lst = $('div:contains("demo")');
        alert(lst.length);
      });
    </script>

  </head>
  <body>
    <div>
      This is a sample demo for contains selector
    </div>
    <div>
      Demo of the selector
    </div>
    <div>
      Sample demo
    </div>
  </body>
</html>
```

Selecting the even and odd rows selectors

These types of selectors work on the rows in a table and are usually used to provide special formatting to the odd or even rows by changing the color of each odd row to make it look more like a grid. We can use this type of selector with the following syntax:

```
$('tr:even');
$('tr:odd');
```

Let's have a look at the following example to change all the row colors in a table to gray:

```html
<!DOCTYPE html>
<html>
  <head>
    <link rel="stylesheet" type="text/css"
      href="Content/bootstrap.css" />
    <script src="http://ajax.aspnetcdn.com/ajax/jQuery/
      jquery-1.12.0.min.js"></script>
    <script>
      $(document).ready(function () {
        $('tr:odd').css('background-color', 'grey');
      });
    </script>

  </head>
  <body>
    <table>
      <thead>
        <tr><th>Product
          Name</th><th>Description</th><th>Price</th>
            </tr>
      </thead>
      <tbody>
        <tr><td>Product 1</td><td>This is Product
          1</td><td>$100</td></tr>
        <tr><td>Product 2</td><td>This is Product
          2</td><td>$500</td></tr>
        <tr><td>Product 3</td><td>This is Product
          3</td><td>$330</td></tr>
        <tr><td>Product 4</td><td>This is Product
          4</td><td>$50</td></tr>
        <tr><td>Product 5</td><td>This is Product
          5</td><td>$1000</td></tr>
```

```
          <tr><td>Product 6</td><td>This is Product
            6</td><td>$110</td></tr>
          <tr><td>Product 7</td><td>This is Product
            7</td><td>$130</td></tr>
          <tr><td>Product 8</td><td>This is Product
            8</td><td>$160</td></tr>
          <tr><td>Product 9</td><td>This is Product
            9</td><td>$20</td></tr>
          <tr><td>Product 10</td><td>This is Product
            10</td><td>$200</td></tr>
        </tbody>
      </table>
    </body>
  </html>
```

Manipulating DOM

In this section, we will see some examples of manipulating DOM through the jQuery methods. The jQuery library provides an extensive library of performing different operations on the DOM elements. We can easily modify the element attributes, apply styles, and iterate through different nodes and properties. We have already seen some examples in the previous section, and this section will focus on the DOM manipulation specifically.

Modifying an element's properties

When working with a client-side scripting language, modifying an element's attributes and reading them is a vital task. In plain JavaScript, this can be achievable by writing a few lines of code; however, with jQuery, it can be achieved in a quicker and nicer way.

Modifying any properties of an element, which is to be selected, can be done with the various options listed in the previous section. Each property listed in the following table provides both the get and set options and takes parameter(s) when setting something and no parameters when reading it.

There are some common methods available to modify an element, namely html, value, and so on, in jQuery. For more methods, you can refer to http://api. jquery.com/category/manipulation/.

The get method	The set method	Description
.val()	.val('any value')	This method is used to read or write any value of the DOM element.

The get method	The set method	Description
`.html()`	`.html('any html string')`	This method is used to read or write any HTML content of the DOM element.
`.text()`	`.text('any text')`	This method is used to read or write the text content. HTML will not be returned in this method.
`.width()`	`.width('any value')`	This method is used to update the width of any element.
`.height()`	`.height('any value')`	This method is used to read or modify the height of any element.
`.attr()`	`.attr('attributename', 'value')`	This method is used to read or modify the value of a specific element's attribute.
`.prop()`	`.prop()`	This method is the same as `attr()` but more efficient when dealing with the `value` property that returns the current state. For example, the `attr()` checkbox provides the default value whereas `prop()` gives the current state, that is, `true` or `false`.
`.css('style-property')`	`.css({'style-property1': value1, 'style-property2': value2, 'style-propertyn':valueN }`	This method is used to set any property of style, such as the font size, font family, and width for a particular element.

Let's have a look at the following example, which uses the `html()`, `text()`, and `css()` modifiers and updates the p element with `html`, `text`, and `increaseFontSize`:

```
<!DOCTYPE html>
<html>
  <head>
    <link rel="stylesheet" type="text/css"
      href="Content/bootstrap.css" />
    <script src="http://ajax.aspnetcdn.com/ajax/jQuery/
      jquery-1.12.0.min.js"></script>
    <script>
      function updateHtml() {
        $('p').html($('#txtHtml').val());
      }
```

```
    function updateText() {
      $('p').text($('#txtText').val());
    }

    function increaseFontSize() {
      var fontSize = parseInt($('p').css('font-size'));
      var fontSize = fontSize + 1 +"px";
      $('p').css({'font-size': fontSize});
    }
  </script>
</head>
<body >
  <form class="form-control">
    <div class="form-group">
      <p>this is a book for JavaScript for .Net
        Developers</p>

    </div>
    <div class="form-group">
      Enter HTML: <input type="text" id="txtHtml" />
      <button onclick="updateHtml()">Update
        Html</button>
    </div>
    <div class="form-group">
      Update Text: <input type="text" id="txtText" />
      <button onclick="updateText()">Update
        Text</button>
    </div>
    <div class="form-group">
      <button onclick="increaseFontSize()">Increase Font
        Size</button>
    </div>
  </form>
</body>
</html>
```

The outcome of the preceding HTML code is as follows:

You can update HTML by clicking on the **Update Html** button and plain text by clicking on the **Update Text** button:

Finally, the font size can be increased by clicking on the **Increase Font Size** button:

Creating new elements

The jQuery library provides a smart way of creating new elements. Elements can be created using the same $() method and passing html as a parameter. Once the element is created, it cannot be shown until it is added to the DOM. There are various methods available that help append, insert after, or insert before any element, and so on. The following table shows the list of all the methods used to add new elements to the DOM:

The get method	Description
.append()	This method is used to insert the HTML content into the element from which it has been called
.appendTo()	This method is used to insert every element at the end from which it has been called
.before()	This method is used to insert the HTML content before the element from which it has been called

The get method	Description
.after()	This method is used to insert the HTML content after the element from which it has been called
.insertAfter()	This method is used to insert the HTML content after every element from which it has been called
.insertBefore()	This method is used to insert the HTML content before every element from which it has called
.prepend()	This method is used to insert the HTML content into the element at the starting position from which it has been called
.prepend()	This method is used to insert the HTML content from the starting position for each element from which it has been called

The following example creates a form with two fields, Name and Description, and a button to save these values:

```
<!DOCTYPE html>
<html>
  <head>
    <link rel="stylesheet" type="text/css"
      href="Content/bootstrap.css" />
    <script src="http://ajax.aspnetcdn.com/ajax/jQuery/
      jquery-1.12.0.min.js"></script>
    <script>
      $(document).ready(function () {
        var formControl = $("<form id='frm'
          class='container' ></form>");
        $('body').append(formControl);
        var nameDiv = $("<div class='form-group'><label
          id='lblName'>Enter Name: </label> <input
            type='text' id='txtName'
              class='form-control' /></div>");
        var descDiv = $("<div class='form-group'><label
          id='lblDesc'>Enter Description: </label>
            <textarea class='form-control' type='text'
              id='txtDescription' /></div>");
        var btnSave = $("<button class='btn
          btn-primary'>Save</button>")
        formControl.append(nameDiv);
        formControl.append(descDiv);
        formControl.append(btnSave);
      });
    </script>
  </head>
  <body>
  </body>
</html>
```

This code will give the following output:

Removing elements and attributes

With the option of using different methods to create and render elements in the DOM, jQuery also provides a few methods to remove elements from the DOM. The following table is a list of methods that we can use to remove a particular element, set of elements, or all child nodes:

Methods	Description
.empty()	This method removes the inner HTML code from the element
.detach()	This method removes the set of matched elements from the DOM
.remove()	This method removes the set of matched elements from the DOM
.removeAttr()	This method removes a particular attribute from the element
.removeClass()	This method removes a class from an element
.removeProp()	This method removes a property from an element

The difference between remove() and detach() is that remove removes the content from the DOM permanently; this means that if the element has specific events or data associated, these events or data will also be removed. However, detach just separates and isolates the element from the DOM and returns the content that you can save in some variable for later attachment:

```
@model WebApplication.ViewModels.Book.BookViewModel
@{
    ViewData["Title"] = "View";
}
```

```
<script src="http://ajax.aspnetcdn.com/ajax/jQuery/
  jquery-1.12.0.min.js"></script>
<script>
  var mainDivContent=undefined
  $(document).ready(function () {
    $('button').click(function () {
      if (mainDivContent) {
        mainDivContent.appendTo('#pageDiv');
        mainDivContent = null;
      } else {
        mainDivContent = $('#mainDiv').detach();
      }
    });
  });
</script>
<div id="pageDiv" class="container">
  <br />
  <div id="mainDiv" class="form-horizontal">
    <div class="form-group">
      <label asp-for="Name" class="col-md-2
        control-label"></label>
      <div class="col-md-10">
        <input asp-for="Name" class="form-control" />
      </div>
    </div>
  </div>
  <div class="form-group">
    <div class="col-md-offset-2 col-md-10">
      <button class="btn btn-primary">
        Detach/Attach</button>
    </div>
  </div>
</div>
```

On detaching, the output will be as follows:

On attaching, the output will be similar to the following screenshot:

Event handling in jQuery

The jQuery event model provides a better way of handling events on the DOM elements. Programmatically, if developers want to register any event of the user's action; for example, a button click event can be a cumbersome process when working with plain JavaScript. This is because different browsers have different implementations and the syntax is somehow different from one another. The jQuery library, on the other hand, provides a cleaner syntax and developers don't have to work on the cross browser issues.

Registering events in jQuery

There are many shortcuts available in jQuery to register events to different elements. The following table shows you a list of all these events with specific descriptions:

Events	Description
click()	This event is used when the mouse click occurs
.dblclick()	This event is used when the double-click occurs
.mousedown()	This event is used when any of the mouse buttons are pressed
.mouseup()	This event is used when any of the mouse buttons are released
.mouseenter()	This event is used when the mouse enters the section
.mouseleave()	This event is used when the mouse leaves the section
.keydown()	This event is used when a keyboard key is pressed
.keyup()	This event is used when the keyboard key is released
.focus()	This event is used when the element is focused
.blur()	This event is used when the element loses focus
.change()	This event is used when the item is changed

There are various other events, which you can check out at `http://api.jquery.com/category/events`.

Registering an event is quite simple using jQuery. First of all, the element has to be selected by choosing any of the selectors and then registering the events by calling a specific event handler; for example, the following code snippet will register the click event for the button:

```
$(document).ready(function({
  $('#button1').click(function(){
    console.log("button has been clicked");
  });
)};
```

After the preceding example code, register the `asp.net` button click event and call the `Contact` action of the controller of `Home` in ASP.NET:

```
<script src="http://ajax.aspnetcdn.com/ajax/jQuery/
  jquery-1.12.0.min.js"></script>
<script>
  var mainDivContent=undefined
  $(document).ready(function () {
    $('#btnSubmit').click(function () {
      window.location.href = '@Url.Action("Contact",
        "Home")';
    });
  });
</script>
<div id="pageDiv" class="container">
  <br />

  <div class="form-group">
    <div class="col-md-offset-2 col-md-10">
      <button id="btnSubmit" class="btn btn-primary">
        Submit</button>
    </div>
  </div>
</div>
```

In the preceding example, we used the HTML helper, `Url.Action`, through the Razor syntax, which generated the URL and set it to the `href` property of the window's current location. Now, click on the button shown in the following screenshot:

The following contact page will be displayed:

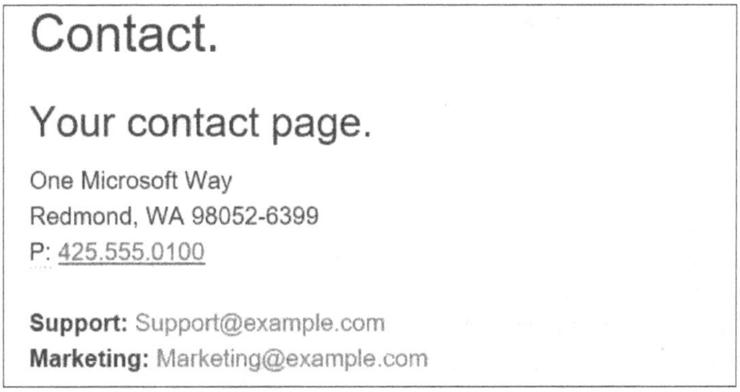

Contact.

Your contact page.

One Microsoft Way
Redmond, WA 98052-6399
P: 425.555.0100

Support: Support@example.com
Marketing: Marketing@example.com

Another example shown here will change the background color of all input controls to aliceblue when the control is focused and change back to white when it blurs:

```
@model WebApplication.ViewModels.Book.BookViewModel
@{
  ViewData["Title"] = "View";
}
<script src="http://ajax.aspnetcdn.com/ajax/jQuery/
  jquery-1.12.0.min.js"></script>
<script>
  var mainDivContent=undefined
  $(document).ready(function () {
    $('#btnSubmit').click(function () {
      window.location.href = '@Url.Action("Contact",
        "Home")';
    });

    $('input').each(function () {
      $(this).focus(function () {
        $(this).css('background-color', 'aliceblue');
      })
      $(this).blur(function () {
        $(this).css('background-color', 'white');

      });
    });
  });
</script>
<div id="pageDiv" class="container">
  <br />
```

```
<div id="mainDiv" class="form-horizontal">
  <div class="form-group">
    <label asp-for="Name" class="col-md-2
      control-label"></label>
    <div class="col-md-10">
      <input asp-for="Name"  class="form-control" />
    </div>
  </div>
  <div class="form-group">
    <label asp-for="Description" class="col-md-2
      control-label"></label>
    <div class="col-md-10">
      <input asp-for="Description" class="form-control"
        />
    </div>
  </div>
</div>
<div class="form-group">
  <div class="col-md-offset-2 col-md-10">
    <button id="btnSubmit" class="btn btn-primary">
      Submit</button>
  </div>
</div>
</div>
```

Binding events using on and off

Apart from registering events directly by calling the event handler, we can also register them using on and off. These events register and deregister the event for specific elements.

Here is a simple example of binding a click event to a button using on:

```
$(document).ready(function () {
  $('#btnSubmit').on('click', function () {
    window.location.href = '@Url.Action("Contact", "Home")';
  });
});
```

This is a very useful technique and can be used in certain conditions where you want to deregister any event. For example, business applications are mostly related to form handling, and forms can be submitted using some button that posts the request to some server. In certain conditions, we have to restrict the user to submit multiple times until the first request has been processed. To handle this problem, we can use the `on()` and `off()` events to register and deregister them when the user clicks the first time. Here is an example that deregisters the button-click event when it is clicked for the first time:

```
<script src="http://ajax.aspnetcdn.com/ajax/jQuery/
  jquery-1.12.0.min.js"></script>
<script>
  $(document).ready(function () {
    $('#btnSubmit').on('click', function () {
      $('#btnSubmit').off('click');
    });
  });
</script>
```

The `preventDefault()` event is just the cancel event that we used to have in .NET. This event is used to cancel the event from execution. It can be used as follows:

```
<script src="http://ajax.aspnetcdn.com/ajax/jQuery/
  jquery-1.12.0.min.js"></script>
<script>
  $(document).ready(function () {
    $('#btnSubmit').on('click', function (event) {
      event.preventDefault();
    });
  });
</script>
```

The `on()` method is equivalent to the `delegate()` method used with the previous version of jQuery. Since jQuery 1.7, `delegate()` has been replaced with `on()`.

There is one more overloaded method, `on`, which takes four parameters:

```
$(element).on(events, selector, data, handler);
```

Here, `element` is the control name, `events` is the event that you want to register, and `selector` is a new thing, which can be the child element of the parent control. For example, for a table element selector, it could be `td`; and on each click event of `td`, we can do something as follows:

```
@model IEnumerable<WebApplication.ViewModels.Book.BookViewModel>
<script src="http://ajax.aspnetcdn.com/ajax/jQuery/
  jquery-1.12.0.min.js"></script>
```

```
<script>
  $(document).ready(function () {
    $('table').on('click','tr', null, function() {
      $(this).css('background-color', 'aliceblue');
    });
  });
</script>

<p>
  <a asp-action="Create">Create New</a>
</p>
<table class="table">
  <tr>
    <th>
      @Html.DisplayNameFor(model => model.Description)
    </th>
    <th>
      @Html.DisplayNameFor(model => model.Name)
    </th>
    <th></th>
  </tr>

  @foreach (var item in Model) {
    <tr>
      <td>
        @Html.DisplayFor(modelItem => item.Description)
      </td>
      <td>
        @Html.DisplayFor(modelItem => item.Name)
      </td>
      <td>
        <a asp-action="Edit"
          asp-route-id="@item.Id">Edit</a> |
        <a asp-action="Details"
          asp-route-id="@item.Id">Details</a> |
        <a asp-action="Delete"
          asp-route-id="@item.Id">Delete</a>
      </td>
    </tr>
  }
</table>
```

The preceding code snippet output would be similar to the following screenshot. When the user clicks on any row, the background color will be changed to Alice blue:

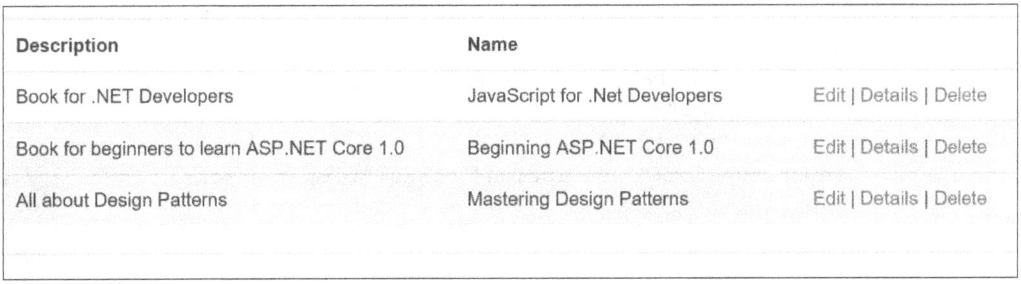

Description	Name	
Book for .NET Developers	JavaScript for .Net Developers	Edit | Details | Delete
Book for beginners to learn ASP.NET Core 1.0	Beginning ASP.NET Core 1.0	Edit | Details | Delete
All about Design Patterns	Mastering Design Patterns	Edit | Details | Delete

Using the hover events

We can use the hover events when the mouse enters or exits a particular element. It can be used by calling the hover() method on any element of the DOM. The syntax of calling this method is as follows:

```
$(selector).hover(mouseEnterHandler, mouseExitHandler);
```

The following example changes the input text control's border color when the mouse enters or exits:

```
@{
    ViewData["Title"] = "View";
}
<script src="http://ajax.aspnetcdn.com/ajax/jQuery/
    jquery-1.12.0.min.js"></script>
<02>
    $(document).ready(function () {
        $("input[type = 'text']").hover(function () {
            $(this).css('border-color', 'red');
        },
        function () {
            $(this).css('border-color', 'black');
        }
    });
</script>
<div id="pageDiv" class="container">
    <br />

<div id="mainDiv" class="form-horizontal">
    <div class="form-group">
        <label asp-for="Name" class="col-md-2
            control-label"></label>
```

```
    <div class="col-md-10">
      <input asp-for="Name" class="form-control" />
    </div>
  </div>
  <div class="form-group">
    <label asp-for="Description" class="col-md-2
      control-label"></label>
    <div class="col-md-10">
      <input asp-for="Description" class="form-control"
        />
    </div>
  </div>
</div>
<div class="form-group">
  <div class="col-md-offset-2 col-md-10">
    <button id="btnSubmit" class="btn btn-primary">
    Submit</button>
  </div>
</div>
</div>
```

The following screenshot will be the output of the preceding code snippet. This will change the border color of the input text control to red when the mouse enters and black when it exits:

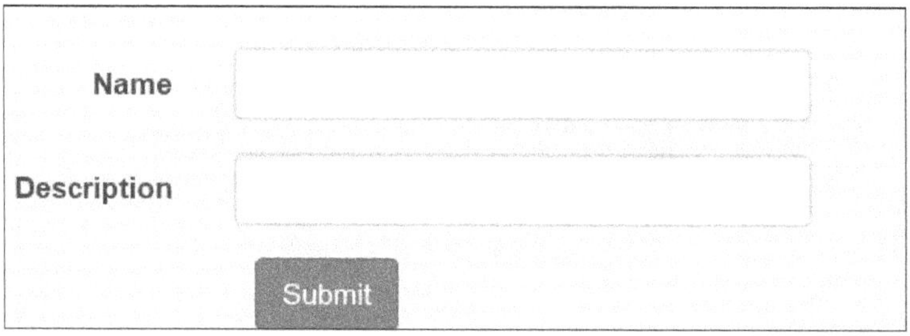

Name	
Description	
	Submit

Summary

In this chapter, you learned about jQuery basics and how to use them in web applications, especially in ASP.NET core 1.0. This is a very powerful library. It eliminates cross-browser issues and provides consistent behavior across all browsers. This library provides simple and easy methods to select elements, modify attributes, attach events, and perform complex operations by writing code in a cleaner and more precise manner. In the next chapter, we will look into the various techniques of doing Ajax requests using jQuery and plain JavaScript to perform server-side operations.

4
Ajax Techniques

One of the core characteristics of making responsive web applications is Ajax. Traditionally, in server-side postbacks, whenever a user performs any action, the information supplied in the form is sent back to the server and the same page loads again, containing all the images, CSS, and JavaScript files loaded again on the client side. This approach is quite heavy in terms of the size of the request and response being sent from the client and server. Thus, the application becomes less responsive and the user has to wait for the page to refresh every time any action is taken. In this chapter, we will discuss how to simplify the whole process and avoid heavy server-side postbacks through Ajax.

Introducing Ajax

Ajax stands for **Asynchronous JavaScript and XML**; it creates asynchronous requests on server without sending and rendering the whole page again on client side, whereas it only sends a bit of information that needs to be sent out to the server and receives response in a specific format to update a specific section or the elements of DOM through JavaScript. This allows developers to develop responsive web applications and dynamically update the content of the page without reloading it every time for a particular action. For example, in a master-child page relationship, the child content is dependent on the parent item selection; and with a classic approach, every time the parent item is selected, the page is being posted back to the server side, where the server does some backend job to fill the child section and returns the HTML code, which is then rendered on the client side. Through Ajax, this can be achieved by making an asynchronous request to send the selected information and update the selected parts of the page content.

How Ajax works

Ajax uses the **XMLHttpRequest** (**XHR**) object to invoke the server-side methods asynchronously. XHR is developed by Microsoft, and it was initially provided with Internet Explorer 5. It was used initially by calling an `ActionXObject` instance to create an instance; however, with modern versions, every browser supports initializing the XHR object through the `XMLHttpRequest` object.

The following diagram shows the architectural view of how Ajax works:

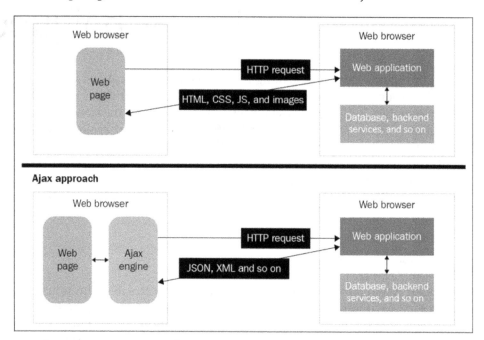

Traditionally, when any action is taken from the client side, the entire data is sent back to the server and is loaded again on the client side once the response is received. Instead of updating the data, which needs to be updated, including all the static files such as CSS, JavaScript, and images, it is loaded from the server again and rendered on the client side, unless some caching mechanism is implemented. With Ajax, we send the data in a JSON string or XML and get the response in a JSON, XML, HTML, or any other format, depending on the server. We can also use request header, such as `Accept`, when sending the request, so the server knows what the client is accepting; and based on the formatter, it can serialize the data into a particular format. In ASP.NET MVC 6, there are two formatters implemented by default for JSON and XML, which send the data, based on the request `Accept` header and serialize the object accordingly. Custom formatters can also be implemented on a server level to handle specific scenarios.

Ajax requests using the classic XHR object

All browsers, including Internet Explorer, Chrome, Firefox, and Safari, provide this object that can be used from JavaScript to execute the Ajax requests.

In JavaScript, we can initialize the XMLHttpRequest object as follows:

```
var xhr = new XMLHttpRequest();
```

Every request could be a GET or POST request. Once the response is received from server, a few properties get populated and event handlers are invoked, which can be configured for the XHR object when making the Ajax request.

Let's look into the details of what methods, properties, and events the XHR object provides.

XHR methods

The XHR object provides various methods as follows, but the two most important methods to initiate an Ajaxified request are open() and send():

- **Sending request**:

  Request can either be GET or POST. When making any request, will we first have to invoke the open method and specify the HTTP method, such as GET or POST, and the URL of the server. Rest of the parameters, such as async bit, user, and password, are optional.

  The signature of the open method is as follows:

  ```
  void Open(

    DOMString method,
    DOMString URL,
    optional boolean async,
    optional DOMString user?,
    optional DOMString password

  );
  ```

  The send method is used to send the request to the server. This is the actual method, which sends the request to the server and it accepts the data in various formats.

The following table shows the overloaded methods available for the send method:

Methods	Description
`void send()`	This method is used when making the GET requests
`void send (DOMString? Data)`	This method is used when passing the data in string
`void send(Document data)`	This method is used when passing the document data
`void send(Blob data)`	This method is used to pass the blob data or data in binary
`void send(FormData data)`	This method is used to pass the whole form

- **Aborting request**:

  There are certain cases in which developers might need to abort the current request. This can be done by calling the `abort()` function of the XHR object:

  ```
  var xhr = new XMLHttpRequest();
  xhr.abort();
  ```

- **Setting request headers**:

  XHR provides several techniques of making an Ajax request. This means that there are cases when we need to send data in the JSON, XML, or some custom format, based on the server implementation. For example, when working with ASP.NET MVC 6, there are two default formatters implemented, JSON and XML, and if you want to implement your own custom formatter, this is also possible. When sending data in a specific format, we need to tell the format to the server through request headers. This helps the server in identifying the formatter that has to be loaded to serialize the response and process the request.

  The following table shows the default headers that can be supplied with the Ajax request:

Headers	Description
`Cookie`	This header specifies any cookie set in the client side
`Host`	This header specifies the domain name of the page
`Connection`	This header specifies the type of connection
`Accept`	This header specifies the content type that the client can handle
`Accept-charset`	This header specifies the character set that the client can display

Headers	Description
Accept-encoding	This header specifies the encodings that client can handle
Accept-language	This header specifies the preferred natural languages accepted as a response
User-Agent	This header specifies a user agent string
Referer	This header specifies the URL of the page

Through the XHR object, we can set the request headers through the setRequestHeader() function, as shown in the following code:

```
var xhr= new XMLHttpRequest();
xhr.setRequestHeader('Content-Type', 'application/json');
```

- **Getting response headers**:

When the response is returned by the server, we can read the response headers by using the following two methods:

```
var xhr= new XMLHttpRequest();
function callback(){
  var arrHeaders = xhr.getAllResponseHeaders();
  //or
  var contentType =
    xhr.getResponseHeader('Content-Type');
}
```

The getAllResponseHeaders() function returns the list of all the response headers, whereas the getResponseHeader() function accepts the header name and returns the value of the header name supplied.

XHR events

The most useful event handler in the XHR object, which is invoked when the value of the readystate property is changed, is the onreadystatechange event. On initiating request, we can associate the function with this event handler and read the response:

```
var xhr= new XMLHttpRequest();
xhr.onreadystatechange = callback;

function callback(){
  //do something
}
```

Another core event handler is `ontimeout`, which can be used in conditions to handle the request timed-out scenario. When initiating an XHR request, there is a `timeout` property through which the timeout can be set in milliseconds, and if the request exceeds the timed-out value, the `ontimeout` event handler will be invoked. The example, where timeout is set to 5,000 milliseconds, if it exceeds the `timeout` property, the `timeout` handler function will be invoked, as shown here:

```
var xhr = new XMLHttpRequest();
xhr.timeout = 5000;
xhr.ontimeout = timeouthandler;
function timeouthandler(){
   //do something
}
```

XHR properties

The list of properties available for the `XMLHttpRequest` object is as follows:

- **GET request state**:

  This property returns the status information about the response. It is normally used to take action based on the request status:

  ```
  var xhr=new XMLHttpRequest();
  xhr.readystate;
  ```

  The list of statuses with their meaning available for the `readystate` property is given in the following table:

Status value	State	Description
0	UNSENT	In this state, the XMLHttpRequest object is created, but the open() method is not called
1	OPENED	In this state, the open method is called
2	HEADERS_RECEIVED	This state occurs once send() is called and headers are received
3	LOADING	This state occurs when the response is downloading
4	DONE	This state occurs when the response is complete

- **Get response data**:

  Response can be retrieved by calling the `response` or `responseText` property. The difference between these properties is that the `responseText` property returns the response as a string, whereas the `response` property returns the response as a `response` object. The `response` object can be a document, blob, or JavaScript object:

  ```
  var xhr= new XMLHttpRequest();
  xhr.response;
  //or
  xhr.responseText;
  ```

- **Get response status**:

  Response status can be retrieved by calling the `status` or `statusText` property. The difference between these properties is that the `status` property returns the numerical value, for example, `200`, if the request is successfully processed by server, whereas the `statusText` property includes the complete text, such as `200 OK` and so on:

  ```
  var xhr= new XMLHttpRequest();
  xhr.status;
  or
  xhr.statusText;
  ```

Let's take a look at the following example that makes the form POST request using the XHR object in ASP.NET MVC 6. The following form has two fields, **Name** and **Description**:

Here is the code snippet that sends the request to server side using the XHR object. This example sends the data in JSON:

```
@model WebApplication.ViewModels.Book.BookViewModel
@{
  ViewData["Title"] = "View";
}
<script>
  var xhr = null;
  function submit() {
    xhr = new XMLHttpRequest();
    xhr.open("POST", '/Book/SaveData');
    var name = document.getElementById("Name").value;
    var description =
      document.getElementById("Description").value;
    var data =
    {
      "Name": name,
      "Description": description
    };
    xhr.setRequestHeader('Content-Type', 'application/json;
      charset=utf-8');
    xhr.onreadystatechange = callback;
    xhr.send(JSON.stringify(data));
  }

  function callback() {
    if (xhr.readyState == 4) {
      var msg = xhr.responseText;r
      document.getElementById("msg").innerHTML = msg;
      document.getElementById("msgDiv").style.display =
        'block';
    }
  }
</script>

<form asp-action="SaveData" id="myForm">
  <p> </p>
  <div id="msgDiv" style="display:none" class="alert
    alert-success">
    <a href="#" class="close" data-dismiss="alert"
      aria-label="close">&times;</a>
    <strong>Success!</strong> <label id="msg"></label>
  </div>
  <div id="pageDiv" class="container">
```

```
<br />
<div id="mainDiv" class="form-horizontal">
  <div class="form-group">
    <label asp-for="Name" class="col-md-2
      control-label"></label>
    <div class="col-md-10">
      <input asp-for="Name" class="form-control" />
    </div>
  </div>
  <div class="form-group">
    <label asp-for="Description"  class="col-md-2
      control-label"></label>
    <div class="col-md-10">
      <textarea asp-for="Description"
        class="form-control" ></textarea>
    </div>
  </div>
</div>
<div class="form-group">
  <div class="col-md-offset-2 col-md-10">
    <button id="btnSubmit" onclick="submit()"
      type="submit" class="btn btn-primary">
        Submit</button>
  </div>
</div>
</div>
</form>
```

In ASP.NET Core, for JSON and XML, we have to explicitly annotate the complex type with the [FromBody] attribute. This is because MVC 6 first searches for the values in the query string irrespective of its type, whether a complex type or a primitive type. For the JSON and XML data, we need to explicitly annotate the method's parameter with the [FromBody] attribute so that the data can be easily bound without any issue:

```
public IActionResult SaveData([FromBody]BookViewModel
  bookViewModel)
{
  return Content("Data saved successfully");
}
```

In the preceding code snippet, we read the form values through document.getElementById and then made a JSON string to pass the form data in a JSON format.

The output will be as follows:

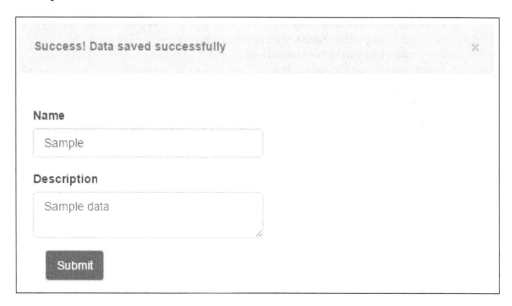

However, there is a library provided by Google, which serializes the form data by calling the `serialize()` function. The only difference is setting the request header `'Content-Type'` to `'application/x-www-form-urlencoded'`, and adding the following script file:

```
<script
  src=http://form-serialize.googlecode.com/svn/trunk/
    serialize-0.2.min.js />
```

The following code is the revised version of the `submit` function, which serializes the form data through the `serialize()` function and sends the data as form-encoded values:

```
function submit() {
  xhr = new XMLHttpRequest();
  xhr.open('POST', '/Book/SaveData');
  xhr.setRequestHeader('Content-Type',
    'application/x-www-form-urlencoded');
  var html = serialize(document.forms[0]);
  xhr.onreadystatechange = callback;
  xhr.send(html);
}
```

For the form-encoded values, we will remove the [FromBody] attribute. This is because the form-encoded values are sent as the name value pairs in the query string:

```
public IActionResult SaveData(BookViewModel bookViewModel)
{
   return Content("Data saved successfully");
}
```

In the previous versions of ASP.NET Web API, if the action method of Web API controller contains a complex type, Web API framework automatically bound the values from the request body. Whereas with ASP.NET Core, the Web API and MVC have become one unified framework, and the model binding is not equivalent to what we has in the previous versions of Web API.

In the preceding examples, we saw how easily we can make a POST request and send data in JSON and form-encoded values. Now, let's see another example in which we will load the partial view based on the JSON response sent from server.

The following screenshot is of the ASP.NET page that contains a button to load the list of books in a table:

Here is the code snippet for the main page:

```
@model WebApplication.ViewModels.Book.BookViewModel
@{
   ViewData["Title"] = "Books";
}
<script>
   var xhr = null;
   function loadData() {
      xhr = new XMLHttpRequest();
      xhr.open('GET', '/Book/Books',true);
      xhr.onreadystatechange = callback;
      xhr.send();
   }
```

```
    function callback() {
      if (xhr.readyState == 4) {
        var msg = xhr.responseText;
        document.getElementById("booksDiv").innerHTML = msg;
      }
    }
  }
</script>
<div class="container">
  <button id="btnLoad" onclick="loadData()" type="submit"
    class="btn btn-primary">Load</button>
  <hr />
  <div id="booksDiv">
  </div>
</div>
```

The following is the partial view that displays the list of books in a table:

```
@{
  Layout = null;
}
@model IEnumerable<WebApplication.ViewModels.Book.BookViewModel>
<script src="http://ajax.aspnetcdn.com/ajax/jQuery/
  jquery-1.12.0.min.js"></script>
<script>
  $(document).ready(function () {
    $('table').on('click','tr', null, function() {
      $(this).css('background-color', 'aliceblue');
    });
  });
</script>

<p>
  <a asp-action="Create">Create New</a>
</p>
<table class="table">
  <tr>
    <th>
      @Html.DisplayNameFor(model => model.Description)
    </th>
    <th>
      @Html.DisplayNameFor(model => model.Name)
    </th>
    <th></th>
  </tr>
```

```
@foreach (var item in Model) {
  <tr>
    <td>
      @Html.DisplayFor(modelItem => item.Description)
    </td>
    <td>
      @Html.DisplayFor(modelItem => item.Name)
    </td>
    <td>
      <a asp-action="Edit" asp-route-id="@item.Id">Edit</a>
        |
      <a asp-action="Details"
        asp-route-id="@item.Id">Details</a> |
      <a asp-action="Delete"
        asp-route-id="@item.Id">Delete</a>
    </td>
  </tr>
}
</table>
```

Here is the code snippet of the ASP.NET MVC Books controller that contains the Books action method that returns a list of books:

```
public class BookController : Controller
{
  // GET: /<controller>/
  public IActionResult Index()
  {
    return View();
  }


  public IActionResult Books()
  {
    List<BookViewModel> books = new List<BookViewModel>();
    books.Add(new BookViewModel { Id = 1, Name = "JavaScript
      for .Net Developers", Description = "Book for .NET
        Developers" });
    books.Add(new BookViewModel { Id = 1, Name = "Beginning
      ASP.NET Core 1.0", Description = "Book for beginners
        to learn ASP.NET Core 1.0" });
    books.Add(new BookViewModel { Id = 1, Name = "Mastering
      Design Patterns", Description = "All about Design
        Patterns" });
    return View(books);
  }
```

```
public IActionResult Create()
{
    return View();
}
}
```

So, with this in place, when the user clicks on the `Load` button, the request will be made to the server and the ASP.NET MVC controller `Books` action method will be invoked, which returns `View` that renders the partial view that will be rendered inside the `booksDiv` element on the main page:

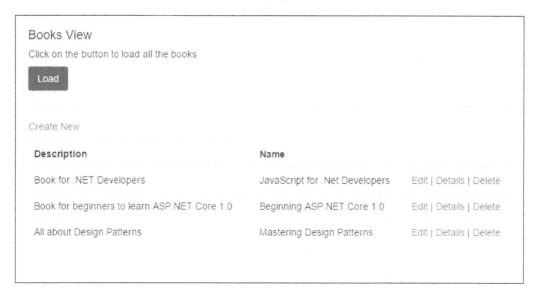

Making an Ajax request using jQuery

In the previous sections, we discussed how to send an Ajax request using a plain `XMLHttpRequest` object, which is available in all browsers. In this section, we will see what jQuery offers in making the Ajax request and how to use the HTTP GET and POST requests through the jQuery object.

jQuery.ajax()

This method is used to make both GET and POST asynchronous requests. The following code is the signature of this method, which takes two parameters: URL and `options`. The URL parameter is the actual server URL, whereas `options` takes the configure request headers and other properties in a JSON representation:

```
$.([URL],[options]);
$.( [options]);
```

The following example shows how to make an asynchronous request on the MVC controller and displays an alert on successful response being returned from server:

```
<script src="http://ajax.aspnetcdn.com/ajax/jQuery/
  jquery-1.12.0.min.js"></script>
<script>
  $(document).ready(function () {
    $.ajax('/Book/Books', {
      success: function (data) {
        $('#booksDiv').html(data);
      },
      error: function (data) {
        $('#booksDiv').html(data);
      }
    });
  });
</script>
```

The `Books` action method returns the ASP.NET MVC view, which passes the list of books that will be populated inside the `booksDiv` DOM element:

Create New

Description	Name	
Book for .NET Developers	JavaScript for .Net Developers	Edit | Details | Delete
Book for beginners to learn ASP.NET Core 1.0	Beginning ASP.NET Core 1.0	Edit | Details | Delete
All about Design Patterns	Mastering Design Patterns	Edit | Details | Delete

Ajax properties

The following table shows some core properties that you can specify to configure the Ajax request:

Name	Type	Description
accepts	PlainObject	This property tells the server about the type of response that the client will accept.
async	Boolean	By default, this property is true (for asynchronous request), but it can be set to false (synchronous).
cache	Boolean	If this property is set to false, force requested pages will not be cached by the browser.

Name	Type	Description
contents	PlainObject	This property is used to specify regular expressions for parsing response.
contentType	String or Boolean	This property tells the server about the type of data passed in the request. The default value is application/x-www-form-urlencoded; charset=UTF-8.
crossDomain	Boolean	This property is set to true if you want to force the cross-domain request.
data	PlainObject, String, or Array	This property can be used to pass the data in JSON, XML, or any other format.
dataType	String	This property specifies the type of data expecting from server. Some core datatypes are XML, JSON, script, and HTML.

Pre-filtering Ajax requests

This is a great feature to filter the existing request options and configuration attributes before they are sent out. It provides two overloaded methods: one that takes a function that injects the options, originalOptions, and jqXHR objects, and the other that takes a string where you can filter out the configuration attributes for specific requests followed with the function accepting parameters as options, originalOptions, and jqXHR. The following code is the signature of both overloaded methods:

```
$.ajaxPrefilter(function(options, originalOptions, jqXHR){
    //Modify options, originalOptions and store jqXHR
}
$.ajaxPrefilter('dataType', function(options, originalOptions,
    jqXHR){
    //Modify options, originalOptions and store jqXHR
}
```

The objects in the preceding code are explained as follows:

- options: These objects are the same as the request options supplied in the Ajax request, but they can be overridden and filtered accordingly.

- originalOptions: These objects provide the actual options being supplied in the Ajax request. They can be used to refer and cannot be modified. Any change in the configuration can be done using the options object.

- jqXHR: This object is equivalent to the XMLHttpRequest object in jQuery.

Let's take a look at the following example, which appends the `fromAjax` parameter to tell the MVC controller that the request is executed from JavaScript:

```
<script>
  $(document).ready(function () {

    $.ajaxPrefilter(function (options, originalOptions, jqXHR)
      {
      options.url += ((options.url.indexOf('?') < 0) ? '?' :
        '&')+ 'fromAjax=true';
    });

    $.ajax('/Book/Books', {
      success: function (data) {
        $('#booksDiv').html(data);
      },
      error: function (data) {
        $('#booksDiv').html(data);
      }
    });
  });
</script>
```

The following code is the controller action method that returns the list of books if the request is an Ajax request:

```
public IActionResult Books(bool fromAjax)
{
  if (fromAjax)
  {
    List<BookViewModel> books = new List<BookViewModel>();
    books.Add(new BookViewModel { Id = 1, Name = "JavaScript
      for .Net Developers", Description = "Book for .NET
        Developers" });
    books.Add(new BookViewModel { Id = 1, Name = "Beginning
      ASP.NET Core 1.0", Description = "Book for beginners
        to learn ASP.NET Core 1.0" });
    books.Add(new BookViewModel { Id = 1, Name = "Mastering
      Design Patterns", Description = "All about Design
        Patterns" });
    return View(books);
  }
  return Content("Request to this method is only allowed from
    Ajax");
}
```

There are various properties for options available, which you can refer at `http://api.jquery.com`.

Setting default values for all future Ajax requests

With the `$.ajax.setup` function, we can set the configuration values for all the future requests to be made through the `$.ajax()` or `$.get()` function. This can be used to set the default settings before calling the `$.ajax()` function, and the `ajax` function will pick the settings defined in the `$.ajaxSetup()` function.

The following is the signature to call `$.ajax.setup`:

```
$.ajaxSetup({name:value, name:value, name:value, …});
```

The following example sets the default URL for the `ajax` request being made through the `$.ajax` function:

```
<script>
  $(document).ready(function () {

    $.ajaxSetup({ url: "/Book/Books"});

    $.ajax({
      success: function (data) {
        $('#booksDiv').html(data);
      },
      error: function (data) {
        $('#booksDiv').html(data);
      }
    });
  });
</script>
```

Loading data through the get functions in jQuery

The jQuery library provides different functions for retrieving data from server. The function, such as `$.get()`, can be used to load the data by using the HTTP GET request, whereas `$.getJSON()` is specifically used to load the JSON-encoded data, and `$.getScript()` is used to load and execute a JavaScript from the server.

Using jQuery.get()

The `$.get()` function is a shorthand function of `$.ajax()` and only allows the GET request. It abstracts most of the configuration values to default values. Similar to the `$.ajax()` function, it returns the data to the `callback` function, but does not provide an error callback. So, if any error occurred during the request processing, it cannot be tracked.

It takes four parameters, URL, data, callback, and type. Where URL is the address to which the request is sent, data that takes a string that is sent to the server when the request is made, callback refers to the function which is executed when the request is succeeded and type denotes the type of data expected from the server like XML, JSON and so on.

The following is the signature of the $.get() function:

```
$.get('URL',data, callback, type);
```

Here is the example that loads the books, which contain a net string in its title:

```
<script>
  $(document).ready(function () {

    $.get('/Book/Books', {filter : "net"}, function (data) {
        $('#booksDiv').html(data);
      }
    );

  });
</script>
```

Using jQuery.getJSON()

The jQuery.getJSON() function is used to load JSON from the server. It can be used by calling the $.getJSON() function:

```
$.getJSON('URL', {name:value, name:value, name:value,…});
```

The following is the example that loads the JSON by calling an action method, which returns the JSON response and displays the book title in the booksDiv element:

```
<script>
  $(document).ready(function () {

    $.getJSON('/Book/Books', function (data) {
      $.each(data, function (index, field) {
        $('#booksDiv').append(field.Name + "<br/> ");
      });
    }
  );
</script>
```

The `Action` method returns the JSON response as follows:

```
public IActionResult Books()
{
    List<BookViewModel> books = new List<BookViewModel>();
    books.Add(new BookViewModel { Id = 1, Name = "JavaScript for
        .Net Developers", Description = "Book for .NET Developers"
        }
    books.Add(new BookViewModel { Id = 1, Name = "Beginning
        ASP.NET Core 1.0", Description = "Book for beginners to
            learn ASP.NET Core 1.0" });
    books.Add(new BookViewModel { Id = 1, Name = "Mastering Design
        Patterns", Description = "All about Design Patterns" });
    return Json(books);

}
```

On the page, the book titles will be rendered as shown in the following screenshot:

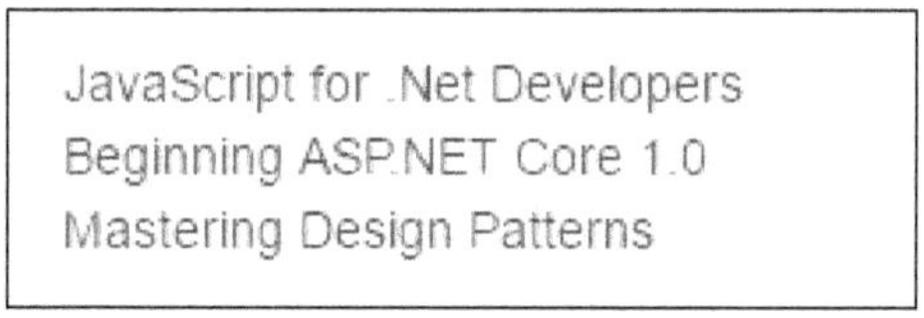

```
JavaScript for .Net Developers
Beginning ASP.NET Core 1.0
Mastering Design Patterns
```

Using jQuery.getScript()

The `jQuery.getScript()` function is a shorthand of `$.ajax()`, and it is specifically designed to load the script from the server. The following is the signature of the `$.getScript()` function:

```
$.getScript(url, callback);
```

The following example loads the custom `.js` file once the document is loaded:

```
<script>
    $(document).ready(function () {

    $.getScript("/wwwroot/js/custom.js");
</script>
```

Posting data to server using the post function

Similar to the `$.get()` function, jQuery also provides a `$.post()` function, which is a shorthand of `$.ajax()`, and is specifically designed to only make the HTTP POST requests.

Here is the signature of the $.post() function:

```
$.post(url, data, callback, type);
```

The following example submits the form data using the $.post() function:

```
<script>

  function submit() {
    $.post('/Book/SaveData', $("form").serialize(), function
      (data) {
      alert("form submitted");

    });
  }
</script>
```

The following is the code snippet of the Book controller's SaveData action method that takes the object and returns the response as a string:

```
public IActionResult SaveData(BookViewModel bookViewModel)
{
  //call some service to save data
  return Content("Data saved successfully")
}
```

Similarly, we can pass data in JSON by specifying the type as json:

```
<script>
  function submit() {
    $.post('/Book/SaveData', {Name:"Design Patterns",
      Description: "All about design patterns"}, function
        (data) {
    },'json' );
  }
</script>
```

Ajax events

Ajax events are categorized into local and global events. Local events can be declared when making an Ajax request using the $.ajax function. Events such as success and error are termed as local events, whereas global events work with every Ajax request executed within the page.

Local events

The following is the list of local events, and it is specifically related to the $.ajax() function. Other shorthand functions, such as $.get() and $.post(), do not have these methods available, as each of them have specific values to pass the parameters and configuration attributes:

- beforeSend: This event is triggered before the ajax request is being made.
- success: This event occurs when the successful response is being made from the server.
- error: This event occurs when an error is occurred during the ajax request.
- complete: This event occurs when the request is completed. It does not check whether an error has occurred or the response was successful and executed when the request is completed.

Global events

The following is the list of global events, and it works with all other shorthand functions as well, such as $.post(), $.get(), and $.getJSON:

- ajaxStart: This event is used when there is no ajax request in the pipeline and the first ajax request is starting up
- ajaxSend: This event is used when an ajax request is sent to the server
- ajaxSuccess: This event is used when any of the successful response returns from the server
- ajaxError: When an error occurs for any ajax request, this event is fired
- ajaxComplete: This event is used when any of the ajax request is completed

The following code is a simple example of ASP.NET that calls the action method, Books, of BookController, which returns the list of books and triggers global and local events:

```
@model WebApplication.ViewModels.Book.BookViewModel
@{
   ViewData["Title"] = "Books";
}
<script src="http://ajax.aspnetcdn.com/ajax/jQuery/
   jquery-1.12.0.min.js"></script>
<script>

  $(document).ready(function () {

    $(document).ajaxComplete(function (e) {
      alert("Ajax request completed");
```

```
  }).ajaxSend(function () {
    alert("Ajax request sending");
  }).ajaxSend(function () {
    alert("Ajax request sent to server");
  }).ajaxStop(function () {
    alert("Ajax request stopped");
  }).ajaxError(function () {
    alert("Some error occurred in Ajax request");
  }).ajaxSuccess(function () {
    alert("Ajax request was successful");
  })
  $('#btnLoad').click(function(){
    $.ajax('/Book/Books', {
      success: function (data) {
        $('#booksDiv').html(data);
      },
      error: function (data) {
        $('#booksDiv').html(data);
      }
    });

  });

});
</script>
<div class="container">
  <br />
  <h4>Books View</h4>
  <h5>Click on the button to load all the books</h5>
  <button id="btnLoad" type="submit" class="btn
    btn-primary">Load</button>
  <hr />
  <div id="booksDiv">
  </div>
</div>
```

Cross-origin requests

Due to security reasons, every browser restricts web applications to make cross-origin request through JavaScript. Cross-origin requests are the requests that make an HTTP request to another server, which is the outside domain. For example, if the application-based URL is `localhost`, and you are going to make a request on `anotherdomain.com`, it will not work. However, there are few differences between browsers' implementation, as in Chrome if the port number differs, it won't allow you to make a request; whereas Internet Explorer ignores this.

Cross-origin request is only restricted to the request being made from the `XMLHttpRequest` object; however, we can still have resources such as CSS, images, and script files loaded from other sources or domains.

The reason for not enabling this is to protect the data from malicious site attacks. However, to handle these scenarios, we can either use JSON-P (an older technique) or CORS, which will be discussed in the following section.

JSON-P

The **JavaScript Object Notation Padding (JSON-P)** technique is used with older browsers. This technique is obsolete now, and alternatively, CORS is safer and neater.

Using JSON-P

JSON-P is a technique that fakes a browser for making cross-origin request. It works by specifying a `<script>` tag that makes a cross-origin request to some other server, and the response returned is actually the function name, which is already defined in the web page. It then passes the data as a parameter to the function when the script is executed.

It can be implemented by adding a `<script>` tag, specifying the request URL in the `src` attribute and JavaScript `callback` function in a query string for the same URL. For example, consider the following request URL:

```
http://otherdomain.com?Id=1
```

Append the function in the request URL, which will be invoked when the script is loaded:

```
http://otherdomain.com?Id=1&callback=jsonPCallback
```

The following code snippet calls the `geo` service and specifies a `callback` parameter, which points to the `jsonCallback` function defined in the script. This script will be loaded when the page loads and executes the `src` URL, which finally calls the `jsonCallback` method and passes the response.

This code snippet is a sample HTTP `GET` request that uses the `Bing` API to get the location information based on the latitude and longitude values provided:

```
<script>
  var scrpt = document.createElement('script');

  scrpt.setAttribute('src','
    http://dev.virtualearth.net/REST/v1/Locations/
      latitudeNo,longitudeNo?o=json&key=BingMapsKey);
  document.body.appendChild(scrpt);
```

```
function jsonCallback(data) {
    alert("Cross Origin request got made");
}
</script>
```

On the other hand, with jQuery, cross-origin requests can be made by specifying the `dataType` attribute as `jsonp` and `crossDomain` as `true` in the `$.ajax` call:

```
$.ajax({
    url: serviceURL,
    type: "GET",
    dataType: "jsonp",
    method:"GetResult",
    crossDomain: true,
    error: function () {
        alert("list failed!");
    },
    success: function (data) {
        alert(data);
    }
});
```

CORS

Alternatively, CORS is a more preferred way when making cross-origin requests. It is a W3C standard and allows a server to send cross-origin requests from any domain. This needs to be enabled on the server side.

ASP.NET Core provides an easy way of enabling CORS on the server side, and this can be done by adding `Microsoft.AspNet.WebApi.Cors` through `NuGet`, or by modifying `project.json` and adding a dependency as follows:

```
"Microsoft.AspNet.Cors": "6.0.0-rc1-final"
```

Enable the CORS service using the `ConfigureServices` method in the `Startup` class:

```
public void ConfigureServices(IServiceCollection services
{
    services.AddCors();
}
```

Add the CORS middleware by using the `UseCors()` method in the `Configure` method. The `UseCors` method provides two overloaded methods: one that takes the CORS policy and other that takes the delegate, which can be used as a builder to build policy.

 Note that `UseCors()` should be added before `UseMVC`.

Through the CORS policy, we can define the allowed origins, headers, and methods. The CORS policy can either be defined at the `ConfigureServices` or `Configure` method when defining middleware.

Specifying the CORS policy at services level

This section will cover the way of defining the policy at the `ConfigureServices` method and referring when adding middleware. The `AddPolicy` method takes two parameters: the name of the policy and a `CorsPolicy` object. The `CorsPolicy` object allows chaining methods and allows you to define origins, methods, and headers using the `WithOrigins`, `WithMethods`, and `WithHeaders` methods.

Here is the sample code snippet that allows all origins, methods, and headers. So, whatever the request origin (domain) and HTTP methods or request headers are passed, the request will be processed:

```
public void ConfigureServices(IServiceCollection services)
{
  services.AddCors(options => {
    options.AddPolicy("AllowAllOrigins", builder =>
      builder.AllowAnyOrigin().AllowAnyMethod().
        AllowAnyHeader());
  });


}
```

In the preceding code, `Origins` represents the domain names, `Method` represents the HTTP methods, and `Header` represents the HTTP request headers. It can be simply used in the `Configure` method as follows:

```
public void Configure(IApplicationBuilder app, IHostingEnvironment
  env, ILoggerFactory loggerFactory
{

  app.UseCors("AllowAllOrigin");
}
```

We can also define multiple policies, as follows:

```
public void ConfigureServices(IServiceCollection services)
{
  services.AddCors(options => {
    options.AddPolicy("AllowAllOrigins", builder =>
      builder.AllowAnyOrigin().AllowAnyMethod().
        AllowAnyHeader());
      options.AddPolicy("AllowOnlyGet", builder =>
        builder.WithMethods("GET").AllowAnyHeader().
          AllowAnyOrigin());
  });
```

Enable CORS at the Configure method

Alternatively, we can define the CORS policy on the `Configure` method itself.
The `UseCors` method has two overloaded methods: one that takes the policy
name that is already defined in the `ConfigureServices` method, and the other is
`CorsPolicyBuilder` through which the policy can define directly on the `UseCors`
method itself:

```
public void Configure(IApplicationBuilder app, IHostingEnvironment
  env, ILoggerFactory loggerFactory)
{
  app.UseCors(policyBuilder =>
    policyBuilder.WithHeaders
      ("accept,content-type").AllowAnyOrigin().WithMethods
        ("GET, POST"));
}
```

Defining on the `ConfigureMethod` class enables the CORS policy throughout the
application. Instead of using the `EnableCors` attribute, we can specifically define the
policy name per controller, and action level as well, and use the policy defined in the
`ConfigureServices` method.

Defining through attribute is an alternative, which refers to the policy name from the
`ConfigureServices` method and ignores the policy defined at the middleware level.
Here are the ways of enabling CORS at controller, action, and global level:

*   Enabling CORS at the controller level:

    The following code enables the CORS policy at the MVC-controller level:

    ```
    [EnableCors("AllowAllOrigins")]
    public class BookController : Controller
    {
      //to do
    }
    ```

- Enabling CORS at the action level:

  The following code enables the CORS policy at the MVC action method level:

  ```
  [EnableCors("AllowAllOrigins")]
  public IActionResult GetAllRecords(
  {
    //Call some service to get records
    return View();
  }
  ```

- Enabling CORS globally:

  Globally, CORS can be enabled by defining at the middleware level, as we have seen through the `Configure` method. Otherwise, if it is defined at the `ConfigureServices` level, enabling it globally can be achieved by using the `CorsAuthorizationFilterFactory` object, as shown here:

  ```
  public void ConfigureServices(IServiceCollection services)
  {
    services.AddCors(options => {
      options.AddPolicy("AllowAllOrigins", builder =>
        builder.AllowAnyOrigin().AllowAnyMethod().
          AllowAnyHeader());
      options.AddPolicy("AllowOnlyGet", builder =>
        builder.WithMethods("GET").AllowAnyHeader().
          AllowAnyOrigin());
    });

    services.Configure<MvcOptions>(options =>
    {
      options.Filters.Add(new
        CorsAuthorizationFilterFactory
          ("AllowOnlyGet"));
    });
  }
  ```

The preceding code snippet contains two policies: `AllowAllOrigins` and `AllowOnlyGet`, and through `CorsAuthorizationFilterFactory`, we can pass the `AllowOnlyGet` policy as the policy name and make it global.

Calling WCF services from JavaScript

To consume the WCF service methods from JavaScript, we need to expose them as the RESTful service methods that accept and return the data in either JSON or XML formats. This helps developers to consume the WCF services as easily as the REST services, and use them with the jQuery $.ajax or $.getJSON (shorthand method of $.ajax) methods. To expose a WCF service as a REST service, we need to annotate the WCF service methods with the WebGet or WebInvoke attributes. The WebGet attribute is mostly used when making any HTTP GET request, whereas WebInvoke is used for all HTTP request methods.

The following code shows the representation of using the WebGet attribute on a WCF operation contract that returns the product based on productCode passed during the method call:

```
[OperationContract]
[WebGet(ResponseFormat = WebMessageFormat.Json, BodyStyle =
  WebMessageBodyStyle.Wrapped, UriTemplate =
    "json/{productCode}")]
Product GetProduct(string productCode);
```

We can also represent the same method using WebInvoke, as shown in the following code:

```
[OperationContract]
  [WebInvoke(Method ="GET",  ResponseFormat =
    WebMessageFormat.Json, BodyStyle =
      WebMessageBodyStyle.Wrapped, UriTemplate =
        "products/{productCode}")]
Product GetProduct(string productCode);
```

The following code shows the representation of using WebInvoke for the HTTP POST request:

```
[OperationContract]
[WebInvoke(Method - "POST", ResponseFormat =
  WebMessageFormat.Json, RequestFormat = WebMessageFormat.Json,
    BodyStyle = WebMessageBodyStyle.Wrapped, UriTemplate =
      "products /SaveProduct")]
bool SaveProduct(Product product);
```

If you notice, the POST method contains both RequestFormat and ResponseFormat attributes that tell the server the type of data provided when making any HTTP POST request and the response will be returned based on the ResponseFormat type defined.

When working with the RESTful services, make sure that the binding is set to `webHttpBinding`, as shown in the following screenshot. Also with the .NET framework 4 and higher, Microsoft introduced another attribute known as `crossDomainScriptAccessEnabled`, which can be set to `true` to deal with cross-origin requests:

```xml
<system.serviceModel>
  <serviceHostingEnvironment multipleSiteBindingsEnabled="true" aspNetCompatibilityEnabled="true" />
  <services>
    <service behaviorConfiguration="Default"
         name="WcfService.ProductService">
      <endpoint address="" behaviorConfiguration="webBehavior"
          binding="webHttpBinding"
          contract="WcfService.IProductService" />
      <endpoint contract="IMetadataExchange" binding="mexHttpBinding"
                address="mex" />
    </service>
  </services>
  <behaviors>
    <endpointBehaviors>
      <behavior name="webBehavior">
        <webHttp helpEnabled="true" />
      </behavior>
    </endpointBehaviors>
    <serviceBehaviors>
      <behavior name="Default">
        <serviceMetadata httpGetEnabled="true" />
      </behavior>
    </serviceBehaviors>
  </behaviors>
```

Moreover, in order to enable CORS, you can specify `standardEndpoints`, as shown in the following screenshot, under `system.serviceModel`:

```xml
<standardEndpoints>
  <webScriptEndpoint>
    <standardEndpoint crossDomainScriptAccessEnabled="true"/>
  </webScriptEndpoint>
</standardEndpoints>
```

Add custom headers as follows. Specifying asterisk (*) allows everything, whereas for security purpose, origin, headers, and methods can be defined explicitly to specific values that are separated by commas:

```xml
<httpProtocol>
  <customHeaders>
    <add name="Access-Control-Allow-Origin" value="http://localhost"/>
    <add name="Access-Control-Allow-Headers" value="Content-Type, Accept"/>
    <add name="Access-Control-Allow-Methods" value="POST, GET, OPTIONS"/>
    <add name="Access-Control-Max-Age" value="1728000"/>
  </customHeaders>
</httpProtocol>
```

The following table shows the description of each access control keys:

Access control key	Description
`Access-Control-Allow-Origin`	This key is used to allow the client's domain from where the service will be invoked
`Access-Control-Allow-Headers`	This key is used to specify the headers permitted when the client is making a request
`Access-Control-Allow-Method`	Using this key, the HTTP methods allowed when the client is making a request
`Access-Control-Max-Age`	This key takes the value in seconds to see how long the response to the preflight request can be cached for without sending the another preflight request

To invoke the `SaveProduct` method, we can use the jQuery `$.ajax()` method and supply the following parameters, as shown in the following code. If you notice, we defined `contentType` as well as `dataType`. The difference is that `contentType` is used to tell the server about the type of data client is sending, whereas `dataType` is used to let the server know the type of data the client is expecting to receive in response. The `dataType` values can be `json`, `jsonp`, `xml`, `html`, or `script`:

```
function SaveProduct(){
  var product = {
    "ProductName":"Product1",
    "ProductDescription":"This is Product A"
  };


  $.ajax({
    type:"POST",
    url:"http://localhost/products/SaveProduct",
    data:JSON.stringify(product),
    contentType: "application/json",
    dataType:"json",
    processData:true,
    success: function(data, status, xhr){
      alert(data);

    },
    error: function(error){
      alert(error);

    }

  });
}
```

In order to make a call to another domain, we can use `jsonp`, so the server wraps the JSON data in a JavaScript function, which is known as a `callback` function, and when the response comes back to the client, it will automatically call the `success` method. The modified version of the preceding method to handle cross-origin request is shown in the following code.

In this code, we modified the URL and passed the `callback=?` query string as a parameter. Moreover, the `crossDomain` attribute is used to ensure that the request will be `crossDomain`. When the server responds, `?` specified in the `callback` query and the string will be replaced by the function name, such as `json43229182_22822992`, and will call the `success` method:

```
function SaveProduct(){
  var product = {
    "ProductName":"Product1",
    "ProductDescription":"This is Product A"
  };


  $.ajax({
    type:"POST",
    url:"
      http://localhost:4958/ProductService.svc/products/
        SaveProduct?callback=?",
    data:JSON.stringify(product),
    contentType: "application/json",
    dataType:"jsonp",
    crossDomain: true,
    processData:true,
    success: function(data, status, xhr){
      alert(data);

    },
    error: function(error){
      alert(error);

    }

  });
}
```

Similarly, we can invoke the `GetProduct` method as shown in the following code:

```
(function () {
  var productCode= "Prod-001";
  var webServiceURL =
    "http://localhost:4958/ProductService.svc/products/
      GetProduct/"+productCode;
  $.ajax({
    type: "GET",
    url: webServiceURL,
    dataType: "json",
    processData: false,
    success: function (data) {
      alert(data);
    },
    error: function (error) {
      alert(error);
    }
  });
});
```

For cross domain, it can be modified as follows:

```
(function () {
  var productCode= "Prod-001";
  var webServiceURL =
    "http://localhost:4958/ProductService.svc/products/
      GetProduct/"+productCode;
  $.ajax({
    type: "GET",
    url: webServiceURL+"?callback=?",
    dataType: "jsonp",
    crossDomain:true,
    processData: false,
    success: function (data) {
      alert(data);
    },
    error: function (error) {
      alert(error);
    }
  });
});
```

Alternatively, for the preceding solution, we can also override the `callback` function name in a `jsonp` request, and the value specified in `jsonpCallback` will be used instead of `callback=?` passed in a URL. The following code snippet calls your local function whose name is specified in the `jsonpCallback` value:

```javascript
function callbackFn(data){

}

(function () {
  var productCode= "Prod-001";
  var webServiceURL =
    "http://localhost:4958/ProductService.svc/products/
      GetProduct/"+productCode;
  $.ajax({
    type: "GET",
    url: webServiceURL,
    dataType: "jsonp",
    crossDomain:true,
    processData: false,
    jsonpCallback: callbackFn,
    success: function (data) {
      alert(data);
    },
    error: function (error) {
      alert(error);
    }
  });
});
```

Summary

In this chapter, we discussed Ajax techniques and concepts of using the `XMLHttpRequest` object. We have seen the basic architecture of how the Ajax request is processed and what events and methods it provides. Similarly, we also discussed what jQuery offers and the extensive library it has for performing different types of the HTTP GET and POST requests. In the next chapter, we will discuss the basics of `TypeScript`, and one of the most popular client-side framework, Angular 2. We will also go through developing a simple application using ASP.NET Core MVC 6 with Angular 2 as a frontend framework and Entity Framework 7 for backend operations.

5

Developing an ASP.NET Application Using Angular 2 and Web API

In this chapter, we will develop a complete application on ASP.NET Core using MVC 6 for MVC views and Web API for web services. For the client side, we will use Angular 2, which is one of the most popular frameworks for client-side development. Angular 2 is written in TypeScript, but it provides the option to write code in JavaScript and Dart. In this chapter, we will use TypeScript because it adheres to the ECMAScript 6 standard, with a provision to generate JavaScript when you build your project in ECMAScript 3, ECMAScript 4, and ECMAScript 5 standards. TypeScript is a superset of JavaScript and most of the things are common to both; in fact, TypeScript provides some features that in JavaScript are not implemented by many browsers, except Mozilla Firefox.

This chapter focuses on the basic concepts and takes you through a sample application to learn how Angular 2 can be used with ASP.NET Core and MVC 6.

TypeScript

TypeScript is a language developed by Microsoft and is a superset of JavaScript. TypeScript transpiles into JavaScript at compile time. Visual Studio 2015 automatically builds the TypeScript into JavaScript files and places them inside a folder configured with the `TypeScript.tsconfig` configuration file. It provides a lot more than JavaScript provides, but developers can still use some of the types and objects in TypeScript that they use in JavaScript. However, TypeScript generates cleaner and more optimized code, which is then run by the Angular 2 framework. So, when the TypeScript compiles, it generates JavaScript and stores a map file to handle debugging scenarios. Suppose you want to debug your TypeScript code from Visual Studio 2015; this mapping file contains the mapping information of the source TypeScript file and generated JavaScript file being run inside your Angular page and the break points can be set on your TypeScript file.

Compilation architecture of TypeScript

The TypeScript compiler goes through several stages to compile TypeScript files and generate JavaScript files.

The compilation process starts with a pre-processor, which determines what files need to be included by following reference `/// <reference path=.../>` tags and `import` statements. Once the files are identified, the parser parses and tokenizes the source code into an **Abstract Syntax Tree (AST)**.

An AST represents the syntactical structure of the source code in a tree format that consists of nodes. The binder then passes over the AST nodes and generates and binds symbols. One symbol is created for each named entity and if there are multiple entities with the same name, they will have the same symbol.

Symbols represent named entities and merge multiple files if several declarations are found. To represent a global view of all the files, a program is build. A program is the main entry point to the type system and code generation. Once the program is created, a type checker and an emitter can be created.

A type checker is the core part of the TypeScript system, consolidates all the symbols from multiple files into a single view, and builds a symbol table. This symbol table contains the types of each symbol identified and merged into a common symbol. A type checker contains complete information about which symbol belongs to which node, the type of a particular symbol, and so on.

Finally, an emitter is used by the TypeScript compiler, through a program, to generate the output file: `.js`, `.js.map`, `.jxs`, or `d.ts`.

Advantages of TypeScript

The following are some core benefits of using TypeScript with Angular 2.

Superset of JavaScript

TypeScript is a typed superset of JavaScript that compiles to JavaScript. The basic advantage of being a superset is that it provides the latest features of JavaScript that many browsers do not support yet. Developers use features such as async functions, decorators, and others during application development, which then compile into a JavaScript file that targets the ECMAScript 4 or ECMAScript 3 versions, which browsers can easily understand and interpret.

Support for classes and modules

Typescript supports `class`, `interface`, `extends`, and `implements` keywords.

Here is how you can define class in TypeScript:

```
class Person {
  private personId: string = '';
  private personName: string = '';
  private dateOfBirth: Date;
  constructor() {}
  getPersonName(): string {
  return this.personName;
  }
  setPersonName(value): void {
  this.personName = value;
}}
```

Here is the transpiled version of TypeScript in JavaScript:

```
var Person = (function () {
function Person() {
  this.personId = '';
  this.personName = '';
}
Person.prototype.getPersonName = function () {
  return this.personName;
};
Person.prototype.setPersonName = function (value) {
  this.personName = value;
};
  return Person;
})();
```

Static type checking

The main benefit of using TypeScript is static type checking. When you build your project, the TypeScript compiler checks the semantics and gives errors at compile time to avoid runtime errors. For example, the following code will give an error at compile time:

```
var name: string
name =2;//give error
```

Here is another example that extends the `Person` class and gives a type mismatched error at compile type:

```
class Person {
  constructor(name: string) {
  }
}
class Employee extends Person{
  constructor() {
  super(2); //error
  }
}
```

ECMAScript 6 feature support

At the time of writing, most browsers still do not support ECMAScript 6 completely, but with TypeScript, we can write code and use ECMAScript 6 features. As ECMAScript 6 supports backward compatibility, we can set the target version through the TypeScript configuration file, which generates the JavaScript based on the version specified. This helps developers to write code using ECMAScript 6 features and the output JS files will be generated in ECMAScript 3, ECMAScript 4, or ECMAScript 5 standards.

Optional typing

TypeScript supports strict typing and validates types at compile type, but using strict typing is not mandatory. You can even declare a variable without specifying its type and it will be resolved when the value is assigned.

Declaring types in TypeScript

Here is an example of declaring a variable without its type:

```
private sNo = 1;
private text = 'Hello world';
```

Here is an example of declaring a variable with types:

```
private sNo: number = 1;
private text: string = 'Hello world';
```

Core elements of TypeScript

This section discusses the core elements of TypeScript:

- Declaring variables
- Types
- Classes and interfaces
- Functions
- Iterators
- Modules and namespaces

Declaring variables

Variable declaration is equivalent to what we do in JavaScript. However, as TypeScript follows the ECMAScript 6 standard, it provides strong types as well. Strong types can be declared by naming a variable followed by a colon (:) and its type.

Here is a simple variable declaration in JavaScript:

```
var name;
```

It can be declared in TypeScript as follows:

```
var name: string;
```

Variables can be initialized in TypeScript as follows:

```
var name: string = "Hello World";
```

Types

Most of the types available in TypeScript are equivalent to JavaScript types. The following table contains a list of all available types, with a code snippet for using them:

Type	Description	Code snippet

Number	TypeScript provides a number type that holds all types of decimal, hexadecimal, binary, and octal values.	`let decimal: number = 2;`
		`let hex: number = 0x001;`
		`let binary: number = 0b1010;`
		`let octal: number = 0o744;`

String	It's the same as we use in any other language. String values can be surrounded with single or double quotes.	`let x: string = 'Hello';` `let y: string = "Hello";`
Array	TypeScript supports simple arrays, and generic arrays as well.	`let countries = ['US', 'UK', 'UAE'];` `let countries<string> = ['US', 'UK', 'UAE'];`

Tuple	Through tuples, we can define an array whose element types are known.	`let val: [string, number, Date];`
		`val = ['Hello World', 10, new Date()];`
		`val[0];//print Hello World`

Enum	Used to give names to the numerical values. By default, the first value specified is 0 but can be set explicitly to any number.	`enum Status {InProcess, Active, Ready, Success, Error}`
		`let s: Status = Status.Active;`
		`//specify values explicitly`
		`enum Status {InProcess=1, Active=2, Ready=3, Success=4, Error=5}`

Any	This type can be used in cases where the type is not known and is dependent on an assignment.	`let x: any;`
		`x=['Hello', 1, 2]; //tuple;`
		`x=1; //number`
		`x='Hello World'; //string`

Classes and interfaces

The following are the ways of defining interfaces, deriving classes and interfaces, and writing generic classes in TypeScript.

Defining interfaces

Just like C#, TypeScript allows you to define interfaces that can be implemented in TypeScript classes and force the implementer class to implement all the members defined in the interface.

Here is the code to define an interface in TypeScript:

```
interface IShape {
  shapeName: string;
  draw();
}
class TodoService implements IShape  {
  constructor(private http: Http) {
  this.shapeName = "Square";
  }

  shapeName: string;

  draw() {
  alert("this is " + this.shapeName);
  }
}
```

Deriving classes and interfaces

Like C#, classes and interfaces can be extended by deriving from base classes or interfaces. To extend any class, we can use the extends keyword, and for an interface we can use implements, as shown here:

```
interface IPerson {
  id: number;
  firstName: string;
  lastName: string;
  dateOfBirth: Date;
}

interface IEmployee extends IPerson{
  empCode: string;
  designation: string;
}

class Person implements IPerson {
  id: number;
  firstName: string;
  lastName: string;
```

```
      dateOfBirth: Date;
}

class Employee extends Person implements IEmployee {
  empCode: string;
  designation: string;
}
```

In the previous code snippet, we have declared two interfaces, `IPerson` and `IEmployee`. `IPerson` contains common properties such as `id`, `firstName`, `lastName`, and `dateOfBirth`, which can be used in all derived interfaces, such as `IEmployee` or any other.

Then, we have implemented the `IPerson` interface in the `Person` class, and finally derived the `Employee` class from `Person` and implemented the `IEmployee` interface. If you have noticed, as the `Person` class already implements the `IPerson` interface, we do not have to implement it again and only implement the properties, such as `empCode` and `designation` in the `Employee` class.

Generic classes

Generic classes are useful to define a particular class whose type is generic and determined when it is called. Generic classes can be defined by using `<T>` followed by the class name.

Here is a simple example that shows the generic class process, which can work as per the type specified during initialization. The `getTypeInfo()` method will print a specific message based on the type of object initialized:

```
class Process<T>{
  value: T;
  getTypeInfo(){
  if (typeof this.value == "string")
    console.log("Type is a string");
  else if (typeof this.value == "number")
    console.log("Type is a number");
  else alert("type is unknown");

  }
}

let pString = new Process<string>();
pString.getTypeInfo(); //print Type is a string
let pNumber = new Process<number>();
pNumber.getTypeInfo(); //print Type is a number
```

Functions

Functions can be defined in the same way as JavaScript. TypeScript supports both named and anonymous functions. In TypeScript, function parameters can be typed parameters, as shown here:

```
function concat(x: string, y: string): string {
   return x +" "+ y;
}
```

Functions can also have optional parameters and can be declared by using `(?)` as shown here:

```
function concat(x: string, y: string, z?: string): string {
   return x + " " + y + " " + z;
}
```

With this option, we can call the function by passing two parameters or three parameters because the third parameter is optional.

Generic functions

TypeScript allows you to define generic functions, which accept any type of argument or return type. Generic functions can be defined by specifying the `<T>` after the function name, as shown in the following code, and the arguments or returned type can also be generic and refer to the same `T` type. This is useful to define a particular function that accepts all types of arguments and works as expected. The following example shows the process function based on the type of argument concatenated or added:

```
function process<T>(x: T, y: T): string{
   if (typeof x == "string")
   return x + " " + y;
   else if (typeof x == "number")
   return "Sum is: "+ x + y ;
   else
   return "Type in unknown";
}
```

Iterators

Apart from standard loops such as for, `while`, TypeScript also provides two types of for statements, `for..of` and `for..in`. Both statements iterate on collections. The difference between these is that the `for..of` statement returns the keys of the object whereas `for..in` returns the values:

```
countries = ['USA', 'UK', 'UAE'];
   //this loop will display keys 0, 1, 2
```

```
for (let index in this.countries) {
  console.log(index);
}
//this loop will display values USA, UK, UAE
for (let index of this.countries) {
  console.log(index);
}
```

Modules and namespaces

ECMAScript 6 introduces the concept of modules. Modules can be thought of as logical containers that have their own scope. Any class, variable, or method declared inside a module is scoped within its own container and accessible to other modules only if it is allowed explicitly. In TypeScript, any file containing imports or exports at a top level are considered modules. Modules import one another using a module loader, and at runtime the module loader is responsible for loading all the dependencies of the module defined within it. Modules can be exported using the `export` keyword and other modules can import it using the `import` keyword.

Here is an example of defining and exporting a module in TypeScript:

```
//BaseManager.ts
export class BaseManager{
}
```

To use the module in some other area requires you to use the `import` keyword, as shown here:

```
//ServiceManager.ts
export class ServiceManager extends BaseManager{
}
```

Modules can be imported by using the `import` keyword. When importing any module, you have to use the `import` keyword, followed by the class name in brackets {}, followed by the actual filename that contains the class. For example, the following code shows the way of importing `ServiceManager` into `Main.ts`:

```
//Main.ts
import {ServiceManager} from "./ServiceManager"
```

We can also give a friendly name to the class, as follows:

```
//Main.ts
import {ServiceManager as serviceMgr} from "./ServiceManager"
```

Namespaces, on the other hand, are the logical modules to categorize classes, methods, and so on. Just like C#, they can be defined by using a `namespace` keyword. One namespace can be split across different TypeScript files and this gives developers a handy way of categorizing specific files to a single namespace. The following example shows the way to categorize TypeScript files into a single namespace and using them:

```
//PersonManager.ts
namespace BusinessManagers{
   export class PersonManager{}
}
//SecurityManager.ts
namespace BusinessManagers{
   export class SecurityManager(){
}
}
//main.ts
/// <reference path="personmanager.ts" />
   /// <reference path="SecurityManager.ts" />
personObj = new BusinessManagers.PersonManager();
securityObj =new BusinessManagers.SecurityManager();
```

If you notice, we have used a triple-slash directive, which is used to refer to the dependent files before executing the code in the TypeScript file. Therefore, as these files persist somewhere else, we have to explicitly reference them in the preceding code.

To summarize, namespaces are a better method to use than modules as they categorize files logically by providing a friendly name, and allow developers to structure code properly when working with medium-to-large-sized projects.

We can also give a shortened name to a namespace if it's unfriendly by using an `import` keyword as shown here:

```
namespace BusinessManagers {
   export class PersonManager {

   }
}

import mgr = BusinessManagers;
let personObj = new mgr.PersonManager();

To LC: Apply code to:
"namespace BusinessManagers {
   export class PersonManager {

   }
```

```
}

import mgr = BusinessManagers;
let personObj = new mgr.PersonManager();
```

So this winds up the core topics of TypeScript. To learn more about TypeScript, you can refer to `http://www.typescriptlang.org/`.

Introduction to Angular 2

Angular 2 is a client-side framework to build web applications. It is very flexible in terms of being used with both mobile and web platforms. The basic advantage of using Angular is that it follows the ECMAScript 6 standard and developers can do object-oriented programming, define classes and interfaces, implement classes, and define data structures using **Plain Old JavaScript Objects** (**POJO**) for binding data. Another big advantage in terms of performance is the unidirectional data flow. Unlike Angular 1.x, Angular 2 provides both the option of doing two-way data binding or unidirectional data binding. In certain cases, unidirectional binding is good for performance. For example, when submitting a form, two way bindings with controls may be overkill.

Angular 2 architecture

Angular2 consist of a number of components. Each component can be bound to the page by either a selector, for example `<my-app> </my-app>`, or a routing module. Each component has a selector, template HTML or template reference link, directives, providers, and a controller class whose properties and methods can be accessed in the associated view. When the web application first starts, `System.import` loads the main component of the application, which bootstraps the root component. Here is a sample main component bootstrapping an Angular app:

```
//Loading module through Import statement
Import {AppComponent} from 'path of my component'
bootstrap(AppComponent, [Providers]);
```

Providers can be defined inside square brackets. There are various providers available, which we will discuss in a later chapter.

This `bootstrap` object is in `angular2/platform/browser`, which can be imported into the TypeScript file with the `import` command:

```
import {bootstrap} from 'angular2/platform/browser';
```

This `bootstrap` object directs Angular to load the component defined in it. When the component is loaded, all the attributes or metadata defined for the component are evaluated. Each component should have the `@Component` annotation, some properties to define metadata about the component, and one or more classes termed as component controllers that contain properties and methods accessible by the template defined in the `@Component template` or `templateUri` properties.

Here is a sample `app.component.ts` that contains a selector, a template, and a class, `AppComponent`:

```
//app.component.ts
import { Component, View} from 'angular2/core';
  import {bootstrap} from 'angular2/platform/browser';
  @Component({
  selector: "my-app",
  template: `<p>This is a first component</p>`,
  })
  class AppComponent  {
  }
  bootstrap(AppComponent);
```

Events of component life cycle

When the component initializes, it goes through several events and has a very structured life cycle process. We can implement these events to do specific operations. The following table shows the list of events we can use in our component controller class:

Event	Description
ngOnInit()	It is called after the component is initialized and the controller constructor is executed.
ngOnDestroy()	It is used to clean up resources when the component is disposed of.
ngDoCheck()	It is used to override the default change detection algorithm for a directive.
ngOnChanges(changes)	It is invoked when any of the component selector property values get modified. (Custom properties of the selectors can be defined through inputs.)
ngAfterContentInit()	It is invoked when the directive's content is initialized. (Directives are defined later.)
ngAfterContentChecked()	It is invoked every time the directive's content is checked.
ngAfterViewInit()	It is invoked when the view is completely initialized.
ngAfterViewChecked()	It is invoked on every check of your component's view.

Modules

A module represents a container that contains classes, interfaces, and more, to export functionality, so other modules can be imported using the `import` statement. For example, here is `math.ts`, used to perform different arithmetic operations:

```
//math.ts
import {Component} from 'angular2/core';
@Component({

})
export class MathService {
  constructor() {
  }
  public sum(a: number, b: number): number {
  return a + b;
  }
  public subtract(a: number, b: number): number {
  return a - b;
  }
  public divide(a: number, b: number): number {
  return a / b;
  }
  public multiply(a: number, b: number): number {
  return a * b;
  }
}
```

Components

A component is a combination of the `@Component` annotation to define metadata properties and the associated controller class that contains the actual code, such as the class constructor, methods, and properties. The `@Component` annotation contains the following metadata properties:

```
@Component({
  providers: string[],
  selector: string,
  inputs: string[],
  outputs: string[],
  properties: string[],
  events: string[],
  host: { [key: string]: string },
  exportAs: string,
  moduleId: string,
```

```
  viewProviders: any[],
  queries: { [key: string]: any },
  changeDetection: ChangeDetectionStrategy,
  templateUrl: string,
  template: string,
  styleUrls: string[],
  styles: string[],
  directives: Array < Type | any[] >,
  pipes: Array < Type | any[] >,
  encapsulation: ViewEncapsulation
})
```

Core properties of Angular 2 components

When defining a component, we can specify various properties, as listed previously. Here we will see some of the core properties that are often required when creating Angular 2 components:

- Templates and selectors
- Inputs and outputs
- Directives
- Providers

Templates and selectors

The following real example contains the template and the selector defined in the component class. When the button is clicked, it will call the logMessage() method, which prints the message in the <p> element. If you notice, we have not used the export keyword with the class because we have already bootstrapped the component on the same file and this component does not need to be referenced anywhere else:

```
import { Component, View } from 'angular2/core';
import {bootstrap} from 'angular2/platform/browser';
@Component({
  selector: "my-app",
  template: "<p> {{message}}</p><button (click)='logMessage()'>Log
    Message</button>"
})
class AppComponent {
  logMessage() {
    this.message = "Hello World";
  }
```

```
    message: string = "";
}
bootstrap(AppComponent);
```

The app selector can be used anywhere in the HTML or `index.cshtml` page if working on an ASP.NET project, and the template will be rendered inside it. Here is an example of using the custom tag `my-app`:

```
<html>
<body>
  <my-app></my-app>
</body>
</html>
```

Once the page runs, it will render the output with this generated source:

```
<html>
<body>
  <p>Hello World</p>
  <button (click)='logMessage()'>Log Message</button>
</body>
</html>
```

Inputs and outputs

Inputs allow developers to specify the custom attributes mapped to some property of the component class downward in the hierarchy of components, whereas outputs are used to define custom event handlers on the component that can be raised upward in the hierarchy of components. In short, inputs are used to send data from parent to child components, whereas outputs are used to invoke events from child to parent components. In the previous example, we saw how selectors can be used, and the associated template is rendered in place of a selector, with the provision of having all the members of the component class available. In certain cases, we have to specify some attributes in our custom selector to pass the value to handle particular actions. For example, we may need some attribute in the previous `<my-app>` tag to specify the logging type, such as to log on to a developer's console or show an alert message.

Using inputs

In this example, we will create two input attributes, `logToConsole` and `showAlert`. We can define input attributes in the `@Component` annotation. The following code snippet is the separate component defined in `child.component.ts` and contains the selector as child; the template displays the Boolean values of the `logToConsole` and `showAlert` attributes specified in the child tag. The inputs contain the list of string variables that will be defined as the child tag attributes:

```
//child.component.ts
import { Component} from 'angular2/core';
@Component({
  selector: 'child',
  template: `<div> Log to Console: {{logToConsole}}, Show Alert:
    {{showAlert}} <button (click)="logMessage()" >Log</button>
    </div>`,
  inputs: ['logToConsole', 'showAlert'],
})
```

Here is the `ChildComponent` class that contains the `logToConsole` and `showAlert` Boolean variables. These variables actually hold the values supplied from the notification tag. Finally, we have the `logMessage()` method that will be invoked on a button click event and either log the message on the developer's console or show an alert message based on the value that has been set by the parent component in the hierarchy:

```
export class ChildComponent {
  public logToConsole: boolean;
  public showAlert: boolean;

  logMessage(message: string) {
    if (this.logToConsole) {
      console.log("Console logging is enabled");
    }
    if (this.showAlert) {
      alert("Showing alert message is enabled");
    }

  }
}
```

In the `app.component.ts` file, where we have the main `AppComponent` defined, we can use the child selector as shown in the following code. When defining the child selector, we can set the values for custom inputs defined in the `ChildComponent`, `logToConsole` and `showAlert`. This way the parent component can specify the values to the child component through inputs. Here is the complete code of `AppComponent`:

```
//app.component.ts
import { Component, View } from 'angular2/core';
import {bootstrap} from 'angular2/platform/browser';
import {ChildComponent} from './child.component';

@Component({
  selector: "my-app",
  template: `<child [logToConsole]=true
    [showAlert]=true></child>`,
  directives: [ChildComponent]
})
export class AppComponent {
}
bootstrap(AppComponent);
```

> When using template to define HTML, we can use a backtick (`` ` ``) rather than the double quotes (" ") or single quotes (' '), as shown the preceding example. This allows the HTML content to span multiple lines.

Using outputs

Outputs are used to invoke events on the parent component from child components in the hierarchy of components. We will modify the preceding example and add the outputs event in the `ChildComponent`, then register it in the `AppComponent` using the `ChildComponent` selector.

Here is the modified code snippet for `ChildComponent`:

```
//child.component.ts
import { Component, EventEmitter, Output} from 'angular2/core';
@Component({
  selector: 'child',
  template: `<div> Log to Console: {{logToConsole}}, Show Alert:
    {{showAlert}}   <button (click)="logMessage()" >Log</button>
    </div>`,
  inputs: ['logToConsole', 'showAlert']
})
```

```
export class ChildComponent {
  public logToConsole: boolean;
  public showAlert: boolean;
  @Output() clickLogButton = new EventEmitter();

  logMessage(message: string) {
    this.clickLogButton.next("From child");
  }
}
```

The `@Output` property lists `clickLogButton` as a custom event that `ChildComponent` can emit, which its parent `AppComponent` will receive.

We have added `EventEmitter` in the `import` statement. `EventEmitter` is a built-in class that ships with Angular and provides methods for defining and firing custom events. Once the `logMessage()` method is executed, it will execute the `clickLogButton.next()` method from the `ChildComponent`, which finally calls the event registered in the `AppComponent`.

We have added the `clickLogButton` in the `AppComponent`, as shown in the following code. In Angular 2, we can specify the event by specifying the event name in brackets `()` followed by the method that will be called when the event is raised. This is how the event is registered. Here, `logMessage` is the local method defined in the `AppComponent`:

```
(clickLogButton)="logMessage($event)"
```

Here is the code snippet for AppComponent:

```
  //app.component.ts
import { Component, View } from 'angular2/core';
import {bootstrap} from 'angular2/platform/browser';
import {ChildComponent} from './child.component';

@Component({
  selector: "my-app",
  template: `<child [logToConsole]=true [showAlert]=true
    (clickLogButton)="logMessage($event)" ></child>`,
  directives: [ChildComponent]
})
export class AppComponent {

  logMessage(value) {
    alert(value);
  }
}
bootstrap(AppComponent);
```

The `logMessage` method is the method that will be invoked when the event is raised from the `ChildComponent`.

Directives

Directives are custom tags that render the HTML at runtime but encapsulate the rendering content in the directive itself. We can relate it to the tag helpers in ASP.NET. There are three kinds of directives, components, structural directives, and attribute directives:

- **Components**: It is a directive with a template.
- **Structural directive**: It is a directive to add or remove DOM elements. There are some built-in structural directives that Angular provides. Directives such as `ngIf`, `ngSwitch`, and `ngFor` are structural directives.
- **Attribute directive**: It changes the appearance of any DOM element.

Creating a simple Hello World directive

Directives can be created in a simple way, as a component is created, and can be referenced in the calling component through its selector tag.

Here is an example of `HelloWorldComponent` that defines a simple directive to display a `"Hello world"` message in the heading format:

```
//helloworld.component.ts
import {Component} from 'angular2/core';

@Component({
  selector: "helloworld",
  template: "<h1>Hello world</h1>"
})

export class HelloWorldComponent {

}
```

The following example is the component that uses this directive. When using any directive, it has to be first imported through the `import` statement, then the `@Component` metadata property needs to be set to access it in the associated template:

```
import { Component, View, provide, Inject } from 'angular2/core';
  import {bootstrap} from 'angular2/platform/browser';
  import {HelloWorldComponent} from './helloworld.component';

  @Component({
```

```
    selector: "my-app",
    template: `<helloworld></helloworld>`,
    directives: [, HelloWorldComponent],
})
export class AppComponent{

}
bootstrap(AppComponent);
```

This directive can be used on the page as follows:

```
<helloworld></helloworld>
```

Structural directives

Structural directives can be used to add or remove DOM elements. For example, we can add the list of countries as a table through *ngFor, as shown in the following code, and hide or unhide the div through the *ngIf directive:

```
<div *ngIf="display">
  <table>
    <thead>
      <tr>
        <th>
          Country
        </th>
        <th>
          Currency
        </th>
      </tr>
    </thead>
    <tbody *ngFor="#country of countries">
      <tr><td>{{country.CountryName}}</td>
        <td>{{country.Currency}}</td></tr>
    </tbody>
  </table>
</div>
```

Here is the backend countries.component.ts, which uses the HTTP module to call the ASP.NET Web API service. It returns a list of countries, which is assigned to the countries array. The display default value is set to true, which generates the table. By setting the display value to false, the table will not be generated:

```
///<reference path="../../node_modules/angular2/
   typings/browser.d.ts" />
import {Component} from 'angular2/core';
```

```
import {Http, Response} from 'angular2/http';

@Component({
  selector: 'app',
  templateUrl: 'Countries'
})
export class TodoAppComponent {
  countries = [];
  display: boolean = true;
  //constructor
  constructor(private http: Http) {
  }

  //Page Initialized Event Handler
  ngOnInit() {
    this.getCountries();
  }
  getCountries() {
    this.http.get("http://localhost:5000/api/todo").map((res:
      Response) => res.json())
      .subscribe(data => {
        this.countries = data;
      },
      err => console.log(err),
      () => console.log("done")
      );
  }

}
```

This is how structural directives can be used in Angular 2. In the following chapter, we develop a sample application and discuss each artifact for making HTTP GET and POST requests using Angular 2.

Attribute directive

An attribute directive requires building a controller class annotated with @Directive and defines a selector to identify the attribute associated with it. In the following example, we will develop a simple myFont directive that changes the text to italic when it is applied to any page elements. Here is the font.directive.ts file:

```
import { Directive, ElementRef, Input } from 'angular2/core';
@Directive({ selector: '[myFont]' })
export class FontDirective {
  constructor(el: ElementRef) {
```

```
        el.nativeElement.style.fontStyle = 'italic';
    }
}
```

For each matching element on the page, Angular creates a new instance and injects `ElementRef` into the constructor. `ElementRef` is a service through which we can directly access the element through its `nativeElement` property and access other attributes. In the preceding code snippet, we are changing the font style to italic for the elements that have the `myFont` directive applied.

On the page level, it can be used as follows:

```
<p myFont>myFont is an Attribute directive</p>
```

Providers

Providers are used to register the types that gets instantiated through the dependency injection framework of Angular 2. When a component is initialized, Angular creates a dependency injector which registers all the types specified in the providers array. Then at the constructor level, if there is any type defined in the providers array, it will get initialized and injected into the constructor.

The following example is `MathComponent`, which will be injected into the main app component constructor and call the sum method to add two numbers together:

```
//math.component.ts
import { Component } from 'angular2/core';
@Component({})

export class MathComponent {

  public sum(a: number, b: number) : number{
    return a + b;
  }
  public divide(a: number, b: number): number {
    return a / b;
  }
  public subtract(a: number, b: number): number {
    return a - b;
  }
  public multiply(a: number, b: number): number {
    return a * b;
  }

}
```

The following example is `AppComponent`, showing how to import a `math` component, then defining the provider and injecting it at the constructor level:

```
//app.component.ts
import { Component, View } from 'angular2/core';
import {bootstrap} from 'angular2/platform/browser';
import {MathComponent} from './servicemanager.component';
  @Component({
    selector: "my-app",
    template: "<button (click)="add()" >Log</button>",
    providers: [MathComponent]
  })
  export class AppComponent  {
    obj: MathComponent;
    constructor(mathComponent: MathComponent) {
      this.obj = mathComponent;
    }
    public add() {
      console.log(this.obj.sum(1, 2));
    }
  }
  bootstrap(AppComponent);
```

Other primitive types can also be injected in a slightly different way using the Inject Angular module. We can also define a type using the `provide` keyword, which takes a key and the value:

```
providers: [provide('Key', {useValue: 'Hello World'})]
```

The preceding syntax can also be used when defining types in providers, as follows:

```
providers: [provide(MathComponent, {mathComponent: MathComponent })]
```

One of the main benefits of defining `providers` with the `provide` keyword is when testing. When testing applications, we can replace the actual components with the mock or test components. For example, suppose we have a class that calls some SMS service to send SMS using some paid gateway, and in the testing cycle we don't want to use the production SMS gateway component, but rather we would like to have some custom test component that just inserts the SMS into a local database. In this case, we can associate some mock class, such as `SMSTestComponent`, to perform testing scenarios.

The following example injects the string value into the constructor. We need to add the Inject module as specified in the following code, and then use `@Inject` to inject the value associated to the key:

```
//app.component.ts
import { Component, View, provide, Inject } from 'angular2/core';
import {bootstrap} from 'angular2/platform/browser';
import {MathComponent} from './servicemanager.component';
@Component({
  selector: "my-app",
  template: `button (click)="logMessage()" >Log</button>`,
  providers: [MathComponent, provide('SampleText', {useValue:
    'Sample Value'})]
})
export class AppComponent{
  obj: MathComponent;
  Val: string;
  constructor(mathComponent: MathComponent,
    @Inject('SampleText') value) {
    this.obj = mathComponent;
    this.Val = value;
  }

public logMessage() {
  alert(this.kVal);
}
}
}
bootstrap(AppComponent);
```

Dependency injection in Angular

Angular chains dependency injection and injects components into the child components if they are defined in the providers array of the parent component. However, a child component can define the same component in its own providers array. The scope of the component travels through the chain of components. However, components that are defined in the `viewproviders` array aren't injected or inherited by the child components in the hierarchical chain.

Let's take a simple example that contains one main component in `app.ts` and `AppComponent` defines two providers: `ChildComponent` and `MathComponent`. `ChildComponent` is the child of the parent component, whereas `MathComponent` is used in both the parent and child components. If you notice, in the following code snippet, we have not specified the `MathComponent` in the `providers` array of the `ChildComponent`, and as it is defined in the `ParentComponent`, it is already injected by the Angular dependency injection module.

Here is the code snippet for `AppComponent` (parent):

```
//app.component.ts
import { Component} from 'angular2/core';
import {bootstrap} from 'angular2/platform/browser';
import {MathComponent} from './servicemanager.component';
import {ChildComponent} from './child.component';
@Component({
  selector: "my-app",
  template: `<button (click)="callChildComponentMethod()">
    Log</button>`,
  providers: [MathComponent, ChildComponent]
})
export class AppComponent  {
  childObj: ChildComponent;
    constructor(childComponent: ChildComponent) {
    this.childObj = childComponent;


}
  public callChildComponentMethod() {
    this.childObj.addNumbers(1, 2);


  }
}
bootstrap(AppComponent);
```

The following is the code snippet for `MathComponent`, which contains some basic arithmetic operations:

```
//math.component.ts
import { Component } from 'angular2/core';
@Component({})
export class MathComponent {

  public sum(a: number, b: number) : number{
    return a + b;
  }
  public divide(a: number, b: number): number {
    return a / b;
  }
  public subtract(a: number, b: number): number {
    return a - b;
  }
  public multiply(a: number, b: number): number {
    return a * b;
  }
}
```

Finally, here is the `ChildComponent` code, which does not have the `MathComponent` provider defined in the `providers` array:

```
//child.component.ts
import {Component} from 'angular2/core';
import {MathComponent} from './servicemanager.component';
@Component({
  selector: 'child-app',
  template: '<h1>Hello World</h1>'
})
export class ChildComponent {
  obj: MathComponent;
  constructor(mathComponent: MathComponent) {
    this.obj = mathComponent;
  }
  public addNumbers(a: number, b: number) {
    alert(this.obj.sum(a, b));
  }
}
```

Routing in Angular

Routing has an essential role when working with large applications. Routing is used to navigate to different pages. Routing can be defined in three steps:

1. Define `@RouteConfig` at any component level:

   ```
   @RouteConfig([
     { path: '/page1', name: 'Page1', component:
       Page1Component, useAsDefault: true },
     { path: '/page2', name: 'Page2', component:
       Page2Component }]
   )
   ```

2. Use the `[routerLink]` attribute on the anchor HTML tag and specify the route name configured in `@RouteConfig`.

3. Finally, add the `<router-outlet>` tag to render the page on the current navigated route.

The following example contains two components, `Page1Component` and `Page2Component`, and the main `AppComponent` has routing defined like this:

```
//app.component.ts
import {Component} from 'angular2/core';
import {RouteConfig, ROUTER_DIRECTIVES} from 'angular2/router';
import {Page1Component} from './page1.component';
```

```
import {Page2Component} from './page2.component';

@Component({
  selector: "my-app",
  template: `{{name}}
    <a [routerLink]="['Page2']">Page 2</a>
    <router-outlet></router-outlet>`,
  directives: [ROUTER_DIRECTIVES],
})
@RouteConfig([
  { path: '/', name: 'Page1', component: Page1Component,
    useAsDefault:true },
  { path: '/page2', name: 'Page2', component: Page2Component }]
)
export class AppComponent {
}
```

In the preceding code, first we imported the `RouteConfig` and `ROUTER_DIRECTIVES` from `angular2/router` and then defined the `RouteConfig` for page 1 and page 2. In the inline template, we placed the anchor tag and defined the route name for page 2. When the application runs, page 1 is set as a default page on a root path /, so the page 1 content will be displayed in place of the router outlet. When the user clicks on the `Page2` link, the page 2 content will be rendered in the same place.

Here is the code of `page1.component.ts`:

```
//page1.component.ts
import {Component} from 'angular2/core';
@Component({
  template:'<h1>Page1 Content</h1>'
})
export class Page1Component {
}
```

Here is the code of `page2.component.ts`:

```
//page2.component.ts
import {Component} from 'angular2/core';

@Component({
  template: '<h1>Page2 Content</h1>'
})

export class Page2Component {
}
```

Developing a to-do application in ASP.NET Core

We have learned the core features of Angular 2 and how to write programs in TypeScript. Now it's time to develop a simple to-do application using Angular 2 and ASP.NET Core. ASP.NET Core is the latest web development platform from Microsoft, which is more optimized and modular than previous versions of ASP.NET. It provides an option to use the machine-wide .NET Framework, or a new .NET Core which runs on an app-by-app basis and even contains the framework binaries in the published web application folder itself. With the new ASP.NET Core, we are not dependent for running our application on IIS, and there are several other servers provided to run cross-platform using Kestrel. To learn more about ASP.NET Core, please refer to `http://docs.asp.net`.

We will go through a step-by-step tutorial that leads to a working to-do application. The following screenshot show a snapshot of the main page. Once the user logs in, it will show a list of all the to-do items available. User can add a new to-do item by clicking a **Create Todo** button and deleting the existing one as well. We will not be covering the security authentication and authorization module in this chapter, instead focusing on how to use Angular 2 with ASP.NET Core:

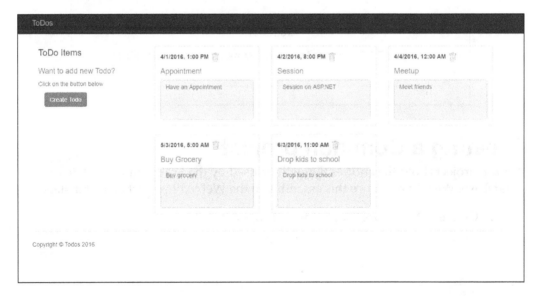

In this application, we will have three projects. TodoWebApp calls the TodoServiceApp, and Common is used by Web API, which holds the entity models. The following diagram shows how to develop these three projects and configure and use Angular 2:

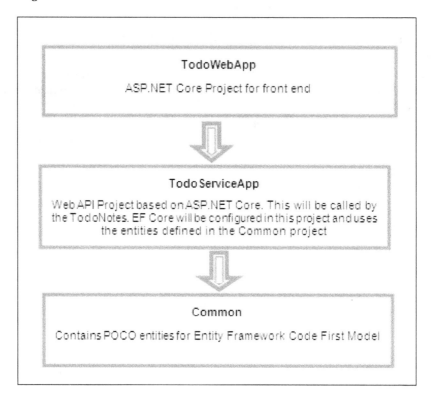

Creating a Common project

Common projects hold the entities that will be used by the Entity framework to create a database. We will reference this assembly in the Web API project at a later stage:

1. Create a .NET Core Class Library project:

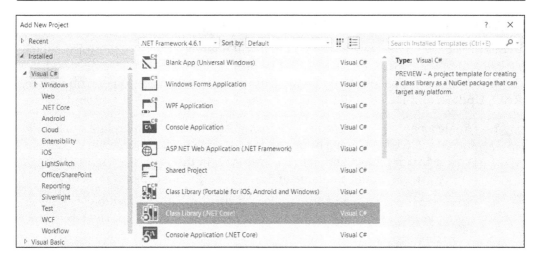

2. Add a new folder, `Models`, and add a `TodoItem` class as follows:

```csharp
using System;
using System.Collections.Generic;
using System.Linq;
using System.Threading.Tasks;

namespace Common
{
  public class TodoItem
  {
    public int Id { get; set; }
    public string Title { get; set; }
    public string Description { get; set; }
    public DateTime DueDateTime { get; set; }
    public int UserId { get; set; }
  }
}
```

The preceding `TodoItem` class contains the `Id` (primary key) and `Title`, `Description`, `DueDateTime`, and the `UserID` to save to-dos for a specific user.

Creating a TodoServiceApp project

In this project, we will create a web API that will reference the Common project which contains the TodoItem POCO model. In this project, we will expose services and create a database repository that will use Entity Framework Core to perform **Create, Read, Update, and Delete (CRUD)** operations in the Microsoft SQL Server database:

1. Create a new Web API project, choosing ASP.NET Core template. Web API and ASP.NET MVC have been merged into one unified framework, so there is no separate project template for Web API. In this case, we will use the Empty Project Model available in the ASP.NET Core project templates.

2. Open project.json and add a reference to our Common assembly:

    ```
    "dependencies": {
      "Microsoft.NETCore.App": {
        "version": "1.0.0-rc2-3002702",
        "type": "platform"
      },
      "Microsoft.AspNetCore.Server.IISIntegration":
        "1.0.0-rc2-final",
      "Microsoft.AspNetCore.Server.Kestrel": "1.0.0-rc2-final",
      "Common": "1.0.0-*"
    }
    ```

Enabling MVC in a Web API project

In order to enable the MVC project, we have to call AddMvc() in the ConfigureServices method, and UseMvc() in the Configure method:

1. Add the MVC package in project.json:

    ```
    "Microsoft.AspNetCore.Mvc": "1.0.0-rc2-final"
    ```

2. Call AddMvc() from the ConfigureServices method:

    ```
    public void ConfigureServices(IServiceCollection services)
    {
        services.AddMvc();
    }
    ```

3. Finally, call UseMvc() from the Configure method:

    ```
    public void Configure(IApplicationBuilder app)
    {
        app.UseMvc();
    }
    ```

Installing Entity Framework

Here are the steps to install Entity Framework:

1. Add two Entity Framework assemblies, `Microsoft.EntityFrameworkCore.SqlServer` and `Microsoft.EntityFrameworkCore.Tools`, as shown in the following code:

```
"dependencies": {
"Microsoft.NETCore.App": {
  "version": "1.0.0-rc2-3002702",
  "type": "platform"
},
"Microsoft.AspNetCore.Server.IISIntegration":
  "1.0.0-rc2-final",
"Microsoft.AspNetCore.Server.Kestrel": "1.0.0-rc2-final",
"common": "1.0.0-*",
"Microsoft.AspNetCore.Mvc": "1.0.0-rc2-final",
"Microsoft.EntityFrameworkCore.SqlServer":
  "1.0.0-rc2-final",
"Microsoft.EntityFrameworkCore.Tools": {
  "type": "build",
  "version": "1.0.0-preview1-final"
}
}
```

Adding AppSettings to store a connection string

ASP.NET Core provides various options for storing application settings. The default configuration file is now `appsettings.json`, which stores the data in a JSON format. However, there are other methods available as well to store data in the environment variables, XML, and INI formats as well. In this project, we will store the connection string in the `appsettings.json` file:

1. Add the ASP.NET configuration file `appsettings.json` and specify the connection string as follows:

```
{
  "Data": {
    "DefaultConnection": {
      "ConnectionString": "Data Source =.;
        Initial Catalog = tododatabase;
        Integrated Security = True;
        MultiSubnetFailover = False; "
    }
  }
}
```

2. Add the following packages in `project.json`:

```
"Microsoft.Extensions.Configuration.Json":
   "1.0.0-rc2-final",
"Microsoft.Extensions.Options.ConfigurationExtensions":
   "1.0.0-rc2-final",
```

Configuring AppSettings in the Startup class

The new configuration system of ASP.NET Core is based on `System.Configuration`. To use settings in our project, we will instantiate a `Configuration` object in our `Startup` class and use the `Options` pattern to access individual settings.

The `Options` pattern converts any class into a settings class and then we can inject that class into the controllers through ASP.NET's built-in dependency injection. Through the `options` class, the developer can access the settings keys and values, as shown in the following steps:

1. In the `Startup` class constructor, we will add the `appsettings.json` file using the `ConfigurationBuilder` object. `ConfigurationBuilder` allows a provision to add different providers and have a build method that builds the configuration stores in different providers and returns the `IConfigurationRoot` instance:

```
public Startup()
  {
    // Set up configuration sources.
    var builder = new ConfigurationBuilder()
      .AddJsonFile("appsettings.json")
    Configuration = builder.Build();
  }

    public IConfigurationRoot Configuration { get; set; }
```

 If multiple providers have the same keys, the last one specified in the `ConfigurationBuilder` will be used.

2. Now we can use the `Configuration` property to access the connection string, as follows:

```
Configuration["Data:DefaultConnection:ConnectionString"];
```

Adding data access in Web API

In this section, we will add a `TodoContext` and `TodoRepository` class to perform CRUD operations:

1. Add a new folder, `DataAccess`, and add the `TodoContext` class, which will be derived from the `DbContext` class. This is the main `TodoContext` class Entity Framework used to create the database:

```
using Common;
using Microsoft.Data.Entity;
using System;
using System.Collections.Generic;
using System.Linq;
using System.Threading.Tasks;

namespace TodoServiceApp.DataAccess
{
  public class TodoContext : DbContext
  {
    public DbSet<TodoItem> TodoItem { get; set; }
  }
}
```

2. We have to now override the `OnConfiguring()` method and call the `UseSqlServer()` method of the `DbContextOptionsBuilder` object. The `OnConfiguring()` method is called every time the `Context` object is initialized and configures the options specified. The `UseSqlServer()` method takes the connection string that is defined in the `appsettings.json` file, which we have configured in the `Startup` class. Now we want to inject the app settings object into this class. In order to do so, we will use the `Options` pattern. As per the options pattern, we shouldn't use the `Configuration` property we have defined in the `Startup` class directly, and instead we will create a custom POCO class that contains the same keys we have in our app settings file and overload the default `TodoContext` constructor, which accepts `IOptions<T>`, where `T` is our custom POCO app settings class.

3. As the connection string is defined in a nested object, our `Data` class will be as follows:

```
using System;
using System.Collections.Generic;
using System.Linq;
using System.Threading.Tasks;

namespace TodoServiceApp
{
```

```
public class Data
{
  public DefaultConnection DefaultConnection
    { get; set; }
}

public class DefaultConnection {

  public string ConnectionString { get; set; }
}
}
```

4. In the `Startup` class, we will call the `services.Configure()` method to populate this `Data` object with the keys specified in the `appsettings.json` file, and inject it in the repository we will be creating next.

5. Create a `TodoRepository` class that contains an `ITodoRepository` interface and its implementation, `TodoRepository`. This class will use the `TodoContext` object to perform database operations. Here is the code snippet for the `TodoRepository` class:

```
using Common;
using System;
using System.Collections.Generic;
using System.Linq;
using System.Threading.Tasks;
using TodoServiceApp.DataAccess;

namespace TodoServiceApp.Repository
{
  public interface ITodoRepository
  {
    void CreateTodo(TodoItem todoItem);
    void DeleteTodo(int todoItemId);
    List<TodoItem> GetAllTodos(int userId);
    void UpdateTodo(TodoItem todoItem);
  }

  public class TodoRepository : ITodoRepository
  {
    private TodoContext context;
    public TodoRepository()
    {
      context = new TodoContext();
    }
```

```
public List<TodoItem> GetAllTodos(int userId)
{
  return context.TodoItems.ToList();
}
public void CreateTodo(TodoItem todoItem)
{
  context.TodoItems.Add(todoItem);
  context.SaveChanges();
}
public void DeleteTodo(int todoItemId)
{
  var item = context.TodoItems.Where(i => i.Id ==
    todoItemId).FirstOrDefault();
  context.Remove(item);
  context.SaveChanges();
}
public void UpdateTodo(TodoItem todoItem)
{
  context.Update(todoItem);
  context.SaveChanges();
}

  }
}
```

6. In the `Startup` class, add the Entity Framework in the
   `ConfigureServices()` method, as shown the following code. Our
   Web API controllers will have an overloaded constructor that takes the
   `ITodoRepository` object. We will use the `services.AddScoped()` method
   to inject `TodoRepository` wherever `ITodoRepository` is required. Finally,
   call the `services.Configure()` method to populate the `Data` object with the
   keys specified in the `appsettings.json` file:

```
public void ConfigureServices(IServiceCollection services)
{
  string connString = Configuration["Data:
    DefaultConnection:ConnectionString"];
  services.AddDbContext<TodoContext>(options =>
  options.UseSqlServer(connString));

  services.AddMvc();

  services.AddScoped<ITodoRepository, TodoRepository>();
  services.Configure<Data>(Configuration.
    GetSection("Data"));

}
```

Enabling CORS in the ASP.NET Web API

We learned about CORS in the previous chapter; we have to enable CORS in our Web API project, so that from Angular services we can make a request to access the `TodoService` methods:

1. Call `services.AddCors()` in the `ConfigureServices` method in the `Startup` class:

    ```
    services.AddCors(options => { options.
    AddPolicy("AllowAllRequests", builder => builder.AllowAnyOrigin().
    AllowAnyMethod().AllowAnyHeader()); });
    ```

2. Call `app.UseCors()` in the `Configure` method in `Startup` class:

    ```
    app.UseCors("AllowAllRequests");
    ```

Running database migration

We are using the Entity Framework Code First model, so now we want to create a database in Microsoft SQL Server. To do so, we will first add the Entity Framework tool support in the `project.json` file of the `TodoServiceApp`, and then run .NET CLI commands to add migrations and create the database:

1. Add `Microsoft.EntityFrameworkCore.Tools` in the `project.json` file, as shown here:

    ```
    "tools": {
      "Microsoft.AspNetCore.Server.IISIntegration.Tools": {
        "version": "1.0.0-preview1-final",
        "imports": "portable-net45+win8+dnxcore50"
      },
      "Microsoft.EntityFrameworkCore.Tools": {
        "imports": [ "portable-net451+win8" ],
        "version": "1.0.0-preview1-final"
      }
    },
    ```

2. Now we can run commands, create migrations, and update the database.

3. To create migrations, go to the command prompt and navigate to the `TodoServiceApp` project where `project.json` resides.

4. Then, run `dotnet ef migrations add Initial`, where `Initial` is the name of the migration created. Running this command will add the `Migrations` folder and a class containing code about the DDL operations.

The following screenshot shows the `Migrations` folder created after running the preceding command, and the creation of the `20160405115641_Initial.cs` file that contains the actual migration code snippets to apply or remove migration from the database:

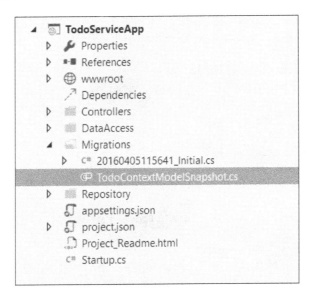

5. To create a database, we need to execute another command in the same folder where `project.json` resides in the `TodoServiceApp` project:

```
dotnet ef database update -verbose
```

6. This will create a database, and we can now go through, adding a controller to handle different HTTP requests and access the database.

Creating a controller

Follow these steps to create a controller:

1. Add a new `Controllers` folder and add a class named `TodoController`.

2. Here is the code snippet for the `TodoController` class:

```
using System;
using System.Collections.Generic;
using System.Linq;
using System.Threading.Tasks;
using Microsoft.AspNetCore.Mvc;
using Common;
```

```csharp
using TodoServiceApp.Repository;


namespace TodoApi.Controllers
{
  [Route("api/[controller]")]
  public class ToDoController : Controller
  {
    ITodoRepository repository;
    public ToDoController(ITodoRepository repo)
    {
      repository = repo;
    }
    // GET: api/values
    [HttpGet]
    public IEnumerable<string> Get()
    {
      return repository.GetAllTodos();
    }
    // GET api/values/5
    [HttpGet("{id}")]
    public IEnumerable<TodoItem> Get(int id)
    {
      return repository.GetAllTodos(id);
    }
    // POST api/values
    [HttpPost]
    public void Post([FromBody]TodoItem value)
    {
      repository.CreateTodo(value);
    }
    // PUT api/values/5
    [HttpPut("{id}")]
    // DELETE api/values/5
    [HttpDelete("{id}")]
    public void Delete(int id)
    {
      repository.DeleteTodo(id);
    }
  }
}
```

Now we have completed our `TodoService` project, so we will develop a todo web application project and configure Angular 2.

Creating a TodoWebApp project

We will develop a single-page application and use the MVC view to render it using Angular 2. This application will have one main page that lists all the to-do items for a particular user, whereas to add a new to-do item, a new page will open in a modal dialog window:

1. To start, let's create an empty project using the ASP.NET Core project template available in Visual Studio 2015, and name it TodoWebApp.

2. Add an MVC reference in project.json:

   ```
   "Microsoft.AspNetCore.Mvc": "1.0.0-rc2-final",
   "Microsoft.AspNetCore.StaticFiles": "1.0.0-rc2-final",
   ```

3. In the Startup class, add the AddMvc() method in the ConfigureServices method and the UseMvc() method in the Configure method. Here is the code snippet of the Startup class:

   ```
   namespace TodoWebApp
   {
     public class Startup
     {
       // This method gets called by the runtime. Use this
         method to add services to the container.
       // For more information on how to configure your
         application, visit
         http://go.microsoft.com/fwlink/?LinkID=398940
       public void ConfigureServices(IServiceCollection
         services)
       {
         services.AddMvc();
       }
       // This method gets called by the runtime. Use this
         method to configure the HTTP request pipeline.
       public void Configure(IApplicationBuilder app)
       {
         app.UseStaticFiles();
         app.UseMvc(routes =>
         {
           routes.MapRoute(name: "default", template:
             "{controller=Home}/{action=Index}/{id?}");
         }
       }
     }
   ```

Configuring Angular 2 in the TodoWebApp project

Angular 2 is part of the Node module, and we can add Node packages through the **Node Package Manager (NPM)** configuration file, `package.json`. In `package.json`, we can add packages through the `devDependencies` node and the `dependencies` node. The `devDependencies` node holds the packages that are used during development, such as `Gulp`, which can be used to concatenate and minify JavaScript and CSS files, TypeScript for developing Angular 2 components, and `rimraf` to delete the files. In the `dependencies` node, we will specify packages such as `angular2`, `systemjs`, `reflect-metadata`, `rxjs`, and `zone.js`, which will be used when the application runs:

1. Add a new `package.json` file from the Visual Studio project template option **NPM Configuration File** and add the following JSON snippet:

```
{
    "name": "ASP.NET",
    "version": "0.0.0",
    "dependencies": {
    "angular2": "2.0.0-beta.9",
    "systemjs": "0.19.24",
    "reflect-metadata": "0.1.3",
    "rxjs": "5.0.0-beta.2",
    "zone.js": "0.6.4"
    },
    "devDependencies": {
      "gulp": "3.8.11",
      "typescript": "1.8.7",
    }
}
```

2. Visual Studio automatically downloads and restores packages specified in the `package.json` file, creates a `node_modules` folder in the project itself, and places all the packages there. The `Node_modules` folder is basically hidden by default in Visual Studio, but can be made visible by enabling the `ShowAllFiles` option.

Dependencies

The following is the list of dependencies with their descriptions:

- `angular2`: It is the Angular 2 package.

- `systemjs`: It provides `System.import` to hook up the main entry point of Angular.

- `reflect-metadata`: It is a proposal to add decorators to ES7. Through this, we can specify the metadata to our class in Angular 2.

- `rxjs`: It is a reactive streams library that allows working with asynchronous data streams.

- `zone.js`: It provides an execution context that persists across asynchronous tasks.

Development dependencies

The following is the list of development dependencies with their descriptions:

- `gulp`: Used to copy the files to the `wwwroot` folder

- `typescript`: Used to write programs in TypeScript

Configuring TypeScript

To configure TypeScript, perform the following steps:

1. Add the `Scripts` folder where all the TypeScript files reside. In the current version of ASP.NET, there is a restriction on naming this folder `Scripts`, and it should be added in the root of the project; otherwise, TypeScript files will not be transpiled to JavaScript files.

2. After adding the `Scripts` folder, add the TypeScript configuration file (`tsconfig.json`) and add the following configuration to it:

```json
{
  "compilerOptions": {
  "noImplicitAny": false,
  "noEmitOnError": true,
  "removeComments": false,
  "sourceMap": true,
  "target": "es5",
  "module": "commonjs",
  "moduleResolution": "node",
  "outDir": "../wwwroot/todosapp",
  "mapRoot": "../scripts",
  "experimentalDecorators": true,
  "emitDecoratorMetadata": true
  },
  "exclude": [
    "node_modules",
    "wwwroot"
  ]
}
```

Configurations defined within the `compilerOptions` node are used by Visual Studio when you build your project. Based on the configuration, the JavaScript files are generated and stored in the output directory. The following table shows the description of each property specified in the preceding code:

Compiler options	Description
noImplicitAny	If `true`, then it warns the expression implied with `any` type
noEmitOnError	If `true`, it does not generate JavaScript if any errors are present in the TypeScript
removeComments	It `true`, removes comments when generating JavaScript files
sourceMap	If `true`, then generates the corresponding map file
Target	Sets the target ECMA script version, such as ES5
modulez	Specifies the module that generated the code, such as `commonjs`, AMD, or `system`
moduleResolution	Specifies the module resolution strategy, such as node
outDir	Path where the generated JavaScript files will be dumped
mapRoot	Path where the map files will be located
experimentalDecorators	If `true`, it enables support for ES7 experimental decorators
emitDecoratorMetadata	If `true`, it emits design-type metadata for decorator declarations in source

Configuring Gulp

In this section, we will use Gulp to minify the JavaScript generated by the TypeScript compiler:

1. Add the Gulp configuration file, `gulpfile.js`.
2. Gulp is used to run tasks, and Visual Studio provides a task runner window that lists all the tasks specified in the `gulpfile.js`, and also allows us to bind those tasks to build events.

3. Let's add the following script in `gulpfile.js`:

```
/// <binding Clean='clean' />
"use strict";

var gulp = require("gulp")

var paths = {
  webroot: "./wwwroot/"
};
var config = {
  libBase: 'node_modules',
  lib: [
    require.resolve('systemjs/dist/system.js'),
    require.resolve('systemjs/dist/system.src.js'),
    require.resolve('systemjs/dist/system-polyfills.js'),
    require.resolve('angular2/bundles/angular2.dev.js'),
    require.resolve('angular2/bundles/
      angular2-polyfills.js'),
    require.resolve('angular2/bundles/router.dev.js'),
    require.resolve('angular2/bundles/http.dev.js'),
    require.resolve('angular2/bundles/http.js'),
    require.resolve('angular2/bundles/angular2'),
    require.resolve('rxjs/bundles/Rx.js')
  ]
};
gulp.task('build.lib', function () {
  return gulp.src(config.lib, { base: config.libBase })
  .pipe(gulp.dest(paths.webroot + 'lib'));
});
```

In the preceding `gulpfile.js`, we have first declared the objects of Gulp. Then the paths variable defines the root folder (`./wwwroot`) for static files. In ASP.NET Core, all the static files should reside under the `wwwroot` folder; otherwise, they cannot be accessed. Now we need to copy the Angular and other related JavaScript files into the `wwwroot` folder. Therefore, we have added the task `build.lib` that calls `gulp.src()` and chains the `gulp.dest()` method to copy the files from the `node_modules/*` folder to the `wwwroot/lib` folder. Here is the screenshot of the `wwwroot` folder, which creates the `lib` folder when you run the preceding steps:

 Tasks can run through the task runner window in Visual Studio.

Adding Angular components

We have installed the Angular packages and configured Gulp to copy the packaged JavaScript files to the `wwwroot` folder. Now we will add Angular components to define our main application selector and render the ASP.NET page inside it:

1. In the `Scripts` folder, create two folders, `app` and `services`. The `app` folder holds the components that we will use in the view, whereas the `services` folder holds the services that will be used to call the Web API methods.

2. Add a main TypeScript file, which will bootstrap the main
   `TodoAppComponent`. Here is the code of `main.ts`:

```
//main.ts
import {bootstrap} from 'angular2/platform/browser';
import {TodoAppComponent} from './apps/todoapp.component';
import {HTTP_PROVIDERS} from 'angular2/http';
import 'rxjs/add/operator/map';

bootstrap(TodoAppComponent, [HTTP_PROVIDERS]);
```

In the preceding code snippet, we have added a `bootstrap` component to bootstrap our first `TodoAppComponent`. `HTTP_PROVIDERS` contains all the providers to make any HTTP request. It is provided while bootstrapping, so the `TodoAppComponent` or the chain of components in the following hierarchy can do HTTP-based operations. `Rxjs/add/operator/map` is a dependent package for `HTTP_PROVIDERS`, which needs to be added as well:

1. Add a new TypeScript file and name it `todoapp.component.ts`.

2. Add the following code snippet for `TodoAppComponent`. In order to first test whether everything is configured properly, we will simply add a sample heading tag that shows `Hello World`:

```
//todoapp.component.ts
///<reference path="../../node_modules/angular2/typings/
browser.d.ts" />
import {Component} from 'angular2/core';

@Component({

  selector: 'todo',
  template: '<h1>{{message}}</h1>'
})

export class TodoAppComponent {
  message: string = "Hello World";

}
```

3. Now we will add two files, `importer.js` and `angular_config.js`. `importer.js` calls `System.import` and points to the main file that bootstraps the application component. `angular_config.js` holds the configuration property to allow default JavaScript extensions to be set to `true`.

Here is the code snippet for `importer.js`:

```
System.import('todosapp/Main')
    .then(null, console.error.bind(console));
```

Here is the code for `angular_config.js`:

```
System.config({ defaultJSExtensions: true });
```

4. Now we need to add the MVC layout page and add all the scripts. Add the following scripts:

```
//_Layout.cshtml

<environment names="Development">
    <link rel="stylesheet"
      href="~/lib/bootstrap/dist/css/bootstrap.css" />
    <link rel="stylesheet" href="~/css/site.css" />
    <script src="~/lib/angular2/bundles/
      angular2-polyfills.js"></script>
    <script src="~/lib/systemjs/dist/system.js"></script>
    <script src="~/lib/custom/angular_config.js"></script>
    <script src="~/lib/rxjs/bundles/Rx.js"></script>
    <script src="~/lib/angular2/bundles/
      angular2.dev.js"></script>
    <script src="~/lib/angular2/bundles/
      router.dev.js"></script>
    <script src="~/lib/angular2/bundles/http.js"></script>
    <script src="~/lib/custom/importer.js"></script>
    <script src="https://ajax.aspnetcdn.com/ajax/jquery/
      jquery-2.1.4.min.js"
      asp-fallback-src="~/lib/jquery/dist/jquery.min.js"
      asp-fallback-test="window.jQuery">
    </script>
    <script src="https://ajax.aspnetcdn.com/ajax/bootstrap/
      3.3.5/bootstrap.min.js"
      asp-fallback-src="~/lib/bootstrap/dist/js/
        bootstrap.min.js"
      asp-fallback-test="window.jQuery &&
        window.jQuery.fn && window.jQuery.fn.modal">
    </script>
</environment>
```

5. Now let's add `HomeController` and view `Index.cshtml`.

6. In `Index.cshtml`, add the to-do selector `todo-app`:

```
@{
    ViewData["Title"] = "Todo Applications";
    Layout = "~/Views/Shared/_Layout.cshtml";

}
<div id="myCarousel" class="container" data-ride="carousel"
    data-interval="6000">
    <todo-app>Loading...</todo-app>
</div>
```

7. Build and run the application and it will show **Hello World**:

Adding the to-do service component

We will now add the components inside the `services` folder that will be responsible for getting data by calling the `Todo` service:

1. First of all, add the `BaseService` component, which contains `baseURL`. All the service components will derive from `BaseService` so they can use the base URL property for making Ajax requests. Add a new TypeScript file and name it `baseservice.component.ts`. Here is the code snippet for `baseservice.component.ts`:

```
//baseservice.component.ts
import {Component} from 'angular2/core';
import {Http, Headers} from 'angular2/http';

@Component({})
export class BaseService {
    baseUrl: string;
    constructor() {
        this.baseUrl = "http://localhost:7105/api/";
    }
}
```

2. Now add `todoservice.component.ts`, which contains the methods to get all to-do items, add a new to-do item, and delete an existing to-do item. Here is the code snippet for `TodoService`:

```
//todoservice.component.ts
import {Component} from 'angular2/core';
import {Http, Headers} from 'angular2/http';
import {BaseService} from
  '../services/baseservice.component';

@Component({
  providers: [TodoService]
})

export class TodoService extends BaseService {
  constructor(private http: Http) {
    super();
  }
  public getTodoItems() {
    return this.http.get(this.baseUrl + 'todo/1');
  }
  public createTodo(item) {
    var path = this.baseUrl + 'todo';
    const headers = new Headers({ 'Content-Type':
      'application/json' });
    return this.http.post(path, JSON.stringify(item), {
      headers: headers });
  }

  public deleteTodo(itemId) {
    var path = this.baseUrl + 'todo';
    return this.http.delete(path + "/" + itemId);
  }
}
```

In the preceding code, we imported the `http` component and injected the constructor. The `http` object provides methods such as `get`, `post`, `put`, and `delete` to read, insert, update, and delete operations. In our `TodoService` Web API project, we have these methods available, which we call as shown in the preceding code. Each method returns a promise, and in the calling components we will check the result and take appropriate actions.

Adding a to-do view component

We have already added `todoapp.component.ts` in the preceding step to check whether Angular is configured properly. Now we will modify the same component to call the `TodoServiceComponent` and display the results on a web page.

Here is the code snippet for `TodoApp.Component.ts`:

```
//todoApp.component.ts
///<reference path="../../node_modules/angular2/typings/browser.d.ts"
/>
import {Component} from 'angular2/core';
import {Http, Response} from 'angular2/http';
import {CreateTodoComponent} from '../apps/createTodo.component';
import {TodoService} from '../services/todoservice.component';

@Component({
  selector: 'todo-app',
  templateUrl: 'Todo',
  directives: [CreateTodoComponent],
  providers: [TodoService]
})
export class TodoAppComponent {
  //member variables
  todos = [
  ];

  //constructor
  constructor(private http: Http, private todoService:
    TodoService) {
  }

  //Page Initialized Event Handler
  ngOnInit() {
    this.getTodoItems();
  }

  //Member Functions
  getTodoItems() {
    this.todoService.getTodoItems().map((res: Response) =>
      res.json())
      .subscribe(data => {
        this.todos = data
        this.parseDate();
      },
```

```
        err  => console.log(err),
        () => console.log('done')
        );
  }
  deleteTodoItem(itemID) {
    var r = confirm("Are you sure to delete this item");
    if (r == true) {
      this.todoService.deleteTodo(itemID)
        .map(r=> r.json())
        .subscribe(result => {
          alert("record deleted");
      });
  }
  this.getTodoItems();
  }

  parseDate() {
    for (let todo of this.todos) {
      let todoDate = new Date(todo.DueDateTime);
      todo.DueDateTime = todoDate;
    }
  }

  handleRefresh(args) {
    this.getTodoItems();
  }
}
```

In `TodoAppComponent`, we have first added the `CreateTodoComponent` directive we will be using in the `Todo/Index.cshtml` page in a later step. We have implemented the `ngOnInit()` event handler that gets the list of to-dos and bound it to the `todos` array object. The `getTodoItems()` method calls the `TodoService` to get the list of to-do items, whereas `deleteTodoItem()` is used to delete the item.

Every request in Angular returns an `Observable` response object that provides a `map` method to tell Angular to parse the response in a specific format. The map also returns the `Observable` object, which can be used to subscribe to the data once it is parsed into the JSON format, as in our case. Finally, we have called the `subscribe` method and sent the JSON response data to the `todos` array. To handle errors, we can chain the call with the `err` method. The anonymous `expression()` method is invoked in every call, irrespective of the response status. That means whether the result is a success or an error, the code defined under the anonymous `expression()` method will be executed.

For creating new to-dos, we will create another `CreateTodoComponent` later, which will call the `handleRefresh()` method through the `Outputs` event to refresh the list and reflect the newly added item on the main page.

Creating the main to-do page

We have created the Angular components that we will use in the MVC view. We have already bootstrapped the Angular components in the previous section and placed the `<todo-app>` tag in the `Home/Index.cshtml` page, which is the landing page of our application. Next, we will create a custom tag helper, then add a `TodoController`, and use this tag helper in the index page.

Creating a custom to-do tag helper

On the main page, we will list all the to-do items for a particular user. For this, we will create a custom tag helper in ASP.NET:

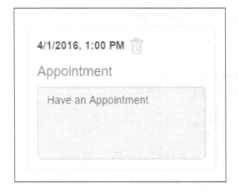

Perform the following steps to create this tag helper:

1. Create a new controls folder in the root of the `TodoWebApp` project and add a `TodoTagHelper` class. Here is the code for `TodoTagHelper`, which uses Angular 2 `ngControl` to bind values from Angular `TodoAppComponent` to the form:

```
[HtmlTargetElement("todo")]
public class TodoTagHelper : TagHelper
{
    public override void Process(TagHelperContext context,
      TagHelperOutput output)
    {
        string todo = "<div class='thumbnail'><div
          class='caption'><nav class='nav navbar-inverse'
          role='navigation'></nav>";
```

```
        todo += "<label class='date'>{{todo.DueDateTime |
          date:'short'}}</label> <img src='images/delete.png'
          (click)=deleteTodoItem(todo.Id)/>";

        todo += "<h4><a href='#'>{{todo.Title}}</a></h4>";
        todo += "<textarea readonly class='form-control'
          style='resize:none;' rows='4' cols='28'>
          {{todo.Description}}</textarea></div></div>";
        output.Content.AppendHtml(todo);
      }
    }
```

2. Add the tag helper in _ViewImports.cshtml:

```
@addTagHelper "*, TodoWebApp"
```

Adding a to-do MVC controller

Add TodoController in the TodoWebApp project and specify two methods for the
index view, which is the main view that displays all the items and creates a new
to-do item:

```
using System.Linq;
using Microsoft.AspNetCore.Mvc;
using TodoNotes.Models;

namespace TodoNotes.Controllers
{
  public class TodoController : Controller
  {
    public TodoController()
    {
      _context = context;
    }
    // GET: Todo
    public IActionResult Index()
    {
      return View();
    }

    // GET: Todo/Create
    public IActionResult Create()
    {
      return View();
    }

  }
```

Generating views for the TodoController action methods

Generate views for the preceding action methods `Index` and `Create`.

Here is the code snippet for `Todo/Index.cshtml`:

```
@{
  Layout = null;
}
<div class="col-md-3">
  <p class="lead">ToDo Items</p>
  <div class="list-group">
    <h4>
      <a href="#">Want to add new Todo?</a>
    </h4>
    <p>Click on the button below</p>
    <div class="col-md-3">
      <a class="btn btn-primary" data-toggle="modal"
        data-target="#todoModal">Create Todo</a>

    </div>
  </div>
</div>
<div id="todoModal" class="modal fade" role="dialog">
  <div class="modal-dialog">

    <!-- Modal content-->
    <div class="modal-content">
      <div class="modal-header">
        <button type="button" class="close"
          data-dismiss="modal">&times;</button>
        <h4 class="modal-title">Insert Todo</h4>
      </div>
      <div class="modal-body">
      <createTodo (refreshTodos)="handleRefresh($event)">
        </createTodo>
      </div>

    </div>
  </div>
</div>
<div class="col-md-9">
  <div class="row" >
    <div class="col-sm-4 col-lg-4 col-md-4" *ngFor="#todo of
      todos">
      <todo></todo>
```

```
        </div>

    </div>
</div>
```

In the preceding HTML markup, we have first defined a button that opens up a modal dialog, todoModal. In the todoModal dialog markup, we have used the createTodo directive, which is defined in the todoapp.component.ts file associated with this page, and the link actually points to the Todo/Create MVC view, which will be rendered at the place of router-outlet. With the combination of the router link and the router outlet, we can render the template. In todoapp.component.ts, we will see how we can use routing in Angular. Finally, we have used the custom tag helper <todo> to display each item available in the to-do list.

Developing the Create Todo component

In this section, we will add the Angular component and name it CreateTodoComponent. This is needed because we will be opening a new MVC view in a modal dialog through a custom createTodo selector, and CreateTodoComponent has a method to save a new to-do in the database, as shown in the following code.

Add a new createtodo.component.ts under the Scripts>apps folder, and then add the following code snippet:

```
//createtodo.component.ts
///<reference path="../../node_modules/angular2/typings/
  browser.d.ts" />
import {Component} from 'angular2/core';
import {Http, Response} from 'angular2/http';
import {FormBuilder, Validators} from 'angular2/common';
import {TodoService} from '../services/todoservice.component';

@Component({
  selector: 'createTodo',
  templateUrl: 'Todo/Create'
})

export class CreateTodoComponent {

  @Output() refreshTodos = new EventEmitter();

  addTodoForm: any;

  constructor(fb: FormBuilder, private todoService: TodoService) {
    this.addTodoForm = fb.group({
      title: ["", Validators.required],
      description: ["", Validators.required],
```

```
      dueDateTime: ["", Validators.required]
    });
  }
  addTodoItem(): void {
    this.todoService.createTodo(this.addTodoForm.value)
      .map(r=> r.json())
      .subscribe(result => {});
    this.refreshTodos.next([]);
    alert("Record added successfully");
  }

}
```

In the preceding code snippet, we have imported the `Http` and `Response` objects to handle the response received from `TodoService`. In the `@Component` annotation, we have defined the selector that is used in the parent `TodoAppComponent` component to render the `Create Todo` view inside the modal dialog.

`FormBuilder` and `Validator` are used to define properties with specific validators that can be bound to the HTML form using the `ngControl` directive. Lastly, we have the `addTodoItem` method, which will be invoked on form submission and make a to-do entry in the database by calling `TodoService`.

Now let's add the following code in `Create.cshtml`:

```
@{
  Layout = null;
}

<form [ngFormModel]="addTodoForm" (submit)="addTodoItem($event)"
  class="container" >
  <div class="form-horizontal">
    <div class="form-group">
      <label class="col-md-2 control-label">Title</label>
      <div class="col-md-10">
        <input ngControl="title" class="form-control" id="Title"
          placeholder="Enter Todo Title" [(ngModel)]="title" />
      </div>
    </div>
    <div class="form-group">
      <label class="col-md-2 control-label">Description</label>
      <div class="col-md-10">
        <textarea ngControl="description"  class="form-control"
          placeholder="Enter Description"></textarea>
        {{description}}
      </div>
    </div>
```

```
    <div class="form-group">
      <label class="col-md-2 control-label">Due Date</label>
      <div class="col-md-10">
        <input ngControl="dueDateTime" class="form-control"
          type="datetime-local" placeholder="Enter Due Date" />
      </div>
    </div>
    <div class="form-group">
      <div class="col-md-offset-2 col-md-10">
        <input type="submit" value="Create"
          class="btn btn-primary" />
      </div>
    </div>
  </div>
</form>
@section Scripts {
  <script src="~/lib/jquery/dist/jquery.min.js"></script>
  <script src="~/lib/jquery-validation/dist/
    jquery.validate.min.js"></script>
  <script src="~/lib/jquery-validation-unobtrusive/
    jquery.validate.unobtrusive.min.js"></script>
}
```

In the preceding code snippet, we have set the ngFormModel to the model we defined in the createtodo.component.ts and the submit form, and we are calling the addTodoItem method, which sends all the values bound with the ngControl directive. ngControl is a new directive introduced in Angular 2 that provides unidirectional binding. With forms, ngControl not only binds the value, but also tracks the state of the control. If the value is invalid, it updates the control with special CSS classes to tell the user that the value is invalid.

Summary

In this chapter, we learned about the core components of TypeScript and writing programs using TypeScript. We also learned the core fundamentals and concepts of the Angular 2 framework and developed a simple to-do application using ASP.NET Core, Angular 2, MVC 6 for Web API, and Entity Framework Core for data access providers. In the next chapter, we will learn about **Windows JavaScript Library (WinJS)**, developed by Microsoft, and see how we can access Windows runtime features, change the appearance of HTML controls, and other options available in this library.

6
Exploring the WinJS Library

Web development has led to revolutionary experiences. With frameworks like bootstrap, material, and others , we are now able to run web applications at their best on different screen sizes and adjust their content accordingly. Developers target web applications to run on different platforms providing a consistent experience to their customers. For example, any web application using bootstrap and other frameworks can run on a browser, tablet, and a mobile device providing the best user experience ever imagined. With these benefits, new prospects were introduced and allow web applications to target different devices bringing the need for accessing client-side device-specific features and layouts as well. With these revolutionary experiences, companies started bringing JavaScript-based libraries that not only changed the look and feel of the applications running on devices but also allowed developers to use device-specific features like sending toast notifications, accessing the camera to upload pictures, and so on, leveraging user experience.

Introduction to WinJS

Windows JavaScript (WinJS) library is an open source JavaScript library developed by Microsoft. It was released in April 2014 during the Microsoft build conference and with Windows 10, Microsoft officially released version 4.0. Currently it's open source and under an Apache 2.0 license.

It was initially targeted for Windows store apps that were based on JavaScript, CSS, and HTML but later supported in modern browsers as well. Today developers can develop mobile applications for any platform including Windows apps, Android apps, and iOS apps using JavaScript, CSS, and HTML and they can use this library to transform the **user interface (UI)** to a native mobile interface with the provision of accessing features of the Windows runtime. The WinJS library exposes not only the Windows runtime modules but also provides Windows UI control setup for use in web applications. WinJS provides Windows runtime features like the classes and runtime components and they can be accessed through JavaScript code. Users can build apps that access device features like the camera, storage, geolocations, filesystems, and style applications that give the best user experience. It also provides a layer of security which keeps the device features safe and protects them from malicious attacks. As far as browser compatibility is concerned, all the modern browsers including Microsoft Edge, Google Chrome, and others support this library. The basic advantage is that now web developers can build Windows store applications using WinJS controls suite and library to use Windows runtime features. Moreover, Microsoft has also empowered WinJS library to integrate with popular client-side frameworks like AngularJS, Knockout, Ember, and Backbone and you can use WinJS directives in your HTML with other controls directives and it works as expected.

WinJS features

WinJS is not only designed to serve universal windows apps that are based on HTML and JavaScript but a generalized JavaScript library that can be used with web applications as well. WinJS brings various features that we will discuss in the following section.

JavaScript coding and language patterns

WinJS provides the coding pattern of defining custom namespaces and classes performing binding implementations and promises.

Stylesheets

It provides two stylesheets, namely UI-dark and UI-light, which can be used with HTML elements to give a particular Windows app a themed appearance. Also, it allows you to handle different screen sizes and orientation like landscape and portrait.

Windows runtime access

We can access the windows runtime features like filesystem, camera, geo-location, and others which are applicable through the native application API.

Security

With the provision of enabling windows runtime features, WinJS also restricts the access to sensitive data on the device.

App model

App model offers events initiated by a Windows application and can be registered in our JavaScript to do a specific operation. For example, suspend, resume, and initialization are some useful events we can use to handle specific tasks through registering them in WinJS.

Databinding

Just like other frameworks like AngularJS, KnockOut, and so on, WinJS also provides specific databinding directives and syntax that is used to bind HTML controls with the data supplied or that exist in your JavaScript code.

Controls

WinJS provides specific controls apart from the extended attributes on HTML elements. These controls are available in the native Windows apps project and with WinJS we can use them in our HTML page to bring the same experience.

Utilities

WinJS provides several utilities to perform localization, animations, and DOM selectors.

Usage of WinJS

Microsoft has developed various applications using WinJS library. Applications like Skype, Store, Weather, News, and others are all developed in HTML, CSS, and JavaScript using WinJS library. The modern era of web development made JavaScript a core framework of developing responsive and rich applications that run on any platform and on any device. This lead Microsoft to invest heavily on WinJS and to make this library useful for web developers who want to create Windows apps or use Windows platform features from web applications. With the release of **Universal Windows Platform (UWP)**, Microsoft released the new **Universal App Platform (UAP)**, a super set of the WinRT platform used by Windows 8 applications. With UWP there is a new Hosted app concept introduced, that allows any web application to convert into the Windows app with a very minimum set of configuration properties.

Adding the WinJS library in the ASP.NET application

WinJS can be added through **Node Package Manager** (**NPM**), NuGet, and by referencing a CDN. This depends on whether you want to keep the files local on the server or as reference from CDN.

CDN

Here is the CDN library that contains JavaScript and CSS files that you can add in your application: `https://cdnjs.com/libraries/winjs`.

NPM

To install it with NPM you can run `npm install winjs` or just add the `winjs` package in the `package.json` file when working in the ASP.NET core application.

NuGet

To install it via NuGet you can add the WinJS package through the NuGet package manager console or just run the following command in the ASP.NET application:

```
Install-Package WinJs
```

The WinJS package comes with a set of JavaScript files and the CSS stylesheets for darker or lighter UI. The following table defines the files and their usage:

File	Type	Usage
`Base.js`	JavaScript	This is a core module and it is used by `UI.js` to provide Windows runtime features
`UI.js`	JavaScript	Contains UI controls
`WinJS.intellisense.js`	JavaScript	Provide intellisense when using WinJS components in JavaScript
`ui-dark.css`	CSS	Stylesheet for darker UI theme
`ui-light.css`	CSS	Stylesheet for lighter UI theme

Getting started with WinJS

Microsoft has provided certain templates in Visual Studio to develop store applications using JavaScript and HTML, on the other hand, we can also add it in our ASP.NET application to bring certain functionalities of Windows runtime features or changing a look and feel accordingly.

Using WinJS in the ASP.NET application

You can start using WinJS by adding the JavaScript to use Windows runtime features and CSS to make UI as Windows applications. In the ASP.NET web application you can add the package through NPM by making an entry, as follows:

```
"dependencies": {
    "winjs": "4.4.0"
}
```

On saving the file, the package will be downloaded automatically in Visual Studio 2015 under the `node_modules\npm` folder.

Here is a screenshot of the folders the WinJS library contains. JS contains `winjs` modules, `css`, and `fonts` that can be used to change UI look and feel:

You can use `Gulp.js` to copy the `css` and `js` files to the `wwwroot` folder and reference them on the page, we can add the following sample code that displays the `You have clicked!` text on a button click event:

```
<!DOCTYPE html>
<html>
<head>
    <meta charset="utf-8" />
    <title></title>
    <script src="lib/winjs/js/base.js"></script>
```

```
        <script src="lib/winjs/js/ui.js"></script>
        <script src="lib/winjs/js/winjs.intellisense-setup.js"></script>
        <script src="lib/winjs/js/winjs.intellisense.js"></script>
        <script src="http://ajax.aspnetcdn.com/ajax/jquery/jquery-
1.9.0.js"></script>
        <link rel="stylesheet" href="lib/winjs/css/ui-dark.css" />
    </head>
    <body>
        <div class="win-container">
            <button class="win-button" id="btn">Show</button>
            <span id="txtMessage"></span>
        </div>
        <script>
            (function () {
                WinJS.UI.processAll().done(function () {
                    $('#btn').click(function () {
                        $('#txtMessage').text("You have clicked!");
                    });
                });
            })();
        </script>
    </body>
</html>
```

The following is the output:

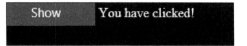

On page load, the function will be executed that registers the click event for the button when all the WinJS controls are processed. The `WinJS.UI.processAll()` method parses whole **document object model (DOM)** and searches for the WinJS controls to process and return a promise after the binding is done for all the controls.

Under the hood, `WinJS.UI.processAll()` only processes those controls which have the `isDeclarativeControlContainer` property set as `true`. This tells WinJS which controls need to be bound with the WinJS library. If you are using custom controls then you need to specify this `isDeclarativeControlContainer` property so it can be processed by WinJS.

Events can be registered through declarative binding or by registering an event from JavaScript. In the preceding code we have registered the button click event through JavaScript however; declaratively you can also set the event and call some JavaScript functions that can be invoked when the button is clicked.

Existing Windows app template in Visual Studio

Windows apps can be developed either using the XAML and C# or by using an HTML, CSS, and JavaScript project template. Visual Studio provides certain templates for both the models and auto configures the WinJS library to start adding features in your application instead of adding packages and configurations for each project manually. You can add the new project form with the following options in Visual Studio 2015. As shown in the following screenshot:

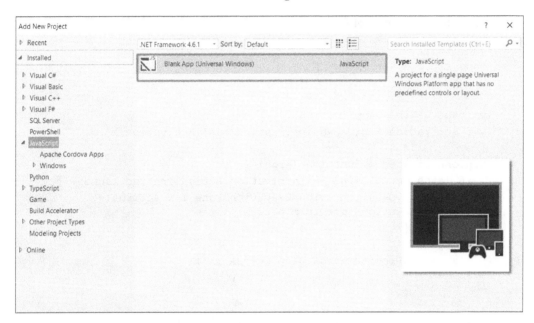

This template adds all the related CSS, JavaScript, and related images that WinJS provides and also adds the default.js file that contains the winJs.ProcessAll() function to bind the HTML elements with WinJS library. The following is the default.html page snippet that contains the WinJS libraries and default.js:

```
<!DOCTYPE html>
<html>
<head>
    <meta charset="utf-8" />
    <title>App1</title>

    <!-- WinJS references -->
    <link href="WinJS/css/ui-dark.css" rel="stylesheet" />
    <script src="WinJS/js/base.js"></script>
```

```
        <script src="WinJS/js/ui.js"></script>

        <!-- App1 references -->
        <link href="/css/default.css" rel="stylesheet" />
        <script src="/js/default.js"></script>
    </head>
    <body class="win-type-body">
        <p>Content goes here</p>
    </body>
    </html>
```

And here is the code snippet for `default.js`:

```
(function () {
    "use strict";


    var app = WinJS.Application;
    var activation = Windows.ApplicationModel.Activation;

    app.onactivated = function (args) {
        if (args.detail.kind === activation.ActivationKind.launch) {
            if (args.detail.previousExecutionState !== activation.
ApplicationExecutionState.terminated) {
            } else {
            }
            args.setPromise(WinJS.UI.processAll());
        }
    };

    app.oncheckpoint = function (args) {
    };

    app.start();
})();
```

Exploring WinJS core fundamentals

Before using WinJS library in any of the projects, it is best to know the core concepts that help us to write quality programs and use the best of what the library offers.

Classes and namespaces

Through WinJS we can create classes and namespace with some special syntax. This is provided in the WinJS library to handle complex scenarios. As we know, classes and namespaces are the features of ECMAScript 6, but unfortunately none of the browsers have proper implementation yet. However, with WinJS we can define classes and namespaces and it's a useful option to use them where needed.

Defining classes in WinJS

Classes in WinJS can be defined through the `WinJS.Class.define()` method. Here is the sample code of a class in WinJS:

```
<script>
        var Logger = WinJS.Class.define(function (value) {
            //constructor
            console.log("Constructor is executing, value passed is: "
+ value );
        }
        );
    //Initializing Logger class object
      var log = new Logger("Hello World");
</script>
```

In the preceding code we have created a class named `Logger`, where the first function's parameter is the constructor, second is for any `instanceMembers` like properties and methods and third for `staticMembers` to define static members and properties. The following is the signature of the `define` method:

Function define(Function constructor, **Object instanceMembers**, Object staticMembers)

Defines a class using the given constructor and the specified instance members.

instanceMembers: *The set of instance fields, properties, and methods made available on the class.*

Now let's add the property `message` and the `LogMessage()` method in the same class `Logger`:

```
<script>
        var Logger = WinJS.Class.define(function (value) {
                this.logName = value;
                this.enabled;
          //constructor
            console.log("Constructor is executing, value passed is " +
value );
          }, {
```

```
            logMessage: function (message) {
                if (this.logEnabled) {
                    alert("The message is" + message);
                }
            },
        logEnabled: {
                get: function () { return this.enabled; },
                set: function (value) { this.enabled = value; }
            }
        }
        );

        var log = new Logger("Sample log");
        log.logEnabled = true;
        log.logMessage("Hello World");
    <script>
```

The syntax of defining the methods for the class is a method name followed with a colon (:) and the function body as follows:

```
logMessage: function (message) {
            alert("The message is" + message);
        }
```

The properties can be defined with get and set function methods as shown in the following code:

```
logEnabled: {
            get: function () { return this.enabled; },
            set: function (value) { this.enabled = value; }
        }
```

Multiple properties and methods can be defined in a same way separated with comma as shown in the following code:

```
    logEnabled: {
                get: function () { return this.enabled; },
                set: function (value) { this.enabled = value; }
            },

        logType: {
                get: function () { return this.loggerType; },
                set: function (value) { this.loggerType = value;}
            }
```

Deriving classes in WinJS

Classes in WinJS can be derived by using the `WinJS.class.derive()` method. Considering the previous example, we can also add the `logEnabled` and `logType` properties on the base class and then derive the `Logger` class from the `BaseLogger` class. Here is the code to derive classes in WinJS:

```
<script>
        var BaseLogger = WinJS.Class.define(function (logName) {
            this.enabled;
            this.loggerType;
            this.loggerName = logName;
        }, {
            logEnabled: {
                get: function () { return this.enabled; },
                set: function (value) { this.enabled = value; }
            },

            logType: {
                get: function () { return this.loggerType; },
                set: function (value) { this.loggerType = value; }
            }
        });

        var Logger = WinJS.Class.derive(BaseLogger, function (logName)
{
            //calling base constructor and passing the LogName to the
base constructor
            BaseLogger.call(this, logName);
        },
        {
            logMessage: function (message) {
                if (Object.getOwnPropertyDescriptor(BaseLogger.
prototype, "logEnabled").get.call(this) == true) {
                    alert("The message is " + message);
                }
            },

        }
        );

        var log = new Logger("Hello World");
        log.logEnabled = true;
        log.logType = "Alert";
        log.logMessage("hello");
</script>
```

In the above script we have taken both the properties `logType` and `logEnabled` to the base class `BaseLogger`. In WinJS, base properties can be accessed through the following syntax:

```
Object.getOwnPropertyDescriptor(BaseLogger.prototype, "logEnabled").
get.call(this)
```

Settings can be done by calling the `set` method after the `getOwnPropertyDescriptor()` method call:

```
Object.getOwnPropertyDescriptor(BaseLogger.prototype, "logEnabled").
set.call(this) = true;
```

Now if you want to take the `logMessage()` method on the `BaseLogger` class, we can do it through prototyping, as follows:

```
BaseLogger.prototype.logMessage.call(this);
```

Namespaces in WinJS

In object oriented programming, namespaces play an important role in organizing classes and categorizing your code. For example, the services can reside under the `ApplicationName.Services` namespace; models can reside under the `ApplicationName.Models` namespace, and so on.

We should always use namespaces where possible as it solves many problems that could occur in mid-size to larger projects. For example, we have two JavaScript files added in our page that have similar names of properties or functions. The one referenced later will supersede the member functions or variables of the previous ones if they have the same name.

WinJS provides an easy way to logically organize classes into namespaces and you can define a namespace by calling `WinJS.Namespace.define("namespace name", {})))`.

Here is the example that encapsulates both the `BaseLogger` and `Logger` class into the `Demo.App.Utilities` namespace:

```
WinJS.Namespace.define("DemoApp.Utilities", {
        //BaseLogger class
        BaseLogger: WinJS.Class.define(function (logName) {
            this.enabled;
            this.loggerType;
            this.loggerName = logName;
        }, {
            logEnabled: {
                get: function () { return this.enabled; },
```

```
                            set: function (value) { this.enabled = value; }
                        },

                        logType: {
                            get: function () { return this.loggerType; },
                            set: function (value) { this.loggerType = value; }
                        },
                    }),

                    //Logger class
                    Logger: WinJS.Class.derive(BaseLogger, function (logName)
{
                        //calling base constructor and passing the LogName to
the base constructor
                        BaseLogger.call(this, logName);
                    },
                    {
                        logMessage: function (message) {
                            if (Object.getOwnPropertyDescriptor(BaseLogger.
prototype, "logEnabled").get.call(this) == true) {
                                alert("The message is " + message);
                            }
                        },

                    })
                });
```

Now the `Log` class can be accessed by specifying its namespace, as shown in the
following code:

```
var log = new DemoApp.Utilities.Logger("Sample Logger");
        log.logEnabled = true;
        log.logType = "Alert";
        log.logMessage("hello");
```

Mixin

Most of the languages do not support multiple inheritance. However, in WinJS we
can do it through mixins. Like class, `mixin` is a collection of methods and properties
but the object of mixins cannot be instantiated. It is used to mix with a class to bring
the methods and properties that mixins have. For example, the following is a Mixin
`logMixin` that contains a `logMessage()` method:

```
var logMixin = {
    logMessage: function (message) {
                alert(message);
            }
```

```
};

var SampleClass = WinJS.Class.define(function(){

});

WinJS.Class.mix(SampleClass, logMixin);

var sample = new SampleClass();

sample.logMessage("Mixin");
```

We can add as many mixins when calling the `mix` method. If two or more have common methods or properties, later one will override the existing one. Let's look into the examples which have two mixins, namely `logMixin` and `logConsoleMixin`. Both the mixins and a `SampleClass` have a same `logMessage()` method. Now based on the specification, the methods will be overridden and when the `logMessage()` is invoked it will write a message on a console log:

```
//First Mixin
var logMixin = {
    logMessage: function (message) {
        alert(message);
    }
};

//Second Mixin
var logConsoleMixin = {
    logMessage: function (message) {
        console.log(message);
    }
}

//Class
var SampleClass = WinJS.Class.define(function () {

},

logMessage= function(message){
var result = confirm(message);
});


WinJS.Class.mix(SampleClass, logMixin, logConsoleMixin);

var sample = new SampleClass();
sample.logMessage("Mixin");
```

Events in WinJS

WinJS provides an `eventMixin` object that can be used to register, unregister, and dispatch events through the following basic steps:

1. First of all, the class from which we need to call the dispatch event needs to have `WinJS.Utilities.eventMixin` added. We can add this through the `WinJS.Class.mix` method, as follows:

   ```
   WinJS.Class.mix(SampleClass, WinJS.Utilities.eventMixin);
   ```

2. Once the `eventMixin` is inherited by the `SampleClass`, we can call the `dispatchEvent()` method to dispatch on a particular action. Here is the code of the `Sample` class that dispatches the event once the `execute` method is called:

   ```
   var SampleClass = WinJS.Class.define(function () {
   },
   {
       execute: function(message){
           this.dispatchEvent("executeInvoked", { message:
   "Executed" });
       }
   });
   ```

3. Next, we can add the `addEventListener()` method and provide the `eventHandler()` that will be invoked once the dispatch message is called:

   ```
   var sampleClass = new SampleClass();
   var sampleEventHandler = function (event) {

       alert(event.detail.message);
   };
   sampleClass.addEventListener("executeInvoked",
   sampleEventHandler);

   sampleClass.execute("hello");
   ```

Databinding

WinJS provides an easy way of binding any JavaScript data source to the HTML element. Any JavaScript data source can be bound using `data-win-bind` attribute on an HTML element. Databinding facilitates in separating the data with the view and allows you to write less code and bind the data with the elements using WinJS, which provides three types of databinding as follows.

One time databinding

One time databinding is used to bind the element on an HTML page from a JavaScript data source. It is unidirectional, that means if the JavaScript data source is updated it will not reflect the change on the HTML to which it is bound to.

Here is the HTML code that has two controls which binds the properties name and description with the view model defined in your JavaScript:

```
<div id="rootDiv">
        <div> Course Name:
            <span id="divForm" data-win-bind="innerText:
name">loading</span>
        </div>
        <div>
            Course Description:
            <span id="divForm" data-win-bind="innerText:
description">loading</span>
        </div>
    </div>
Below is the JavaScript code which defines the view model
let ViewModel = WinJS.Class.define(function () {
                this.nameProp;
                this.descProp;
            },
            {
            name: {
                get: function () { return this.nameProp; },
                set: function (value) { this.nameProp = value; }
            },
            description: {
                get: function () { return this.descProp; },
                set: function (value) { this.descProp = value; }
            }
        });

        let viewModel = new ViewModel();
        viewModel.name = "WinJS databinding";
        viewModel.description = "Introduction to WinJS
    databinding";
        var personDiv = document.querySelector('#rootDiv');
        WinJS.Binding.processAll(personDiv, viewModel);
```

One way databinding

One way databinding is a unidirectional binding. Once the HTML element is bound to the JavaScript data source, any changes in the data source will reflect the change on the HTML page but if something is updated on the HTML element, it will not update the backend JavaScript data source. One way databinding can be done by making the source model observable. So if anything changes on the source object it will update the UI element to which it is bound to. It can either be done by using the `WinJS.binding.as()` method or adding the `observableMixin` with the source class.

The following is an example of one way databinding that binds the properties `Name` and `Description` and on the button click event, updates the HTML element and sets the value set from the backend data source. Adding a button in the previous HTML page added in the *One time databinding* section:

```
//HTML markup
<button id="btnUpdate">Click</button>

//JavaScript
   let ViewModel = WinJS.Class.define(function () {
                      this.nameProp;
                      this.descProp;
            },
            {
  name: {
     get: function () { return this.nameProp; },
     set: function (value) { this.nameProp = value; }
         },
  description: {
     get: function () { return this.descProp; },
     set: function (value) { this.descProp = value; }
         }
  });

let viewModel = new ViewModel();
viewModel.name = "WinJS databinding";
viewModel.description = "Introduction to WinJS databinding";
var personDiv = document.querySelector('#rootDiv');

let observableViewModel = WinJS.Binding.as(viewModel);

   WinJS.Binding.processAll(personDiv, observableViewModel);

document.querySelector('#btnUpdate').onclick = function () {
   observableViewModel.name = "new name";
  observableViewModel.description ="new description";
}
```

Two way databinding

Two way databinding works in both directions. Once the JavaScript object is bound to the HTML control, any changes done on the control itself or if the value of the JavaScript object gets changed, the control value will be updated and vice versa. Implementing two way binding in WinJS is not straight forward. We need to have the one way binding in place to reflect any change happening on the backend data source to reflect on the frontend, as well as to update the backend data source from any changes done on the UI element. This can be done by implementing `onPropertyChange()`, `onKeyDown()`, `onChange()`, or `onClick()` and others based on the HTML element:

```
someTextboxElement.onpropertychange=function(){
    someModel.property = someTextboxElement.value;
}
```

Another approach is to implement a custom binding initializer which can be used as highlighted in the following code:

```
<input type="text" data-win-bind="value: someProperty Binding
twoWayBinding" />
```

Let's create a custom two way binding initializer and extend the same `viewModel` to accept the name and description updates through textboxes. Here is the code of our custom two way binding initializer:

```
//Defining Binding initializer to support two way binding
WinJS.Namespace.define("Binding.Mode", {
    twoway: WinJS.Binding.initializer(function
                        (source, sourceProperties, destination,
destinationProperties) {
        WinJS.Binding.defaultBind(source, sourceProperties,
destination, destinationProperties);
        destination.onchange = function () {
            var destValue = destination[destinationProperties[0]];
            source[sourceProperties[0]] = destValue;
        }
    })
});
```

Then create a class that contains two properties, namely `name` and `description`:

```
//Defining class
let ViewModel = WinJS.Class.define(function () {
                    this.nameProp;
                    this.descProp;
                },
```

```
{
name: {
get: function () { return this.nameProp; },
set: function (value) { this.nameProp = value; }
},
description: {
get: function () { return this.descProp; },
set: function (value) { this.descProp = value; }
}
});


//Initializing class Instance
let viewModel = new ViewModel();
viewModel.name = "WinJS databinding";
viewModel.description = "Introduction to WinJS databinding";


var rootDiv = document.querySelector('#rootDiv');
let observableViewModel = WinJS.Binding.as(viewModel);
WinJS.Binding.processAll(rootDiv, observableViewModel);
```

In the above code, we have first defined the binding initializer using `WinJS.Binding.initializer`. When defining this initializer we have to pass four properties namely source element and its properties object and destination element and its properties. So for example, in our case the source element is a textbox and the source property is its value, whereas the destination element will be a span and `innerText` as its destination property. `WinJS.Binding.defaultBind` creates the one way binding and then we can register the `onchange()` event of the source property which updates the destination property. Then we defined a class and then initialized the values by initializing an instance. And finally, we have transformed the model into the observable model to provide two way binding.

Now, in the HTML element, we can add the binding as follows:

```
<div id="rootDiv">
        <div
 <input type="text" data-win-bind="value: name Binding.twoWayBinding"
/>
        </div>
        <div>
            Course Name:
            <span id="spanName" data-win-bind="innerText:
name">loading</span>
        </div>
        <div>
```

```
<input type="text" data-win-bind="value: description Binding.
twoWayBinding" />
        </div>
        <div>
            Course Description:
            <span id="spanDesc" data-win-bind="innerText:
description">loading</span>
        </div>
    </div>
```

A databinding working model

When the databinding is done in WinJS, the `WinJS.processAll()` method has to be called if it's done using WinJS. This method scans all the elements which specify the `data-win-bind attributes`. For each element, it checks if the data bound with the element is observable or not. This is a crucial step which identifies the type of binding and declares whether the binding is a one way binding, one time binding, or two way binding.

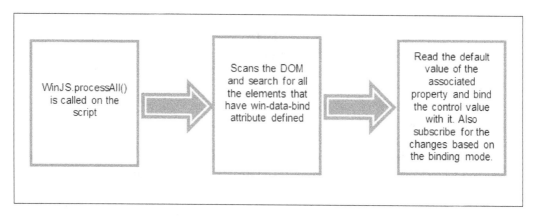

Promises

Promises represent an object that contains a value that might be available at any time. It's a promise which satisfies the consumer that the resource will be available and the consumer can do the rest of the work without waiting for the resource in an asynchronous manner.

It works as an async/await feature of C#. Promises allow consumers to do other work rather than waiting for the value to return and provides certain methods to acknowledge the consumer once the promise is received. In certain cases, there is a chance of not having the response return due to some error and that can also be handled by implementing specific callbacks.

In WinJS, promise is an object with functions `then` and `done`. We can initialize promise as follows:

```
var promise = new WinJS.Promise(function (completed, error, progress)

//Call if we need to update consumer that still in progress
progress("progress");

//Call if any error occurs
error("error");

//Call when the function is completed
completed("completed");
}
);
```

The preceding code is the way of defining a function that returns a promise. We can then call a `progress` method if the method is not completed and we need to notify the consumer if something is in progress. Once the promise is defined, we can use the `then` and `done` methods to implement callback methods that will be triggered by promise. The `then` method returns a promise and denotes the intermediate stage of the operation whereas `done` is the final stage of the operation and does not return a `promise`:

```
promise.then(
function () { console.log("completed"); },
function () { console.log("error") },
function () { console.log("promise") }
);
```

The following example shows the function that displays the table in a console window and returns completed once the promise is processed:

```
function executeTable(table, max)
{
   return new WinJS.Promise(function(completed, error, progress){
   for (i = 1; i < max; i++) {
      console.log(table +' X '+ i +' = ' + (table * i ));
   }
   completed("executed table")
});
};

   executeTable(2, 10).then(
            function (completedVal) {
                    console.log(completedVal);
```

```
        }, function (errorVal) {
                console.log(errorVal);
        },
        function (onProgressVal) {
                console.log(onProgressVal);
        }


    )
```

The following is the output:

```
2 X 1 = 2
2 X 2 = 4
2 X 3 = 6
2 X 4 = 8
2 X 5 = 10
2 X 6 = 12
2 X 7 = 14
2 X 8 = 16
2 X 9 = 18
2 X 10 = 20
executed table
```

Now let's modify the same example and invoke progress to send intermediate results to the consumer on each iteration. The preceding method is synchronous and returning promise doesn't mean the method will be executed asynchronously. To make this method run asynchronously we can wrap the block of code through the setImmediate() function.

setImmediate() is the JavaScript function which is used to interrupt the execution of the function and returns the callback function immediately, that eventually invokes the onProgress() function of promise in our case. Here is the modified version with the setImmediate() and onProgress() methods:

```
function executeTable(table, max)
        {
            return new WinJS.Promise(function (completed, error,
    onProgress) {
                window.setImmediate(function () {
                    for (i = 1; i <= max; i++) {
                        var row = table + ' X ' + i + ' = ' +
    (table * i);
```

```
                    onProgress(row);
              }
              completed("executed table")
          }, 0);
        });
      };


  executeTable(2, 10).then(
        function (completedVal) {
              console.log(completedVal);
        }, function (errorVal) {
              console.log(errorVal);
        },
        function (onProgressVal) {
              console.log(onProgressVal);
        }


  )
```

The result of the preceding code snippet will be the same as shown in the previous example. However, the use of the `setImmediate()` function allows the `onProgress()` method to write messages to the console window asynchronously and is more efficient in terms of performance.

Other operations of promises

There are several other methods on promises that can be used to cancel any promises, chain promises, timeout, wrap, and so on. Let's look over each method and see how it can be used.

Chaining promises and handling errors

Multiple promises can be chained using `then` and based on the order they are chained, get executed one by one sequentially. Here is the simple example that loads the web page using the `WinJS.xhr()` method. This method is the built in method that returns a promise and we can use this method to make HTTP requests:

```
var promise1 = function () { return WinJS.xhr({ url: "http://
microsoft.com" }) };
        var promise2 = function () { return WinJS.xhr({ url:
"http://google.com" }) };
        var promise3 = function () { return WinJS.xhr({ url:
"http://techframeworx.com" }) };
        var promise4 = function () { return WinJS.xhr({ url:
"http://msdn.microsoft.com" }) };
```

```
promise1().then(function (dataPromise1) {
    console.log("got the response from promise 1");
    return promise2();
}).then(function (dataPromise2) {
    console.log("got the response from promise 2");
    return promise3();
}).then(function (dataPromise3) {
    console.log("got the response from promise 3");
    return promise4();
}).done(function (dataPromise4) {
    console.log("got the response from promise4");
    console.log("completed the promise chain");
});
```

In the preceding code we are returning the next promise on every promise chain execution block. This is required when chaining promises otherwise it would not call the next promise in the pipeline. For the last promise in the pipeline, we have used done instead of then which actually tells us that there isn't a promise next in the chain and no chaining can be done now. Another benefit is to perform error handling. In the done method, we can get all the errors being thrown by any of the promises in the chain. If we don't use done then we will not be able to access any errors thrown in the promise chain. The following example is the modified version of the previous example with error handling:

```
var promise1 = function () { return WinJS.xhr({ url:
"http://microsoft.com" }) };
var promise2 = function () { return WinJS.xhr({ url:
"http://google.com" }) };
var promise3 = function () { return WinJS.xhr({ url:
"htt://techframeworx.com" }) };
var promise4 = function () { return WinJS.xhr({ url:
"http://msdn.microsoft.com" }) };

promise1().then(function (dataPromise1) {
    console.log("got the response from promise 1");
    return promise2();
}).then(function (dataPromis2) {
    console.log("got the response from promise 2");
    return promise3();
}).then(function (dataPromise3) {
    console.log("got the response from promise 3");
    return promise4();
}).done(function (dataPromise4) {
    console.log("got the response from promise 4");
    console.log("completed the promise chain");
```

```
}, function (error) {
    console.log("some error occurred, cause: " + error);
});
```

In the preceding example we have used `done` in the final promise in the chain. Now, if you have noticed, the promise 2 URL is not valid and there is a typo mistake. Now if we execute the preceding code, `promise1` and `promise2` will be executed and will write the messages in the console log window. Whereas, the promise will not be executed but the `error` method will be invoked and defined under the `done` method and will write the error description in the console log window:

```
got the response from promise 1
got the response from promise 2
some error occurred, cause: [object XMLHttpRequest]
```

Canceling promises

Promises can be canceled by calling the `cancel` method on the `promise` object. The following is an example to cancel any promise:

```
var promiseGoogle = function. () { return WinJS.xhr({ url: "http://
google.com" }) };
            googlePromiseObj = promiseGoogle();
            googlePromiseObj.cancel();
```

Promises can only be canceled if it's not completed and went into the error state once it was canceled.

Joining promises

Multiple promises can be joined together and return when all of them are finished. We can join promises, as shown in the following code:

```
var promise1 = function () { return WinJS.xhr({ url: "http://
microsoft.com" }) };
            var promise2 = function () { return WinJS.xhr({ url:
"http://googe.com" }) };
            var promise3 = function () { return WinJS.xhr({ url:
"http://techframeworx.com" }) };
WinJS.Promise.join([promise1, promise2, promise3])
.done(function(){
  console.log("All the promises are finished");
});
```

`Promise.any()` can be used in cases when we need to know if any of the defined promises inside the `any` method have executed:

```
var promise1 = function () { return WinJS.xhr({ url: "http://
microsoft.com" }) };
var promise2 = function () { return WinJS.xhr({ url: "http://googe.
com" }) };
var promise3 = function () { return WinJS.xhr({ url: "http://
techframeworx.com" }) };
WinJS.Promise.any([promise1, promise2, promise3])
.done(function(){
  console.log("One of the promises is finished");
});
```

Checking promise

`WinJS.Promise.is()` is a method that takes a value as a parameter and checks if that value is a promise or not. For example, calling `WinJS.xhr` in the `WinJS.Promise.is()` method will return `true`:

```
WinJS.Promise.is(WinJS.xhr({ url: "http://microsoft.com" }));
```

Wrapping non-promise into promise

Any function can be wrapped into the promise using the `WinJS.Promise.as()` method. The following code wraps the non-promise `displayMessage()` method into a promise:

```
function displayMessage() {

                console.log("This is a non promise function")
        }
        var promiseDisplayMessage = WinJS.Promise.
as(displayMessage);
        promiseDisplayMessage.done(function () { console.
log("promise is executed") });
```

Exploring WinJS controls and styles

Windows library for JavaScript provides a rich set of controls, databinding options, and promises and in this section we will explore a few popular controls and styling options.

None of the WinJS controls have separate markup, instead WinJS library provides several attributes that can be used with the existing HTML elements.

Adding WinJS controls

As we have seen, there are no any markups for WinJS controls and they can be added through attributes on the HTML elements. WinJS controls can be added by adding any HTML element and setting its `data-win-control` attribute value to the name of the WinJS control.

In the following example, we are changing a simple HTML button element into the back button usually seen in store apps. And this can be done by adding the `data-win-control` attribute and setting a fully qualified name to `WinJS.UI.BackButton`.

Here is the HTML markup:

```
<button data-win-control="WinJS.UI.BackButton">WinJS button</button>
```

When you run it, it will render a back button on the page, as shown in the following figure:

Also it does not only change the look but also provides the backward navigation functionality out of the box.

Setting properties of WinJS controls

Every HTML element has several properties which can be addressed by specifying values through attributes. For example, rating control allows a user to rate any item and we can set the properties, like the `max` and `min` range of stars to be displayed:

```
<div id="ratingControl" data-win-control="WinJS.UI.Rating"
        data-win-options="{minRating: 1, averageRating : 5,
maxRating: 10}"></div>
```

The output of the preceding mark-up will generate a rating control like the following figure:

There are other Windows specific controls like `ListView`, `FlipView`, and `Zoom` that you can use in your page and bring high performance on large collections or objects. You can learn more about controls at the Windows Dev Center website at: `https://msdn.microsoft.com/en-us/library/windows/apps/mt502392.aspx`

Using Windows runtime features

WinJS provides a complete API to use Windows runtime features and device specific features. When accessing the device specific features using WinJS, the web application should run as a windows application and accessing it from a browser will result in an error. Also, Microsoft has released the concept of Hosted apps which enable any web application to host as a windows application with a few configuration steps.

Hosted apps and accessing the camera

Hosted apps were introduced with the launch of UWP. Let's create a simple example to convert a simple ASP.NET core application into a Windows application using the Hosted app concept and access the camera.

Creating the ASP.NET core application

Create a simple ASP.NET core application in Visual Studio 2015 and add the WinJS packages through NPM. Here is the code snippet of `package.json`:

```
{
  "version": "1.0.0",
  "name": "ASP.NET",
  "private": true,
  "dependencies": {
    "winjs": "4.4.0"
  },
  "devDependencies": {
    "gulp": "^3.9.1"
  }
  }
```

We can add WinJS under the dependencies section and on saving the `package.json` file, the package will be downloaded automatically. We have to add gulp as well to copy the related libraries and CSS files in the `wwwroot` folder. After this, add the `gulpfile.js` and add the following script:

```
/// <binding Clean='clean' />
"use strict";
var gulp = require("gulp");
```

```
var paths = {
    webroot: "./wwwroot/"
};
var config = {
    libBase: 'node_modules',
    lib: [
        require.resolve('winjs/js/base.js'),
        require.resolve('winjs/js/ui.js'),
        require.resolve('winjs/js/winjs.intellisense.js'),
        require.resolve('winjs/js/winjs.intellisense-setup.js')
    ],
    libCss: [require.resolve('winjs/css/ui-dark.css'),
        require.resolve('winjs/css/ui-light.css')
    ]
};
gulp.task('build.lib', function () {
    return gulp.src(config.lib, { base: config.libBase })
    .pipe(gulp.dest(paths.webroot + 'lib'));
});
gulp.task('build.libCss', function () {
    return gulp.src(config.libCss, { base: config.libBase })
    .pipe(gulp.dest(paths.webroot + "lib"));
});
```

When you run the `build.lib` and `build.LibCss` tasks through a task runner tab in Visual Studio 2015, it will copy the WinJS libraries and CSS files inside the `wwwroot` folder:

In this application, we will have a simple HTML page that we can directly add into the `wwwroot` folder, for this we need to call the `app.UseStaticFiles()` method in the `Configure()` method and add the package in `project.json`:

```
"Microsoft.AspNet.StaticFiles": "1.0.0-rc1-final"
```

Let's add the `Index.html` page inside the `wwwroot` folder and add the following scripts in the HTML head element:

```
<script src="lib/winjs/js/base.js"></script>
<script src="lib/winjs/js/ui.js"></script>
```

```
<script src="lib/winjs/js/winjs.intellisense-setup.js"></script>
<script src="lib/winjs/js/winjs.intellisense.js"></script>
<script src="http://ajax.aspnetcdn.com/ajax/jquery/jquery-
1.9.0.js"></script>
```

We will be using the light Windows theme so add ui-light.css, as follows:

```
<link rel="stylesheet" href="lib/winjs/css/ui-light.css" />
```

Now add the page content which contains a button Capture to capture the image and an image element to display the captured image:

```
<div id="rootDiv">
    <div class="col-md-4">
        Click to capture image <input type="button" value="Capture"
onclick="return CaptureCamera();" />
    </div>
    <br />
    <img id="imgPhoto" width="500" height="500"
style="border:dotted;" />
</div>
```

The following is the output of the page:

Now add the following script to access the camera and attach the captured image with the image element:

```
<script>
    if (window.Windows) {
        function CaptureCamera() {
            var notifications = Windows.UI.Notifications;
            var dialog = new Windows.Media.Capture.
CameraCaptureUI();
            var aspectRatio = { width: 1, height: 1 };
            dialog.photoSettings.croppedAspectRatio =
aspectRatio;
            dialog.captureFileAsync(Windows.Media.Capture.
CameraCaptureUIMode.photo).done(function (capturedImage) {
                if (capturedImage) {
                    var imageURL = URL.
createObjectURL(capturedFile, { oneTimeOnly: true });
                    document.getElementById("img").src =
imageURL;
                }
                else {
                    WinJS.log && WinJS.log("No image captured
yet", "WinJSTestApp", "Status");
                }
            }, function (err) {
                WinJS.log && WinJS.log(err, "WinJSTestApp",
"Error");
            });
        }
    } else {
        function CaptureCamera() {
            alert("Cannot access camera, it should be hosted
as a windows application");
        }
    }
</script>
```

Converting an ASP.NET application into Windows application using the Hosted app concept

Converting any web application into the Windows application is very simple. In Visual Studio 2015 you can start creating a simple JavaScript based Windows application using the **Blank App (Universal Windows)** template as shown in the following screenshot:

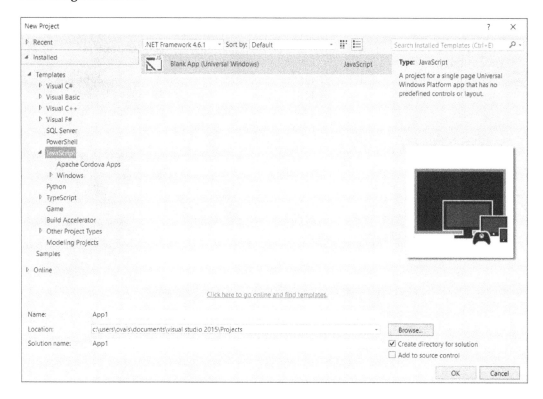

When you add a project it will add the css, images, js, and winjs folders. We have to delete the css, js, and winjs folders as we will not be using any of the files in this project and configure the web application created above and transform it to a Windows application.

Open the `package.appxmanifest` window. Add the URL in the **Start Page** textbox as shown in the following screenshot. Our sample ASP.NET application created above was hosted on port `41345`:

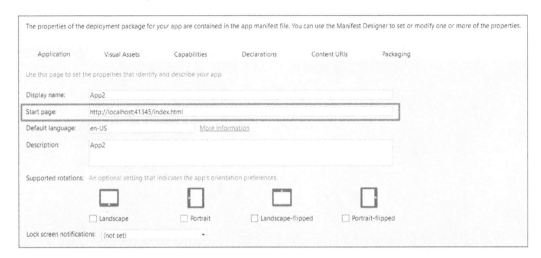

In the **Content URIs** tab, add the URI of our web application and select **All** under **WinRT Access**. You can specify the URL of any web application which should be hosted somewhere. In the preceding screenshot we are using localhost which actually points to a web application hosted locally:

This window allows us to specify access rules to WinRT features and we can set it to `None`, `All`, or `Allow for web only`.

Building and running the application will show the windows application dialog hosting our web application `index.html` page:

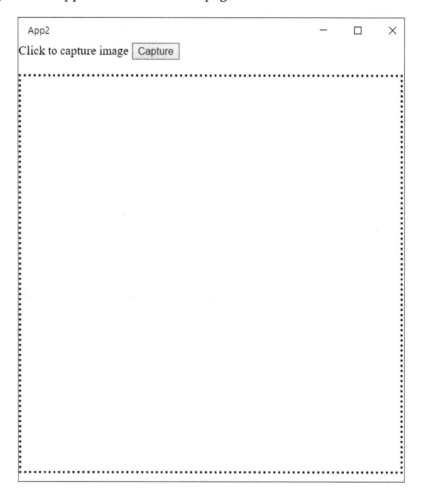

Clicking on the **Capture** button will provide a popup of another dialog to take a snapshot, as shown in the following screenshot:

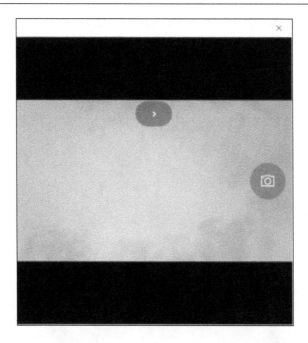

After taking the desired shot, it will ask you to save or reject through tick and cross buttons:

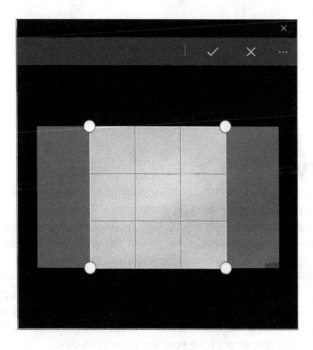

Selecting tick will render the photo in the `img` HTML element, as shown in the following screenshot:

Summary

In this chapter, we explored the WinJS Windows library for JavaScript library which is open source and under an Apache license. We learned the core concepts of defining classes, namespaces, deriving classes, mixins, and promises. We also looked into the databinding techniques and how to use the windows controls or attributes in HTML elements to change the behavior and look and feel of the control. And finally, we used the WinRT API to access the device camera in our web application and learned the concept of Hosted app and transforming any web application into the Windows apps using the Universal Window template in Visual Studio 2015. In the next chapter, we will learn about a few good design patterns that can be implemented in JavaScript to achieve specific requirements.

7
JavaScript Design Patterns

In every mid- to large-sized projects, good architecture and design always plays an important role in handling complex scenarios and increasing the maintainability of the product. Design patterns are best practices developed and used by professional developers to solve a particular problem. If a design pattern has been used in the application for specific scenarios, it evades many of the issues one could face during development or when running the application in production. Design patterns solve the problems by providing the guidelines which are industry best practices to handle problems or to achieve or implement any requirement. A singleton pattern, for example, is used to create only one instance that is shared among all, whereas a prototype is used to extend the existing functionality of an object by adding more properties and methods and so on. Design patterns are classified into three categories, namely creational, structural, and behavioral patterns. The topics which we will cover in this chapter are as follows:

- **Creational patterns**: The following are the creational patterns we will discuss in this chapter:
    - Singleton pattern
    - Factory pattern
    - Abstract factory pattern
    - Prototype pattern

- **Structural patterns**: The following are the list of structural patterns we will discuss in this chapter:
    - Adapter pattern
    - Decorator pattern
    - Facade pattern
    - Bridge pattern

- **Behavioral patterns**: The following are the list of behavioral patterns we will discuss in this chapter:
  - Chain of responsibility
  - Observer pattern
  - Pub/sub pattern
  - Promises

Creational patterns

Creational patterns are used for object instantiation. They are used in situations where the basic form of object creation could result in design problems or increase complexity to the design. In the following section, we will discuss all four creational patterns mentioned previously, and how to implement them in JavaScript.

Singleton design pattern

Singleton is the most widely used pattern. It is used in scenarios where we need to share the same instance of a class or function (in terms of JavaScript) between different objects. It ensures that there is only one instance of particular object which can be accessed globally at any point:

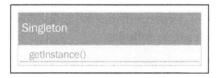

In a singleton pattern, the constructor should be private which restricts the user to create objects using a `new` keyword and exposes one method that creates an instance and verifies that only one instance exists. A simple example could be a logger object that writes the log to the browser's console window:

```
<script>
    var Logger = (function () {

        //private variable
        var instance;

        //private method
        function initializeInstance() {
            //closure returns the public access to the writeLog
function that can be accessible by the singleton object
            return {
```

```
                       writeLog: function (message) {
                            console.log(message);
                       }
                  };
            };
         //closure that returns the public access to the getInstance
   method that returns the singleton object
         return {
                  //This is a public method that returns the singleton
   instance
              getInstance: function () {
                    if ( !instance ) {
                         instance = initializeInstance();
                    }
                    return instance;
              },
         };
      }) ();

    var logger = Logger.getInstance();
    logger.writeLog("Hello world");
</script>
```

 In JavaScript (ES5 standard), classes are still represented through functions.

In JavaScript, to implement a singleton, we can use closures. Closures are inner objects that have access to the private members of the function, such as accessing variables and methods defined within a parent function, and are accessible from closures.

Brackets () in the last statement are specified to assign the object returning to the logger variable rather than the function itself. This actually restricts the object from initializing through a new keyword.

In the preceding script, the function first returns the closure that has one getInstance() method, which actually checks the private member variable instance and if it is not initialized it calls the initializeInstance() method that returns another closure containing the writeLog() method. We can add more methods or variables separated by commas and they will be accessible with the logger object. Here is the modified version of the initializeInstance() method that has one more method, showAlert(), and a variable, logEnabled:

```
function initializeInstance() {
            //closure returns the public access to the writeLog
   function that can be accessible by the singleton object
```

```
            return {
                writeLog: function (message) {
                    if(this.logEnabled)
                        console.log(message);
                },
                showAlert: function (message) {
                    if(this.logEnabled)
                        alert(message);
                },
                logEnabled: false
            };
        };
```

Factory pattern

The factory pattern delegates object instantiation to the centralized class. Instead of instantiating the object using a `new` keyword, we call the `factory` method that returns the type of the object requested:

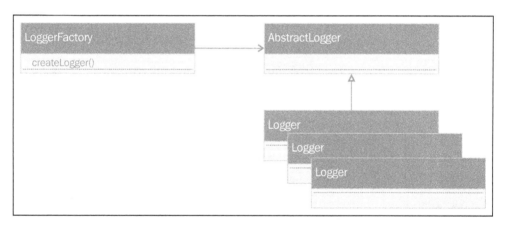

Here is an example of the `LoggerFactory` that creates the logger instances based on the logger type:

```
//LoggerFactory to instantiate objects based on logger type
    function LoggerFactory() {
        var logger;
        this.createLogger = function (loggerType) {
            if (loggerType === "console") {
                logger = new ConsoleLogger();
            }
            else if (loggerType === "alert") {
```

```
            logger = new AlertLogger();
        }
        return logger;
    }
}

//Console logger function
var ConsoleLogger= function(){
    this.logMessage=function(message){
        console.log(message);
    }
};

//Alert logger function
var AlertLogger= function(){
    this.logMessage= function(message){
        alert(message);
    }
};

var factory = new LoggerFactory();

//creating Console logger object using LoggerFactory
var consoleLogger = factory.createLogger("console");
consoleLogger.logMessage("Factory pattern");

//create Alert logger object using LoggerFactory
var alertLogger = factory.createLogger("alert");
alertLogger.logMessage("Factory pattern");
```

In our example, the factory class is LoggerFactory that creates instances
of ConsoleLogger and AlertLogger objects. LoggerFactory exposes a
createLogger() method that takes the type of logger as a parameter to determine
which object needs to be instantiated. Each type of logger has its own logMessage()
method to either log on the console window or show an alert message.

Abstract factory pattern

The abstract factory pattern encapsulates the collection of factories to create instances. The instance exposes the same method that can be invoked by the factory. The following is an example of two factories, ShapeFactory and CarFactory and each one returns two types of instance. ShapeFactory returns Circle and Square instances whereas CarFactory returns HondaCar and NissanCar instances. Each of the instance have the same method make() that can be called for any instance:

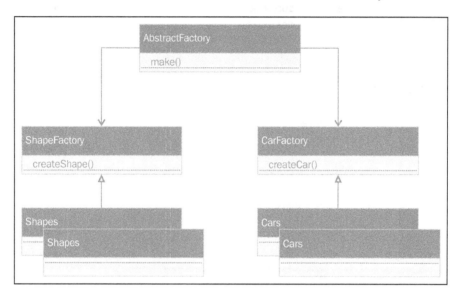

Here is the code for ShapeFactory:

```
<script>
    //Shape Factory to create instances of Circle and Square
    var ShapeFactory = function() {
        var shape;
        this.createShape = function (shapeType) {
            if (shapeType === "circle") {
                return new CircleShape();
            }
            else if (shapeType === "square") {
                return new SquareShape();
            }
        }
    }

    //Circle object to draw circle
```

```
var CircleShape = function () {
    this.make = function () {
        var c = document.getElementById("myCanvas");
        var ctx = c.getContext("2d");
        ctx.beginPath();
        ctx.arc(100, 75, 50, 0, 2 * Math.PI);
        ctx.stroke();
    }
}

//Square object to draw square
var SquareShape= function () {
    this.make = function () {
        var c = document.getElementById("myCanvas");
        var ctx = c.getContext("2d");
        ctx.beginPath();
        ctx.rect(50, 50, 50, 50);
        ctx.stroke();
    }
}
```

The following is the code for `CarFactory` that creates instances of Honda and Nissan cars:

```
//Car factory to create cars
var CarFactory= function() {
    var car
    this.createCar = function (carType) {
        if (carType === "honda") {
            return new HondaCar();
        }
        else if (carType === "nissan") {
            return new NissanCar();
        }
    }
}

//Honda object
var HondaCar = function () {
    this.make = function () {
        console.log("This is Honda Accord");
    }
}

//Nissan object
```

```
var NissanCar = function () {
    this.make = function () {
        console.log("This is Nissan Patrol")
    }
}
```

We call the `execute` method on a button click event which creates the instances and holds them in an array. Eventually the objects `make()` method will be executed that draws the circle on a HTML canvas and writes messages on the console. As in JavaScript, we cannot define abstract methods; we have to explicitly define the same method, such as `make()` in our case that completes our abstract factory pattern:

```
function execute() {
    //initializing an array to hold objects
    var objects = [];

    //Creating Shape Factory to create circle shape
    var shapeFactory = new ShapeFactory();
    var circleShape = shapeFactory.createShape("circle");

    //Creating Car Factory to create cars
    var carFactory = new CarFactory();
    var hondaCar= carFactory.createCar("honda");
    var nissanCar = carFactory.createCar("nissan");

    //Adding all the instances created through factories
    objects.push(circleShape);
    objects.push(hondaCar);
    objects.push(nissanCar);

    //Calling make method of all the instances.
    for (var i = 0; i < objects.length; i++) {
        alert(objects[i]);
        objects[i].make();
    }
}

</script>
```

Here is the HTML code containing a canvas and a button:

```
<div>
    <input type="button" onclick="execute()" value="Execute" />
</div>
<div>
    <canvas id="myCanvas"></canvas>
</div>
```

The output will be as follows on a button click event. The circle will be drawn and two messages will be printed on the console window for Honda and Nissan car objects:

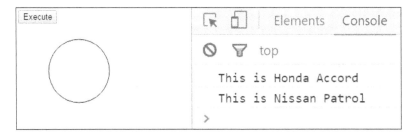

Prototype pattern

The prototype pattern is used to create instances that are clones of existing instances. It is used in scenarios where we need to auto configure the object with some specific values or properties and users don't have to explicitly define:

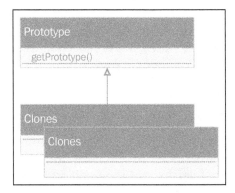

The following is the code that implements the prototype pattern:

```
<script>

    function Car(make, model, year, type)
    {
        this.make = make;
        this.model = model;
        this.year = year;
        this.type = type;

        this.displayCarDetails = function(){
```

```
            }

      }


      function CarPrototype(carPrototype) {
          var car = new Car();

          this.getPrototype = function () {
              car.make = carPrototype.make;
              car.model = carPrototype.model;
              car.year = carPrototype.year;
              car.type = carPrototype.type;
              return car;
          }

      }

      (function () {
          var car = new Car("Honda", "Accord", "2016","sedan");
          var carPrototype = new CarPrototype(car);
          var clonedCar = carPrototype.getPrototype();

      })();
    </script>
```

In the preceding code snippet, there is a car object that accepts four parameters, make, model, year and type. CarPrototype() is a function that accepts the car object and returns the cloned version of the car object. This pattern is performance efficient and saves developers time creating a clone copy of the object by just calling the prototype object's clone method. The user does not need to care about populating the properties after object instantiation; it initializes when the object is created and gets the same values as the original object. It is used in conditions where we need to clone instances of objects when they are in a specific state and can be easily cloned by calling the getProtoype() method.

Structural patterns

Structural patterns are used to simplify the relationships between objects. In the following sections, we will discuss all four structural patterns mentioned previously, and how to implement them in JavaScript.

Adapter pattern

The adapter pattern is used in situations in which our application is dependent on any object whose properties and methods change frequently and we want to avoid modifying the code to use them. The adapter pattern allows us to wrap the interface of a specific object as what the client expects and rather than changing the whole implementation we can just call the wrapper object which contains the code as per the modified version. This wrapper object is called an adapter. Let's have a look at a basic example that uses the `PersonRepository` to save the `person` object by performing an Ajax request:

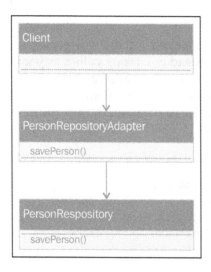

The following is the old interface of the `PersonRepository` object:

```
// old interface
    function PersonRepository(){
        this.SavePerson= function(name, email, phoneNo){
            //Call ajax to save person
            console.log("Name: " + name + ", Email: " + email + ",
Phone No: " + phoneNo);
        }
    }
```

The preceding interface has one `SavePerson()` method that takes three parameters: name, email, and phoneNo. Here is the original code for using the `SavePerson()` method:

```
var execute = function () {

        var personRepository = new PersonRepository();
        personRepository.SavePerson("John", "john@email.com",
"1201111111");



    }
```

Suppose this interface has changed and the new person repository interface accepts the person JSON object, instead of passing values as parameters. One way is to modify the function here itself and encapsulate these parameters in the JSON object and send. Alternatively, we can implement an adapter pattern which contains an adapter function that takes three parameters, calls the new `PersonRepository` object and passes the JSON object.

The following is the new interface of `PersonRepository`:

```
function PersonRepository() {
        this.SavePerson = function (person) {
            //call ajax to send JSON person data
            console.log("Name: " + person.name + ", Email: " + person.
email + ", Phone No: " + person.phoneNo);
        }
    }
```

Here is the adapter pattern that encapsulates the parameters in a JSON object and calls the new `PersonRepository` interface:

```
function PersonRepositoryAdapter() {
        this.SavePerson = function (name, email, phoneNo) {
            var person = { "name": name, "email": email, "phoneNo":
phoneNo };

            var personRepository = new PersonRepository();
            //calling new Person Repository
personRepository.SavePerson(person);
        }
    }
```

Here is the modified version that calls the adapter pattern rather than calling the old `PersonRespository` interface:

```
    var execute = function () {

    //old interface
// var personRepository = new PersonRepository();
  // personRepository.SavePerson("John", "john@email.com",
"1201111111");

    //calling adapter pattern
        var personAdapter = new PersonRepositoryAdapter();
        personAdapter.SavePerson("John", "john@email.com",
"1201111111");

    }
```

Decorator pattern

The decorator pattern is used to change the behavior of the object at runtime. Decorators are like annotation attributes in C#. Likewise, we can add multiple decorators on one object as well. The decorator pattern can be implemented by creating a decorator object and associating that with the target object whose behavior needs to be changed:

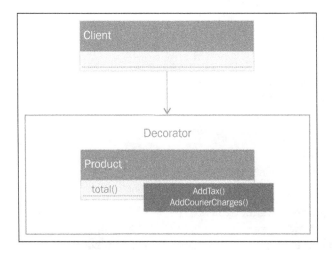

The following is an example of a decorator that adds the `Tax` and `Courier` charge decorators on the `Product` object:

```
<script>

    var Product= function (code, quantity, price) {
        this.code = code;
        this.quantity = quantity;
        this.price = price

        this.total = function () {
            this.price = price * quantity;
            return this.price;
        }

    }

    //Decorator that takes product and percent as parameter to apply
Tax
    function AddTax(product, percent) {
        product.total = function () {
            product.price = product.price + (product.price * percent
/ 100);
            return  product.price;
        }
    }

    //Decorator to add Courier charges in the total amount.
    function AddCourierCharges(product, amount) {
        product.total = function () {
            product.price = product.price + amount;
            return product.price;
        }
    }

    var execute = (function () {
        var prod = new Product("001", 2, 20);
        console.log("Total price: " + prod.total());
        AddTax(prod, 15);
        console.log("Total price after Tax: " + prod.total());
        AddCourierCharges(prod, 200);
        console.log("Total price after Courier Charges: " + prod.
total());
    })();
```

The `product` object takes three parameters, `code`, `quantity`, and `price`, and calculates the total price based on `quantity` and `price`. `AddTax()` and `AddCourierCharges()` are two decorator objects product object followed with a parameter to apply specific calculation on change the total price. The `AddTax()` method applies the tax based on the value supplied, whereas `AddCourierCharges()` will add the courier charge amount to the total price. The `Execute()` method will be called immediately when the page renders and displays the following output in the console window:

```
Total price: 40
Total price after Tax: 46
Total price after Courier Charges: 246
```

Facade pattern

The façade pattern is used to simplify various interfaces or subsystems into one unified interface. It simplifies things to the user and rather than understanding the complexities of different subsystems, the user can call the `façade` interface to perform a specific operation.

Let's see the following example, which has three methods to load permissions, the user profile, and the user chat window on successful login. It has three interfaces, and with façade we can simplify it to one unified interface. This allows the user to call `UserFacade` only once if the login is successful and it will load the permissions, user chat, and user profile from one interface:

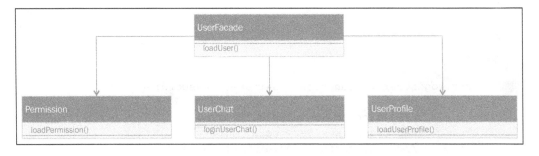

```
<script>
    var Permission = function () {
        this.loadPermission = function (userId) {
            //load user permissions by calling service and populate
    HTML element
            var repo = new ServiceRepository();
            repo.loadUserPermissions(userId);
```

```
            }
        }


    var Profile = function () {
        this.loadUserProfile = function (userId) {
            //load user profile and set user name and image in HTML
page
            var repo = new ServiceRepository();
            repo.loadUserProfile(userId);
        }
    }



    var Chat = function () {
        this.loginUserChat = function (userId) {
            //Login user chat and update HTML element
            var repo = new ServiceRepository();
            repo.loadUserChat(userId);
        }
    }

    var UserFacade = function () {
        this.loadUser = function (userId) {
            var userPermission = new Permission();
            var userProfile = new Profile();
            var userChat = new Chat();

            userPermission.loadPermission(userId);
            userProfile.loadUserProfile(userId);
            userChat.loginUserChat(userId);


        }
    }

    var loginUser = (function (username, password) {

            //Service to login user
            var repo = new ServiceRepository();
            //On successfull login, user id is returned
            var userId = repo.login(username, password);

            var userFacade = new UserFacade();
            userFacade.loadUser(userId);

    })();
    <
```

Bridge pattern

The bridge pattern is used to decouple the abstraction from its implementation and make concrete implementation independent from the interface. This is achieved by providing a bridge between the interface and the concrete implementer:

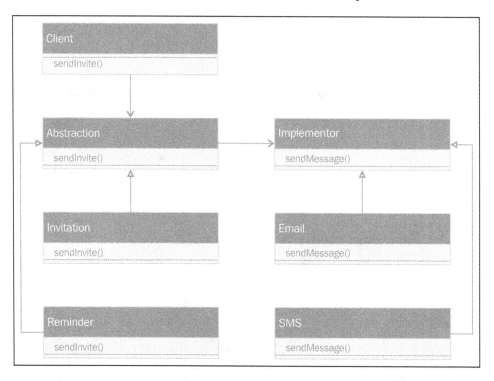

The following code shows the bridge pattern implementation:

```
<script>

    var Invitation = function (email) {
        this.email - email;
        this.sendInvite = function () {
            this.email.sendMessage();
        }
    }

    var Reminder = function (sms) {
        this.sms = sms;
        this.sendReminder = function () {
            this.sms.sendMessage();
        }
```

```
        }

    var SMS = function () {
        //send SMS
        this.sendMessage = function () { console.log("SMS sent"); }

    }

    var Email = function () {
        //send email
        this.sendMessage = function () { console.log("Email sent");}
    }


    var execute = (function () {
        var email = new Email();
        var sms = new SMS();

        var invitation = new Invitation(email);
        var reminder = new Reminder(sms);

        invitation.sendInvite();
        reminder.sendReminder();
    })();
</script>
```

The objective of the preceding example is to separate the notification types
(Invitation and Reminder) from the notification gateway (Email and SMS). So any
notification can be sent through any gateway and can handle any notification that
separates the gateway to the notification types and disable the bounding with the
type of the notification.

Behavioral pattern

Behavioral patterns are used to delegate responsibilities between objects. In the
following section, we will discuss all four behavioral patterns mentioned previously,
and how to implement them in JavaScript.

Chain of responsibility pattern

The chain of responsibility pattern provides a chain of objects executed in order as they are chained to fulfill any request. A good example for ASP.NET developers is the OWIN pipeline that chains the components or OWIN middleware together and is based on the appropriate request handler being executed:

Let's look into a very basic example that executes the chain of objects and displays the table for 2, 3 and 4:

```
<script>

    //Main component
    var Handler = function (table) {
        this.table = table;
        this.nextHandler = null;
    }

    //Prototype to chain objects
    Handler.prototype = {
        generate: function (count) {
            for (i = 1; i <= count; i++) {
                console.log(this.table + " X " + i + " = " + (this.
table * i));
            }
            //If the next handler is available execute it
            if (this.nextHandler != null)
                this.nextHandler.generate(count);
        },
        //Used to set next handler in the pipeline
        setNextHandler: function (handler) {
            this.nextHandler = handler;
        }
    }

    //function executed on Page load
    var execute = (function () {

        //initializing objects
        var handler1 = new Handler(2),
```

```
        handler2 = new Handler(3),
        handler3 = new Handler(4);

    //chaining objects
    handler1.setNextHandler(handler2);
    handler2.setNextHandler(handler3);

    //calling first handler or the component in the pipeline
    handler1.generate(10);

})();
<script>
```

Let's get into a more practical example which takes the amount and checks the budget owner in the objects chained in the pipeline. The following code have a main handler object that takes the budget amount and the budget owner to set the budget amount for Line Manager, Head of Department, CTO, and CEO. Finally, we can set the main entry point in the chain by calling the handler1 method, which first checks whether the amount is under the line manager's budget, then the head of department's, then the CTO's, and finally the CEO's:

```
<script>

    //Main component
    var Handler = function (budget, budgetOwner) {
        this.budget = budget;
        this.budgetOwner = budgetOwner;
        this.nextHandler = null;
    }

    //Prototype to chain objects
    Handler.prototype = {
        checkBudget: function (amount) {
            var budgetFound = false;
            if (amount <= this.budget) {
                console.log("Amount is under " + this.budgetOwner + "
level");

                budgetFound = true;
            }

            //If the next handler is available and budget is not found
            if (this.nextHandler != null && !budgetFound)
```

```
                this.nextHandler.checkBudget(amount);
        },

        //Used to set next handler in the popeline
        setNextHandler: function (handler) {
            this.nextHandler = handler;
        }
    }

    //funciton executed on Page load
    var execute = (function () {

        //initializing objects
        var handler1 = new Handler(10000, "Line Manager"),
         handler2 = new Handler(50000, "Head of Department"),
         handler3 = new Handler(100000, "CTO"),
         handler4 = new Handler(1000000, "CEO");

        //chaining objects
        handler1.setNextHandler(handler2);
        handler2.setNextHandler(handler3);
        handler3.setNextHandler(handler4);

        //calling first handler or the component in the pipeline
        handler1.checkBudget(20000);

    })();
</script>
```

And the following is the output:

```
Amount is under Head of Department level
```

Observer pattern

The observer pattern is widely used to implement a publisher/subscriber model in which if a state of any object changes, it notifies all the observers subscribed. Observer patterns have three methods, namely to add, remove, and notify observers:

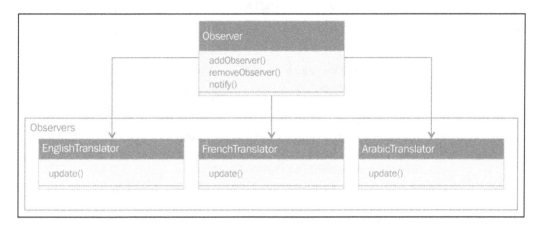

The following is the code snippet that implements the observer pattern:

```
<script>

    //Sample function to convert text to French language
    function translateTextToFrench(value) {
        // call some service to convert text to French language
        return value;
    }

    //Sample function to convert text to Arabic language
    function translateTextToArabic(value) {
        //cal some service to convert text to Arabic language
        return value;

    }

    //Helper function used by the Observer implementors
    var HelperFunction = function (type) {

        var txtEntered = document.getElementById("txtEntered");

        var englishText = document.getElementById("englishText");
        var frenchText = document.getElementById("frenchText");
        var arabicText = document.getElementById("arabicText");

        if (type == "english") {
            englishText.innerText = txtEntered.value;
```

```
        } else if (type == "french") {
            frenchText.innerText = translateTextToFrench(txtEntered.
value);
        } else if (type == "arabic") {
            arabicText.innerText = translateTextToArabic(txtEntered.
value);
        }
    }

    var EnglishTranslator = {
        update: function () {
            //Call helper function to change text to English
            HelperFunction("english");
        }
    }

    var FrenchTranslator = {
        update: function () {
            //Call helper function to change text to French
            HelperFunction("french");
        }
    }


    var ArabicTranslator = {
        update: function () {
            //Call helper function to change text to Arabic
            HelperFunction("arabic");
        }
    }

    //Observer function that contains the list of observer handlers
    function Observer() {
        this.observers = [];
    }

    //to add observer
    Observer.prototype.addObserver = function (object) {
        console.log('added observer: ' + object);
        this.observers.push(object);
    };

    //to remove observer
    Observer.prototype.removeObserver = function (object) {
        console.log("removing observer");
        for (i = 0; i < this.observers.length; i++) {
            if (this.observers[i] == object) {
                this.observers.splice(object);
                return true;
            }
```

```
        }
        return false;
    };

    //To notify all observers and call their update method
    Observer.prototype.notify = function () {
        for (i = 0; i < this.observers.length; i++) {
            this.observers[i].update();
        }
    }
}


    //Adding objects as observers that implements the update method
    var observer = new Observer();
    observer.addObserver(EnglishTranslator);
    observer.addObserver(FrenchTranslator);
    observer.addObserver(ArabicTranslator);


    //Execute will be called on button click to notify observers
    var execute = function () {
        observer.notify();
    };


</script>
<body>
    <div>
        Specify some text: <input type="text" id="txtEntered" />
        <input type="button" onclick="execute()" value="Notify" />
    </div>
    <div>
        <span id="englishText"></span>
        <span id="frenchText"></span>
        <span id="arabicText"></span>
    </div>
</body>
```

In the above example, we have taken a scenario that translates the text for all the languages added as observer objects. We extended the Observer object and defined three methods, namely addObserver(), removeObserver(), and notify() through a prototype. Adding methods through a prototype consumes less memory and each method is shared among all instances. These methods are created once and then inherited by each instance. On the other hand, methods that are defined inside the constructor function are created every time the new instance is created and consume more memory.

The addObserver() method is used to add any object in an observer list, removeObserver() is used to remove a specific object from observer list, and notify() executes the observer's update() method.

EnglishTranslator, FrenchTranslator and ArabicTranslation are objects that have implemented the update() method which is called when notify() is executed. On page load we have registered all the translator objects as observers and provided a textbox with a button through which the user can type any text on the textbox and on a button click event it will call the observer's notify() method that eventually calls the registered observer's update() method.

Pub/sub pattern

The pub/sub pattern is an alternative pattern to the observer pattern with a slight difference in its implementation. In the observer pattern, the Observer object can invoke the notify() method of all the observers, whereas in the publisher/ subscriber pattern, there is a centralized event system which is used to publish events to the subscribers. In this pattern, publishers and subscribers are loosely tied and neither the publisher nor the subscriber know to whom the message was sent or received.

The following example implements a pub/sub pattern that holds a two-dimensional array. The user can add events based on an event name and a callback function. It has three methods: subscribe() to subscribe to events in an events array, unsubscribe() to remove events from an array, and publish() to call the callback functions for a specific event name:

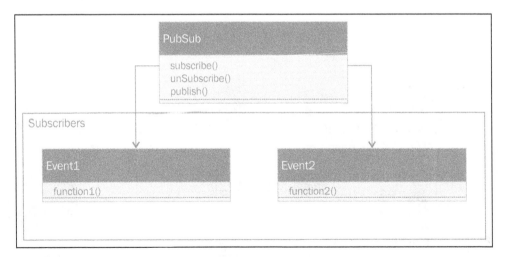

The following is a code snippet to implement the pub/sub pattern in JavaScript:

```javascript
var PubSub = function () {
        this.events = [];
        this.subscribe = function (eventName, func) {
            this.events[eventName] = this.events[eventName] || [];
            this.events[eventName].push(func);
        };

        this.unsubscribe = function (eventName, func) {
            if (this.events[eventName]) {
                for (i = 0; i < this.events[eventName].length; i++) {
                    if (this.events[eventName][i] === func) {
                        this.events[eventName].splice(i, 1);
                        break;
                    }
                }
            }
        };

        this.publish = function (eventName, data) {
            console.log(data);
            if (this.events[eventName]) {
                this.events[eventName].forEach(function (event) {
                    event(data);
                })
            }
        };
    };


    var execute = (function () {
        var pubSub = new PubSub();
        pubSub.subscribe("myevent1", function () {
            console.log("event1 is occurred");
        });

        pubSub.subscribe("myevent1", function () {
            console.log("event1 is occurred");
        });

        pubSub.subscribe("myevent2", function (value) {
            console.log("event2 is occurred, value is "+ value);
```

```
    });


    pubSub.publish("myevent1", null);

    pubSub.publish("myevent2", "my event two");
})();
```

In the preceding example, we have one `PubSub` object that provides three methods to `subscribe`, `unsubscribe`, and `publish` events. The `Subscribe()` method is used to subscribe for any event and takes two parameters, the event name and function, and adds them to the array for a specific event name. If the event name does not exist a new array will be initialized for that event name, otherwise the existing instance will be retrieved to add the item. The user can register as many events as they want, by passing the event name and the anonymous function body that will be executed when the event is published. To publish events, the `publish()` method can be called that takes the event name and the data you want to pass to the corresponding function, which has been executed.

Promises

Promises are one of the most popular patterns extensively used in JavaScript APIs and frameworks to make asynchronous calls simpler. An asynchronous operation in JavaScript needs to have a callback function register, which invokes when the value is returned. With promises, when you make any asynchronous call, it immediately returns a promise and provides objects such as `then` and `done` to define a function when the resultant value is resolved. In the real world, promises are just like a token or a receipt for the food you order in a fast food restaurant, and that receipt guarantees you to have the food delivered when it is ready. Promises are tokens that confirm you get a response to a specific request:

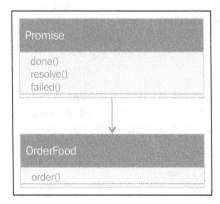

In JavaScript, promises are widely used by APIs and frameworks such as AngularJS, Angular 2, and more. Let's have a look at the following example that implements the promise pattern:

```
//Defining Promise that takes a function as a parameter.
    var Promise = function (func) {
        //Declared member variable
        var callbackFn = null;

        //Expose done function that can be invoked by the object
returning promise
        //done() function takes a callback function which can be
define when using done method.
        this.done = function (callback) {
            callbackFn = callback;
        };

        function resolve(value) {
            setTimeout(function () {
                callbackFn(value)
            },3000)
        }

        //Here we are actually executing the function defined when
initializing the promise below.
        func(resolve);
    }

    //Object that is used to order food and returns a promise
    var orderFood = function (food) {
        //returns the Promise instance and pass anonymous function
that call resolve method which actually serve the request after
delaying 3 seconds.
        return new Promise(function (resolve) {
            resolve(food);
        });
    }


    //Initialized orderFood that returns promise
    var order = new orderFood("Grilled Burger");
    //Calling done method which will be invoked once the order is
ready
    order.done(function (value) {
        console.log(value);
    });
```

In the preceding example, we have developed a `Promise` function that contains `done` and `resolve` methods, where `done` is used to invoke the callback function implemented by the consumer object and `resolve` is called internally to execute the actual task. The second function is `orderFood`, which returns a `promise` object and calls the `resolve` method to actually run the task when `orderFood` is initialized by the consumer. The following snapshot shows the steps of how this code is executed:

```
//Defining Promise that takes a function as a parameter.
var Promise = function (func) {

    //Declaring local variable
    var callbackFn = null;

    //Expose done function that can be invoked by the object returning promise
    //done() function takes a callback function that copy the function passed as a parameter to the callbackFn
    this.done = function (callback) {
        callbackFn = callback;
    };

    //Delay for 3 seconds and execute callbackFn
    function resolve(value) {
        setTimeout(function () {
            callbackFn(value)
        }, 3000)
    }

    //Here we are actually executing the function defined when intializing the promise below      step 3
    func(resolve);
}

//Object that is used to order food and returns a promise     step 2
var orderFood = function (food) {
    //returns the Promise and pass function that calls resolve() function that serves the request
    return new Promise(function (resolve) {
        resolve(food);       step 4
    });
}

//Initialized orderFood that returns a promise
var order = new orderFood("Grilled Burger");     step 1

//Calling done() function that will be invoked once the order is ready
order.done(function (value) {
    console.log(value);     step 5
});
```

If you have noticed, in the preceding example we have used the `setTimeout()` function to delay the response for 3 seconds. We have to use `setTimeout()` to represent an asynchronous scenario where `setTimout()` and the registering of the `done` callback handler are executed in parallel.

The preceding code snippet is a very basic implementation of a promise pattern. However, there are other parts of the promise pattern that we can implement to make it robust. Promises have states and the following is the modified version that not only maintains the states for inprogress, done, and failed but also provides the failed handler to catch exceptions. The following is the description of the states:

- **In progress**: When the resolve method is called the state will be set to in progress. This state will persist until we register the handlers for done and failed scenarios.

- **Done**: When done is invoked, the status will be set to done.

- **Failed**: When any exception occurs, the status will be set to fail.

The following is the modified version of the orderFood example:

```
//Defining Promise that takes a function as a parameter.
var Promise = function (func) {

    //Default status when the promise is created
    var status = 'inprogress';
    var error = null;

    //Declared member variable
    var doneCallbackFn = null;
    var failedCallbackFn = null;

    //Expose done function that can be invoked by the object
returning promise
    this.done  = function (callback) {
        //Assign the argument value to local variable
        doneCallbackFn = callback;
        if (status === "done") {
            doneCallbackFn(data);
        } else {
            doneCallbackFn(status);
        }
        //return promise to register done or failed methods in
chain
        return this;
    };

    //Expose failed function to catch errors
    this.failed = function (callback) {
        if (status === "failed") {
            failedCallbackFn(error);
        }
```

```
            //return promise instance to register done or failed
methods in chain
            return this;
    };

    function prepareFood() {
        setTimeout(function () {
            status = "done";
            console.log("food is prepared");
            if (doneCallbackFn) {
                doneCallbackFn(data);
            }
        }, 3000);


    }

    function resolve(value) {
        try {
            //set the value
            data = value;

            //check if doneCallbackFn is defined
            if (doneCallbackFn) {
                doneCallbackFn(value);
            }
            prepareFood();

        } catch (error) {
            //set the status to failed
            status = "failed";
            //set the exception in error
            error = error;
            //check if failedCallbackFn is defined
            if (failedCallbackFn) {
                failedCallbackFn(value);
            }
        }
    }
    //Here we are actually executing the function defined when
initializing the promise below.
    func(resolve);
}

//Object that is used to order food and returns a promise
```

```
    var orderFood = function (food) {
        //returns the Promise instance and pass anonymous function
that call resolve method which
        //actually serve the request after delaying 3 seconds.
        return new Promise(function (resolve) {
            resolve(food);
        });
    }

    //Initialized orderFood that returns promise
    var order = new orderFood("Grilled Burger").done(function
(value) { console.log(value); }).failed(function (error) { console.
log(error);})
```

Summary

In this chapter, we have learned the importance of design patterns in small-to-large scale applications and how we can use them effectively to resolve specific problems. We have covered four types of design patterns for each category, such as when creating objects, structuring objects, and adding a behavioral change or states to objects. There are various more design patterns available and documented, which can be referred to here: http://www.dofactory.com/javascript/design-patterns.

In the next chapter, we will learn about Node.js that runs JavaScript on the server side. We will see how web applications can be developed in Node.js using Visual Studio 2015 and explore some popular frameworks and view the engines it provides.

8

Node.js for ASP.NET
Developers

JavaScript has become one of the most prevalent languages that not only runs on the client side, but also runs on the server side as well. Node.js empowers JavaScript to run on the server side and provide non-blocking I/O, an event driven model that makes it more lightweight, scalable and efficient. Today, it is more widely used in performing real-time operations, developing business applications, database operations, and more. JavaScript on Node.js can relate to ASP.NET that runs on IIS or any other web server.

Introduction to Node.js

Node.js is a powerful platform to build server-side applications using JavaScript. Node.js itself is not written in JavaScript but provides a runtime environment to run JavaScript code. It allows JavaScript code that runs on the server side, providing the runtime built on the Google V8 JavaScript engine, which is an open source JavaScript engine written in C++, and used by Google Chrome, to compile JavaScript code into machine code, at the time of executing through the V8 JIT compiler.

Node.js works on a single thread; unlike other server-side technologies that create a separate thread for each request, Node.js uses the event callback system that processes the request using a single thread. If multiple requests arrive they have to wait until the thread becomes available and then acquire it. In the case of errors, Node.js does not throw an error and this is an essential technique to avoid error bubbling and the abortion of the single thread. If any error arises while serving a request, Node.js sends the error log, in the callback parameters, in the response itself. This allows the main thread to propagate the error and delay the response. Node.js is good for writing network applications. It consists of HTTP requests, other network communications tasks, and real-time client/server communications using web sockets.

Request processing by the Node.js web server

The Node.js web server maintains a limited thread pool to handle client requests. When the request gets to the server, the Node.js web server places that request into an event queue. The request is then picked up by the event loop component that works in an infinite loop and processes the request when it is free. This event loop component is single-threaded, and if the request involves I/O blocking operations such as filesystem access, database access, or others, it checks the availability of the thread in the internal thread pool and assigns the request to the available thread. Otherwise, it processes the request and sends the response back to the client in a single go. When the I/O blocking request is completed by the internal thread, it sends the response back to the event loop first, which sends the response back to the client.

Comparison of Node.js with .NET

Both ASP.NET and Node.js are server-side technologies. The following diagram shows the comparison of Node.js with .NET:

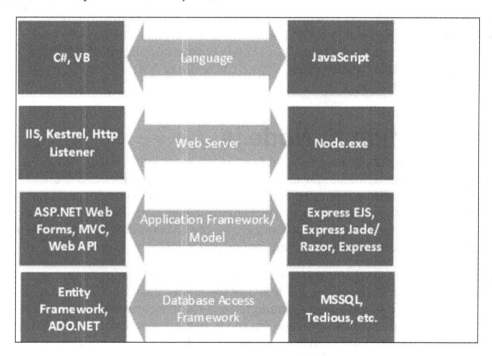

NPM

Node Package Manager (**NPM**) is the Node.js package manager used to install Node modules. Node.js provides a way to write modules in JavaScript, and with NPM we can add and reuse those modules in other applications. With ASP.NET Core, we already use some modules, such as Gulp and Grunt for minifying the CSS and JavaScript files, and doing copying and merging operations. The `package.json` file is the configuration file that holds the metadata information about the application and Node modules used in our project. Here is the sample screenshot of the `package.json` file:

```
{
    "dependencies": {
        "angular2": "2.0.0-beta.9",
        "systemjs": "0.19.24",
        "reflect-metadata": "0.1.3",
        "rxjs": "5.0.0-beta.2",
        "zone.js": "0.6.4"
    },
    "devDependencies": {
        "gulp": "3.8.11",
        "gulp-concat": "2.5.2",
        "gulp-cssmin": "0.1.7",
        "gulp-uglify": "1.2.0",
        "rimraf": "2.2.8",
        "typescript": "1.8.7",
        "concurrently": "2.0.0"
    },
    "name": "nodeconfiguration",
    "version": "0.0.0"
}
```

Dependencies can be installed by executing the following command:

```
npm install NAME_OF_THE_PACKAGE -save
```

Example:

```
npm install gulp -save
```

`--save` is used to update the `package.json` dependencies section and add the packages downloaded.

Installing Node.js

Visual Studio provides great support for developing programs using Node.js. To configure the Node.js development environment on the Windows platform, download and install Node.js from `http://nodejs.org`. There are various installers available as per the platform, as shown in the following screenshot:

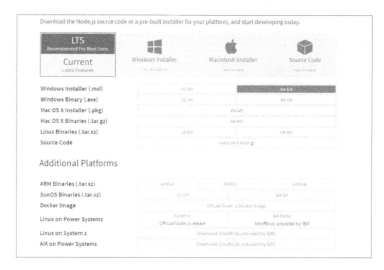

For Windows, we will download the 64-bit Windows installer that downloads the `.msi` package and take you through some simple wizard screens. You will notice that the Node.js installer contains a runtime to run node programs and NPM to reference other Node modules in your program. This can be seen in the following screenshot:

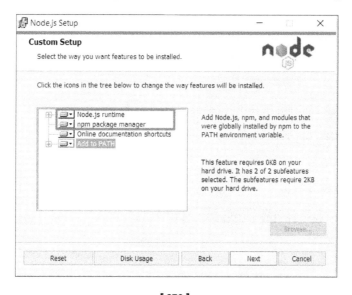

Commands such as npm and node are already added in the environment path and we can execute these commands directly from the command prompt. Therefore, if we open the command prompt and write node, it will give you the Node prompt, which allows you to write JavaScript code on the fly and execute, as shown in the following screenshot:

```
C:\Program Files (x86)\Microsoft Visual Studio 10.0\VC>node
> a=1
1
> str = 'Node Test'
'Node Test'
> b = a + '. ' + str
'1. Node Test'
>
```

Alternatively, we can also run the .js file by calling node javascriptfile.js.

The following is the sample example1.js file that sums the numbers defined in an array:

```
console.log("NodeJs example");


var numbers= [100,20,29,96,55];


var sum=0;
for(i=0; i< numbers.length; i++)
{
    sum += numbers[i];
}
console.log("total sum is "+ sum);
```

The following is the output:

```
E:\Authoring\Chapter8>node example1.js
NodeJs example
total sum is 300
```

Using Node.js with Visual Studio 2015

There are many **Integrated Development Environments (IDEs)** available in the market that have Node.js tooling support. IDEs such as Visual Studio Code, Sublime, Komodo and Node Eclipse are popular IDEs to work with Node.js, but in practice, most .NET developers are more comfortable and familiar working with the Visual Studio IDE. Therefore, we will be using the Visual Studio 2015 Community edition in this chapter.

Node.js templates can be installed in Visual Studio 2015 by installing its extensions. Extensions can be installed from the Visual Studio menu option **Tools | Extensions and Updates**:

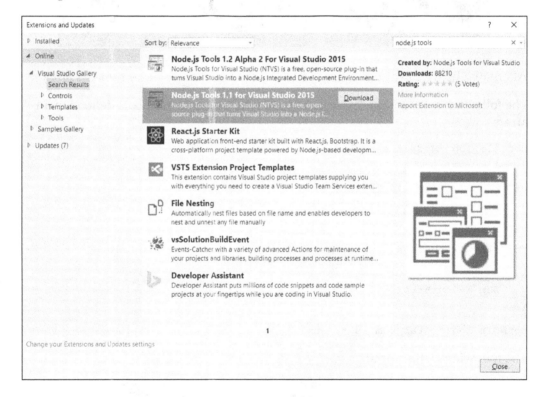

This extension of Node.js is installed with various templates to start developing applications using Node.js. There is a template to develop console applications using the blank Node.js console application template, a web application using Node.js express templates, and so on:

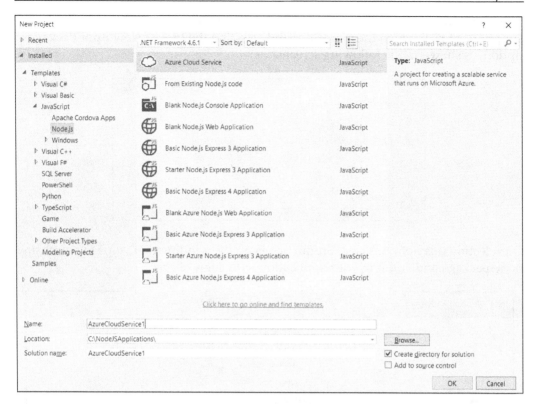

The basic advantage of using these templates is to save time in configuring things manually, and these templates facilitate developers by providing the basic project structure to kick-start the Node.js application right away.

Let's start by creating a basic console application template. The basic console application has an `npm` folder, containing node packages, `package.json` that contains the metadata information and other configuration attributes, and `app.js`, which contains actual JavaScript code:

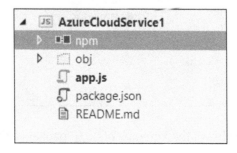

This extension for Node.js provides a handy feature for adding Node modules by simply right-clicking on the npm folder and selecting the **Install New npm Packages** option, as shown in the following screenshot:

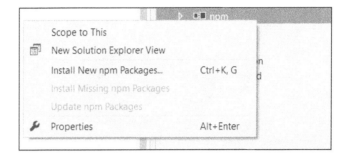

On selecting this option, Visual Studio opens up the window that helps to search any node package and add it to your application with a few clicks:

The preceding diagram shows the versions of Gulp packages that can be added through this option.

Interactive Window is another nice feature in Visual Studio, which opens up the command prompt integrated in the Visual Studio tab, and you can write JavaScript code and execute commands instantly, as shown in the following screenshot:

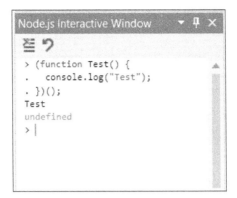

There are several other benefits of using Visual Studio: you can use the Git or TFS version repositories, debug your code and enable breakpoints on your JavaScript files, and so on. The Visual Studio-specific project file for Node.js is known as `.njsproj` and resides in the root folder of your project.

Simple console application using Node.js

A Node.js application consists of one or more JavaScript files that provide specific functionality to the application. Writing thousands of lines of code in one JavaScript file is not practically possible, and also increases maintainability issues. In Node.js, we can create multiple JavaScript files and use them through `require` and `export` objects, which are parts of the Common JS module system:

```
export: used to export variables, functions and objects

//exportexample.js
module.exports.greeting = "Hello World";

require: To use the objects resides in different JavaScript files
using require object.

//consumerexample.js - referencing through file
var obj = require('./exportexample.js');
```

Alternatively we can also call `require` without specifying the `.js` file extension, and it automatically loads the file that exists on a particular path. If the path corresponds to a folder, all the JavaScript files will be loaded:

```
//consumerexample.js - referencing through file
var obj= require('./exportexample');
```

The main entry point when the application is bootstrapped is defined under `package.json`. In the following screenshot, `app.js` is the main entry point file that is loaded first and executed by Node.js:

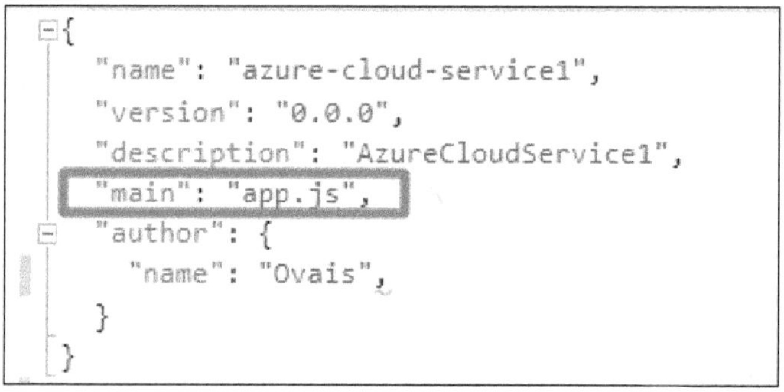

Let's implement a basic example that has two files, namely `app.js` (main entry) and `cars.js`, and returns a few properties of the car object, such as `name`, `model`, and `engine`. To start, create a console application project and add one `cars.js` file.

Here is the code for `cars.js`:

```
module.exports.cars = [
{name:"Honda Accord" , model:"2016", engine: "V6"},
{name:"BMW X6", model:"2015", engine: "V8"},
{name:"Mercedez Benz",model:"2016", engine:"V12"}
];
```

Through `module.exports`, we can export any object. Whether it's a variable, a function, or a JSON object, it can be exported through this. Furthermore, the objects exported can be used through the `require` object in `app.js`, as shown in the following code:

```
var cars = require('./cars.js');
console.log(cars);
```

The following is the output:

```
C:\NodeJSApplications\AzureCloudService1\AzureCloudService1>node app.js
{ cars:
  [ { name: 'Honda Accord', model: '2016', engine: 'V6' },
    { name: 'BMW X6', model: '2015', engine: 'V8' },
    { name: 'Mercedez Benz', model: '2016', engine: 'V12' } ] }
```

The preceding code displays the JSON output as defined in the cars.js file. In order to initialize the cars object, and loop through the car items defined in the list, we need to export it as a function and define it through the this keyword. Specifying it through this will make the list accessible from the cars object we create in the app.js file.

Here is the modified version of cars.js:

```
module.exports = function () {
  this.carsList =
  [
    { name: "Honda Accord" , model: "2016", engine: "V6" },
    { name: "BMW X6", model: "2015", engine: "V8" },
    { name: "Mercedez Benz", model: "2016", engine: "V12" }
  ];
};
```

And here is the modified version of the app.js file that initialized the cars object and loops through the list:

```
var cars = require('./cars.js');
var c = new cars();
var carsList = c.carsList;
for (i = 0; i < carsList.length; i++) {
  console.log(carsList[i].name);
}
```

Web applications with Node.js

There are various Node.js web frameworks available. Frameworks such as Express and Hapi.js are powerful frameworks and have different architectures and designs. In this section, we will use the Express framework, which is one of the most widely used web frameworks for Node.js, for both web and mobile applications, and also provides the application framework model to develop web **Application Programming Interfaces (APIs)**.

Creating blank Node.js applications

An extension of Node.js for Visual Studio provides various templates to develop web applications. We will start by creating a blank Node.js web application, as shown in the following screenshot:

A blank Node.js application template creates one `server.js` file and sets the `main` attribute in the `package.json` file to load `server.js`. The content of `server.js` is as follows:

```
var http = require('http');        Statement 1

var port = process.env.port || 1337;     Statement 2

http.createServer(function (req, res) {      Statement 3
    res.writeHead(200, { 'Content-Type': 'text/plain' });
    res.end('Hello World\n');
}).listen(port);
```

The first statement adds the dependency of an `http` module of Node.js, the second statement is the port number at which the server will listen for HTTP requests, and the third statement creates the server using an `http` object, once it is started and returns the response as `Hello World`. When the server starts, a request can be made by calling `http://localhost:1337`.

The preceding code snippet chains the `listen()` method that actually listens for the incoming requests, and sends the response using the `res.end()` method. Alternatively, we can also specify the content we are returning using the `res.write()` method. Here is the more simplified version of the same code, to understand how the pieces fit together:

```
//Initialized http object
var http = require('http');

//declared port
var port = process.env.port || 1337;

//Initialized http server object and use res.write() to send actual
response content
var httpServer= http.createServer(function (req, res) {
    res.writeHead(200, { 'Content-Type': 'text/plain' });
    res.write('Hello World\n');
    res.end();
});

//listening for incoming request
httpServer.listen(port);
```

Using the Express framework for web applications in Node.js

In any programming language, a framework has an important benefit that minimizes the effort required to develop web applications. The framework plays the important role of processing requests, such as loading a specific view, injecting models into a view, and more. As with ASP.NET, where w have two web-application frameworks, ASP.NET Web Forms and ASP.NET MVC, Node.js provides Express EJS, Jade, and many other web application frameworks to build robust web applications.

Extend simple Node.js to use Express

With the Node.js extension for Visual Studio, you can get all the templates to start working with the Express 3.0 and Express 4.0 application frameworks. Express 4.0 is the most recent version and has some new features and improvements. We can use the template that bootstraps most of the configuration-level stuff for you but, in order to get more clarity, we will extend the simple Node.js example created previously, and use the Express framework to develop a simple web application on top of it.

To use `Express`, we have to add its package dependency using NPM, as shown in the following screenshot:

Once you add the Express package, you can add the following code snippet to kick start the Express app:

```
//Initialized http object
var http = require('http');

//adding express dependency
var express = require('express');

//creating express application
var expressApp = express();

//Configuring root call where '/' represents root path of the URL
expressApp.get("/", function (req, res) {
    res.send("<html><body><div>Hello World</div></body></html>");
});


//declared port
var port = process.env.port || 1337;

//Initialized http server object and use res.write() to send actual
response content
var httpServer = http.createServer(expressApp);

//listening for incoming request
httpServer.listen(port);
```

This is a simple `Hello World` example that returns the HTML content. Now, in scenarios where we want to return a specific view instead of the static HTML content, we achieve this by using Express view engines, which will be discussed next.

Express view engines

Express has various view engines, although Jade and EJS are the most widely used. We will go through these one by one and see what the differences are.

EJS view engine

In the EJS view engine, views are HTML pages and the model properties can be bound using scriptlets: `<% %>`.

To start using EJS, we need to add the EJS package through the NPM package manager option in Visual Studio, or by executing the `npm install ejs -save` command:

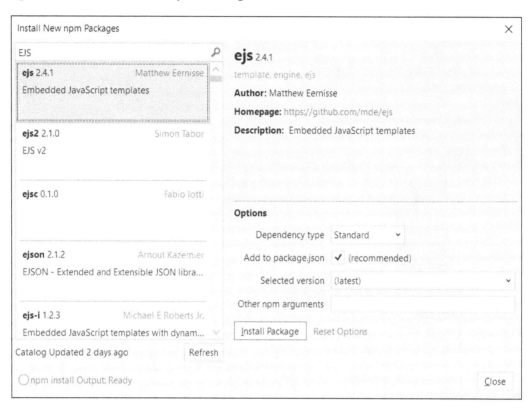

Once this is added, we can set the view engine to `ejs`, as shown in the following code snippet:

```
//Initialized http object
var http = require('http');

//adding express dependency
var express = require('express');

//creating express application
var expressApp = express();

//Set jade for Node.js application
expressApp.set('view engine', 'ejs')
```

Set the path of the ejs view by calling the response object render() method, as shown in the following code:

```
//Configuring root call where '/' represents root path of the URL
expressApp.get("/", function (req, res) {
    res.render("ejsviews/home/index");
});
```

Add the index.ejs file inside the home folder. All the views should reside under the root Views folder, otherwise they won't be loaded when the application is run. Therefore, the ejsviews folder should be defined under the Views folder and home inside the ejsviews folder, as shown in the following screenshot:

The following is the content of the EJS view that will be rendered when the application starts:

```
<html>
 <body>
  <div> <h1> This is EJS View </h1> </div>
 </body>
</html>
```

Add the code at the bottom of the ejsserver.js file that creates the server which listens for requests on port number 1337:

```
//declared port
var port = process.env.port || 1337;

//Initialized http server object and use res.write() to send actual
response content
var httpServer = http.createServer(expressApp);

//listening for incoming request
httpServer.listen(port);
```

When the application runs, `index.ejs` will be loaded and will render the HTML content as shown in the following figure:

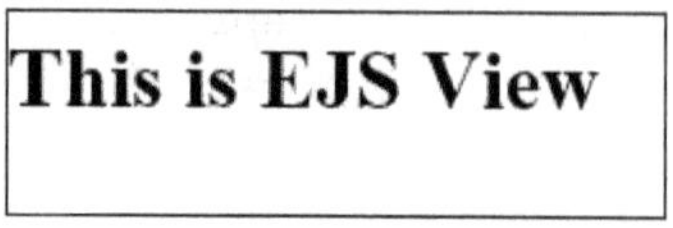

> # This is EJS View

We can also pass the model in the representation of the JSON object. Suppose we need to pass the application name and description; we can pass these values when calling a `render()` method of the response object, as shown in the following code:

```
//Configuring root call where '/' represents root path of the URL
expressApp.get("/", function (req, res) {
    res.render("ejsviews/home/index", { appName: "EJSDemo", message:
"This is our first EJS view engine example!" });
});
```

In `index.ejs`, we can use and bind these values with HTML controls using scriptlets:

```
<html>
 <body>
   <h1> <%= appName %> </h1>
   <p> <%= message %></p>
 </body>
</html>
```

EJS also supports layout pages that contain the static content, such as the header and footer of the web application. So, a developer doesn't need to define the main layout content again and again on every page, and we can keep it centralized, just like we do in ASP.NET MVC using `_layout.cshtml` and `Site.master` in ASP.NET web forms.

To work with master pages, we need to add one more package, known as `ejs-local`. This package can be added using the NPM package manager window in Visual Studio, or by running the `npm` command as `npm install ejs-local --save`:

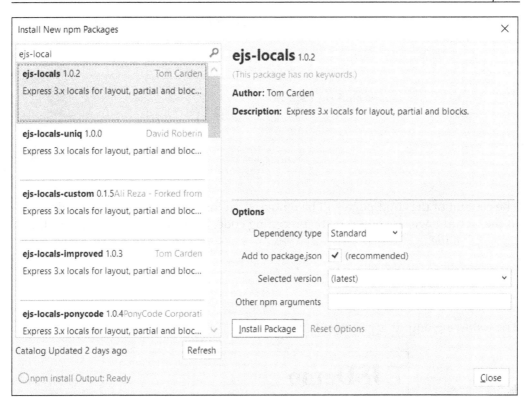

After adding this package, we can add `ejs-locals`, as shown in the following code. It has to be set before setting the view engine:

```
//Initialized http object
var http = require('http');

//adding express dependency
var express = require('express');
var ejsLocal = require('ejs-locals');
//creating express application
var expressApp = express();


//Add engine that supports master pages
app.engine('ejs', ejsLocal);
```

Add the `layout.ejs` page in the same `ejsviews` folder and specify the HTML content:

```
<html>
<head>
  <title> <%= appName %> </title>
</head>
<body>
  <%= body %>
</body>
</html>
```

The content of the child page will be rendered on the line where the body is defined in the layout page, as shown in the preceding code. Here is the code snippet of the `index.ejs` file:

```
<% layout('../layout.ejs') -%>
<h1><%= appName %></h1>
<p> <%= message %></p>
```

The following output is generated:

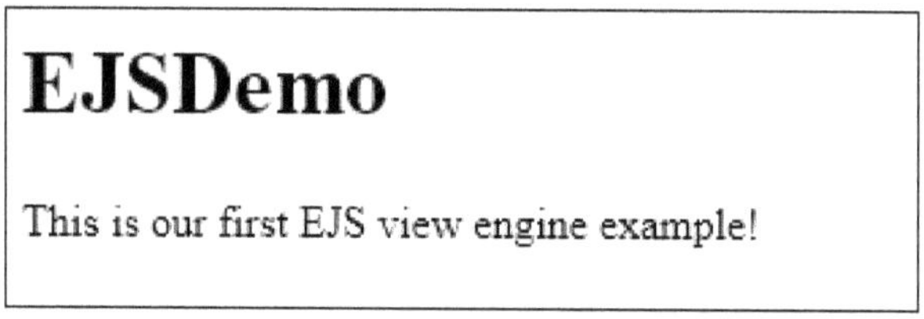

EJSDemo

This is our first EJS view engine example!

Jade view engine

The Jade view engine is another Node.js view engine and the syntax is quite different, when defining views, than we have seen in EJS. To start with the Jade view engine, we need to install the Jade view engine node package using NPM. We can install this from the Visual Studio NPM package manager or by running the `npm install jade -save` command:

When you install it, it will add the Jade package in the `package.json` dependencies section. We will start by setting the Jade view engine in the `app.js` file (the main entry point to kick start the Node.js project).

Here is the code to set up the Jade view engine in `app.js`:

```
//adding express dependency
var express = require('express');

//creating express application
var expressApp = express();

//Set jade for Node.js application
expressApp.set('view engine', 'jade');
```

You will notice that we have not specified the Jade reference through the `require` object. This is because when the Express framework is loaded, it will automatically register the dependencies of Jade. The following code snippet loads the Jade view:

```
//Configuring root call where '/' represents root path of the URL
expressApp.get("/", function (req, res) {
res.render("home/index",
{
appName: "JadeDemo",
message: "This is our first Jade view engine example!"
}
);
});
```

The Jade view syntax is typically different from HTML and all the view extensions should be `.jade`. In the preceding code, we are pointing to `index.jade`, where Jade is not required to be specified explicitly. `Index.jade` should reside under the `views/home` folder. Let's create a folder called `views` and then the `home` folder inside it. Add a new Jade file and named it `index.jade`. Here is the code that displays the `appName` and `message` in HTML elements:

```
doctype
html
    body
        h1= appName
        p= message
```

With Jade syntax, you don't have to define the complete HTML tags, you simply specify it through their names, followed by the value assigned to them. For example, in the preceding example, we are setting the `appName` and `message` values passed as a JSON object to this view through the response `render()` method. However, there are many more attributes that HTML elements support, such as setting control width, font color, font style, and so on. In a later section, we will see how we can achieve this in Jade.

The equal to (=) operator is only required if you are binding to any value injecting in to the view. If you want to specify a hardcoded static value, then it can easily be set without using the equal to operator, as shown in the following code:

```
doctype
html
    body
        h1 Jade App
        p This is Jade View
```

Here are a few examples of using Jade syntax for HTML-specific scenarios:

Attributes	Jade	HTML
Textbox	`input(type='text' name='txtName')`	`<input type='text' name='txtName'/>`
Anchor tag	`a(href='microsoft.com') Microsoft`	`<a href="microsoft.com">Microsoft</a>`
Checkbox	`input(type='checkbox', checked)`	`<input type="checkbox" checked="checked"/>`
Anchor with style attributes	`a(style = {color: 'green', background: 'black'})`	`<a style="color:green;background:black"></a>`
Link button	`input(type='button' name='btn')`	`<input type="button" name="btn"/>`

You can learn more about the Jade language here: `http://jade-lang.com/`.

Jade's framework also supports layout pages. Layout pages hold the static information of the website, which is mostly placed in the header, footer, or side bars, and the content actually changes as per the page requested. In ASP.Net web forms, we define master pages with `<asp:ContentPlaceHolder>` tags, which render the content of the page reference to that master page. In ASP.NET MVC, this can be done using the Razor `@RenderBody` element. In Jade, we can define the content block using a `block` keyword followed by the name of the block. For example, the following is the `layout.jade` that contains the `block contentBlock` statement, where `block` represents where the content of the child page renders, and `contentBlock` is the name of the block that has to be defined in the child page. Multiple blocks can also be defined in a single view.

The following is the content of the layout page:

```
doctype html
html
  head
    title Jade App
  body
  block contentBlock
```

The layout page can be used with the `extends` keyword followed by the layout page name. The Jade view engine automatically searches the page with that name and if it's found, searches for the block name and places the content there. Here is the child page `index.jade` that uses the layout page `layout.jade`:

```
extends layout
block contentBlock
        h1= appName
        p= message
```

The output will be as follows:

JadeDemo

This is our first Jade view engine example!

Routing in the Express application

We have now learned the basics of the EJS and Jade view engines. Both offer similar features, but the syntax is different. In the previous examples, we sent a response that points to a specific page which renders the content on the client side.

The Express framework provides several methods that correspond to HTTP methods, such as `get`, `post`, `put`, `delete`, and so on. We can use the `get` method to retrieve something, `post` to create a record, `put` to update, and so on. Pages can reside anywhere within the `Views` folder, but the routing actually defines which page has to be loaded when the request is made on a specific URL path.

Let's create an EJS page inside the `Views/ejsviews/home` folder and name it `about.ejs`.

Routing can be defined using the Express application object, as shown in the following code:

```
expressApp.get("/About", function (req, res) {
    res.render("ejsviews/home/about");
});
```

When the user browses to `http://localhost/About`, it shows the **About** page.

Middleware

Node.js Express also provides a special routing method, `all()`, which is not mapped to any HTTP method. But it is used to load Middleware at a path, irrespective of the HTTP method being requested. For example, making HTTP GET and POST requests at `http://localhost/middlewareexample` will execute the same `all()` method shown in the following code:

```
expressApp.all('/middlewareexample', function (req, res) {
    console.log('Accessing the secret1 section ...');
});
```

Just like in .NET, we have OWIN middleware that can be chained in the request pipeline. In the same way, Node.js Express middleware can also be chained and can be invoked by calling the next middleware with a little change in the function signature. Here is the modified version that takes the `next` parameter after the response object which provides a handler to the next middleware in the pipeline, defined in a sequence for a particular request path:

```
expressApp.all('/middlewareexample', function (req, res, next) {
    console.log('Accessing the secret1 section ...');
    next();
});
```

For example, suppose we have two middlewares and the first middleware just logs the information to the console window, whereas the second returns the HTML content back to the client. Here is the `server.js` file that contains the two middlewares in the EJS view engine:

```
//Initialized http object
var http = require('http');
//adding express dependency
var express = require('express');

//creating express application
var expressApp = express();

expressApp.all('/middlewareexample', function (req, res, next) {
    console.log('Middleware executed now calling next middleware in
the pipeline');
    next(); // pass control to the next handler
});
expressApp.all('/middlewareexample', function (req, res) {
    res.send("<html><body><div>Middleware executed</div></body></
html>");
});


//declared port
var port = process.env.port || 1337;

//Initialized http server object and use res.write() to send actual
response content
var httpServer = http.createServer(expressApp);

//listening for incoming request
httpServer.listen(port);
```

Now when we access the URL path `http://localhost/middlewareexample`, the message will be printed on the console and renders the HTML content in the browser:

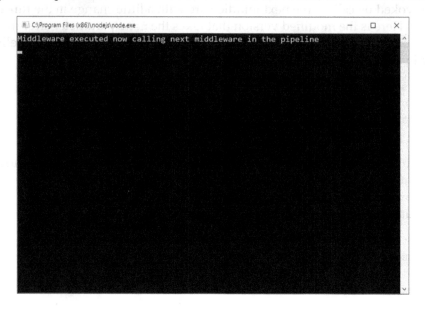

Here is the HTML content that will render in the browser:

Middleware executed

MVC with the Express framework

Almost every application consists of numerous pages, and defining all the logic and routing on the main `server.js` is not practical or maintainable. In this section, we will see how the **Model View Controller** (**MVC**) pattern can be implemented with the Express framework. We will develop a simple application to see how controllers and data services can be developed, and how the controller loads the view and injects the model using the Express framework.

MVC pattern

MVC is a software architectural pattern used to separate an application's concerns. The model represents the entity that contains properties to hold information, whereas the controller is used to inject the model into the view and load the view. The controller is also used to store the model in the database, whereas the view is the page that renders the model injected by the controller and uses it wherever needed.

Creating a controller

We will start by creating a simple `homeController` to render a home page. Let's extend the EJS view engine example developed above, and create a `Controllers` folder at the root of your project. Inside the `Controllers` folder, create a `HomeController.js` file and place the following code snippet there:

```
(function (homeController) {
    homeController.load = function (expressApp) {
        expressApp.get('/', function (req, res) {
            res.render("ejsviews/home/index", {appName: "EJS
Application", message:"EJS MVC Implementation"})
        });
    };
}) (module.exports);
```

In the preceding code, there is an anonymous JavaScript function that takes the `module.export` object and binds it to the `homeController` when it is executed. The basic advantage of implementing it in this way is that every method or property defined with the `homeController` object will be exportable and accessible by the calling object. In the preceding example, we have defined a `load()` method that defines the routing at the root path (/) and returns the **Index** page to the client.

In the main `ejsserver.js` file, we can use the controller by using the `require` object as shown in the following code:

```
//Initialized http object
var http = require('http');

//adding express dependency
var express = require('express');

//adding ejs locals
var ejsLocal = require('ejs-locals');

//creating express application
var expressApp = express();

//Add engine that supports master pages
expressApp.engine('ejs', ejsLocal);

//Set jade for Node.js application
expressApp.set('view engine', 'ejs');

//Initializing HomeController
var homeController = require('./Controllers/HomeContoller.js');
```

```
homeController.load(expressApp);

//declared port
var port = process.env.port || 1337;

//Initialized http server object and use res.write() to send actual
response content
var httpServer = http.createServer(expressApp);

//listening for incoming request
httpServer.listen(port);
```

In the preceding code, we have added the HomeController object using the require object and called the load() method to define the routing that navigates to the index page when the website runs.

Creating data services

Every business application involves lots of CRUD (create, read, update, and delete) operations. For a better design, these operations can be separately implemented in data service objects, so if multiple controllers wanted to use the same service, they can use them without writing the same code repeatedly. In this section, we will create a data service JavaScript file that reads the data and passes it in the routing function. To start with, let's create a folder name DataServices at the root of the application and create ProductService.js inside it. Here is the code for ProductService.js, which returns the products array:

```
(function(data){
    data.getProducts = function () {
        return [{
                name: 'Product1',
                price: 200,
            },
            {
                name: 'Product2',
                price: 500
            },
            {
                name: 'Product3',
                price: 1000
            }
        ];
    };
})(module.exports);
```

We can use this `ProductService` inside `HomeController` through the `require` object:

```
(function (homeController) {
    var productService = require('../DataServices/ProductService');

    homeController.load = function (expressApp) {
        expressApp.get('/', function (req, res) {
            var products = productService.getProducts();
            res.render("ejsviews/home/index", { appName: "EJS
Application", message: "EJS MVC Implementation", data: products });
        });
    };
})(module.exports);
```

And here is the `index.ejs` file, which loops through the products and displays the product name and price:

```
<% layout('../layout.ejs') -%>
<h1><%= appName %></h1>

<p> <%= message %></p>

<div>

  <% data.forEach(function(product) { %>
    <li><%= product.name %> - <%= product.price %></li>
  <% }); %>

</div>
```

Finally, the output looks like the following:

EJS Application

EJS MVC Implementation

- Product1 - 200
- Product2 - 500
- Product3 - 1000

Accessing the Microsoft SQL server in Node.js

Node.js provides different database drivers that can be added as node packages. There are packages for the MongoDB driver, the Microsoft SQL Server driver, and more. We will use the MS SQL driver for Node.js to connect with Microsoft SQL server databases. To install `mssql` you can run the `npm install mssql -save` command, or add it from the NPM package manager window, as shown in the following screenshot:

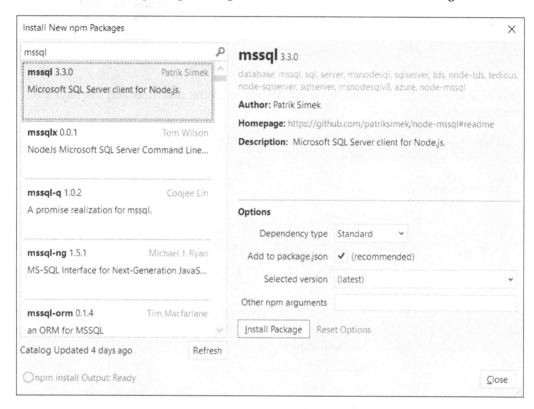

 With the MSSQL driver, TCP/IP should be enabled for a corresponding SQL server instance.

Reading a record from the Microsoft SQL server database

In the `DataService.js` file, we will add the `getProducts()` method, which loads the list of products from the SQL Server database.

The following is the `getProducts()` method, which accepts the callback function, so as soon the products list is fetched from the database, it will be passed in the callback function on the caller side:

```
(function(data){
data.getRecords = function (callbackFn) {
        //loaded SQL object
        var sql = require('mssql');

        //database configuration attributes to connect
        var config = {
            user: 'sa',
            password: '123',
            server: 'ovais-pc', // You can use 'localhost\\instance'
to connect to named instance
            database: 'products'
        }

        var products = null;
        //Connect to SQL Server returns a promise and on successfull
connection executing a query using Request object
        sql.connect(config).then(function () {
            new sql.Request().query('select * from products', function
(err, recordset) {
                callbackFn(recordset);
            });
        });


    };
})(module.exports);
```

In the preceding code, we initialized the `sql` object using the `require` object. The `Config` variable contains the connection attributes, such as `username`, `password`, `server`, and `database`. This is passed while calling the `sql connect()` method. The `Connect()` method returns a `then()` promise, through which we can initiate the SQL query request using the `sql.Request()` method. If the request is successful, we will get the result set in the `recordset` object that will be returned to the caller through its callback function.

Here is the modified version of `HomeController.js` that calls the `DataService` `getRecords()` method and passes the products list retrieved as a model to the index view:

```
(function (homeController) {
    var productService = require('../DataServices/ProductService');

    homeController.load = function (expressApp) {
        expressApp.get('/', function (req, res) {
            var products = productService.getRecords(function
(products) {
                console.dir(products);
                res.render("ejsviews/home/index", { appName: "EJS
Application", message: "EJS MVC Implementation", data: products });
            });
        });
    };
}) (module.exports);
```

The following is the `index.js` file, which loops through the list of products and displays the product name and price:

```
<% layout('../layout.ejs') -%>
<h1><%= appName %></h1>
<p> <%= message %></p>

<table>
<th>
<td> Product Name </td>
<td> Description </td>
<td> Price </td>
</th>
 <% data.forEach(function(product) { %>
   <tr> <td><%= product.Name %> </td> <td> <%= product.Description %>
</td><td> <%= product.Price %> </td></tr>
 <% }); %>
</table>
```

Creating a record in the Microsoft SQL server database

To create a record in the database, we can define the HTML input elements wrapped within the HTML form tag, and on submission of the form, we can make a post request by defining a `post` method in our `HomeController.js` file. When the form is submitted, the values can be retrieved using the `request.body` object. This is the parser that parses the DOM and makes a list of elements wrapped under the form tag. We can access it like `req.body.txtName`, where `txtName` is the HTML input element and `req` is the request object.

Express 4.0 unbundled the `body-parser` object into a separate package and can be downloaded separately using the `npm install body-parser -save` command or through the NPM package manager window, as shown in the following screenshot:

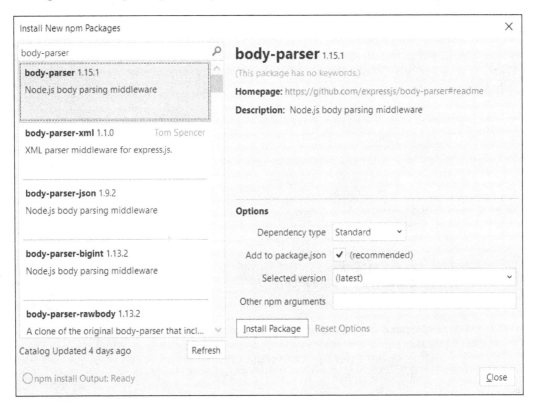

In your main `ejsserver.js` file, add the `body-parser` using the `require` object and pass it in the `expressApp` object by calling the `expressApp.use()` method:

```
var bodyParser = require('body-parser');

expressApp.use(new bodyParser());
```

Once this is added, we can modify `HomeController.js` and define a POST method that will be called once the form is submitted:

```
expressApp.post('/', function (req, res) {
        console.log(req.body.txtName);
        productService.saveProduct(req.body.txtName, req.body.
txtDescription, req.body.txtPrice, function (result) {
                res.send("Record saved successfully");
        });
});
```

The preceding method calls the data service `saveProduct()` method and passes the values filled by the user as parameters. The last parameter is the callback function, which will be executed if the record saved successfully. Here is the `saveProduct` code snippet of the `DataService.js` file:

```
data.saveProduct = function (name, description, price, callbackFn) {

        //loaded SQL object
        var sql = require('mssql');

        //database configuration attributes to connect
        var config = {
            user: 'sa',
            password: '123',
            server: 'ovais-pc', // You can use 'localhost\\instance'
to connect to named instance
            database: 'products'
        }

        //Connect to SQL Server returns a promise and on successfull
connection executing a query using Request object
        sql.connect(config).then(function () {
            new sql.Request().query("INSERT into products (Name,
Description, Price) values('"+ name +"', '"+ description+"',"+
price+")", function (err, recordset) {
                    callbackFn(recordset);
            });
        });

    };
```

And finally, here is the `Index.ejs` view that contains a form with the `Name`, `Description`, and `Price` fields:

```
<form method="post">
<table>
<tr>
  <td> Product Name: </td>
  <td> <input type='text' name='txtName'  /> </td>
</tr>
<tr>
  <td> Description: </td>
  <td><input type='text' name='txtDescription'  /></td>
</tr>
<tr>
  <td> Price: </td>
  <td><input type='number' name='txtPrice' /></td>

</tr>
<tr>
<td>   </td>
<td><input type="submit" value="Save" /> </td>
</tr>
</table>
</form>
```

To learn more about the `mssql` node package, please use this link: `https://www.npmjs.com/package/mssql`.

Summary

This chapter focused on the basics of Node.js and how to use them in developing server-side applications using JavaScript. We have learned about two view engines, EJS and Jade, and how to use them. We have also learned the usage of controllers and services to implement an MVC pattern. And finally, we finished by looking at examples of accessing the Microsoft SQL server database to perform, create, and retrieve operations on a database. In the next chapter, we will focus on best practices for using JavaScript in large-scale applications.

9
Using JavaScript for Large-Scale Projects

Large-scale web application projects comprise of several modules. With continuous improvements and advancements in the development of various JavaScript frameworks, developers use JavaScript frequently in an application's presentation or frontend layer, and server-side operations are only performed when required. For example, when saving or reading the data from server or doing some other database or backend operations, an HTTP request is made to the server that returns the plain JSON object and updates the DOM elements. With these developments in place, most of the application frontend code resides on the client side. However, when JavaScript was first developed, it was targeted to be used for doing some basic operations, such as updating the DOM elements or showing confirm dialogs and other relative operations. The JavaScript code mostly exists on the page itself within the `<script>` scripting tag. However, large-scale applications consist of many lines of code and need proper attention when designing and architecting the frontend. In this chapter, we will discuss a few concepts and best practices that help to make the application frontend more scalable and maintainable.

Think before proceeding

Large-scale applications consist of many JavaScript files and proper structuring of these files brings greater visibility. JavaScript frameworks such as AngularJS, EmberJS, and others already provide proper structuring and guidelines to define controllers, factories, and other objects, as well as provide best practices of using them. These frameworks are very popular and already adhere to the problem of higher scalability and maintainability. However, there are certain scenarios where we want to strictly rely on plain JavaScript files and may develop our own custom framework to remedy particular requirements. To acknowledge these, there are certain best industry-wide practices being used, which make our JavaScript-based frontend more maintainable and scalable.

When working on large scale applications, we need to think ahead of what the scope of the application is all about. We need to think how easily our application can be extended and how quickly the incorporation of other modules or functionality can be achieved. If any module fails, would it affect the behavior of the application or crash other modules? For example, if we are using any third-party JavaScript library that modify some of their method's signatures. In this case, if any third-party library is used frequently everywhere in our application, we have to modify the method at each point, and it may be a cumbersome process to not only change, but also test. On the other hand, if some Facade or wrapper has been implemented, it would only require us to change at one place instead of updating it everywhere. Therefore, designing an application architecture or framework is a thoughtful process, but it makes the application more robust and healthy.

Developing highly scalable and maintainable applications

The following are the factors that we should consider to make highly scalable and maintainable web applications that rely heavily on JavaScript.

Modularization

With big applications, writing everything in a single JavaScript file is not a good practice. Nonetheless, even if you have separate JavaScript files for different modules and referencing them through the scripting `<script>` tag bloats the global namespace. A proper structuring should be done to keep JavaScript files into separate module-wise folders. For example, an ERP application consists of several modules. We can create separate folders for each module and use specific JavaScript files to provide certain functionality for specific views or pages. However, the common files can reside in the common folder.

Here is the sample project structuring to arrange JavaScript files based on an ERP module. Each module has a `service` folder that contains some files to do some read or write operations on the server side, and the `Views` folder to manipulate DOM elements of specific views once the data is loaded or any control event is invoked. The `common` folder may contain all the helper utilities and functions that are used by all the other modules. For example, to log messages on console, or make an HTTP request on the server side, functions can be defined in the common JavaScript files and they can be used by the services or view JavaScript files:

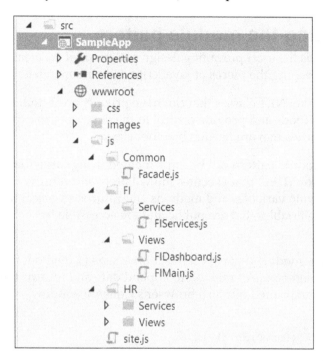

In the preceding structure, the `Services` folder can have the functions related to perform **create, retrieve, update, and delete (CRUD)** operations on the database by calling some Web API or web services, whereas a view file such as `FIMain.js` contains page-specific function.

To make an HTML page clean, it is a better approach to keep JavaScript files separate from the HTML page. So in the preceding screenshot, `FIMain.js` contains the JavaScript function corresponding to the main page, whereas `FIDashboard.js` contains the JavaScript function corresponding to the dashboard page, and so on.

These files can simply be added through the `<script>` scripting tag, but in JavaScript world, adding JavaScript files directly on the page itself is not good practice. Modules can be defined in JavaScript by implementing a module pattern. However, mostly developers prefer using RequireJS API to define modules to make module loading simpler and provide a better scoping of variables and functions defined in this module. It is equivalent to the CommonJS system, but it is recommended because of an asynchronous behavior. It loads the JavaScript modules in an asynchronous way and make the page-load cycle faster.

Implementing the module pattern

A module pattern is the most prevailing design pattern used for creating loose-coupled architecture and keeping the pieces of JavaScript code independent of other modules.

Modules are just like .NET classes that can have private, protected, and public properties and methods and provide control to the developer to expose only those methods or properties that are needed by other classes.

In JavaScript, a module pattern can be implemented using **immediately invoked function expression (IIFE)** that executes immediately and returns a closure. Closure actually hides private variables and methods and returns an object that contains only those methods or variables that are public and are accessible by other modules.

Here is the `Logger` module that exposed a `logMessage()` method, which calls one private `formatMessage()` method to append date and returns the formatted message that is then printed out on a browser's **Console** window:

```
<script>
  var Logger= (function () {

    //private method
    var formatMessage = function (message) {
      return message + " logged at: " + new Date();
    }

    return {
      //public method
      logMessage: function (message) {
        console.log(formatMessage(message));
      }
    };
```

```
    }) ();

    Logger.logMessage("hello world");
  </script>
```

In the preceding code, the `logMessage()` method returns an object that is invoked through a `Logger` namespace.

A module can contain multiple methods and properties, and to implement this scenario, let's modify the preceding example and add one more method to show alert message and a property to access the logger name and expose them through an object literal syntax. Object literal is another representation of binding methods and properties as name value pairs separated by commas and offers a cleaner representation. Here is the modified code:

```
<script>
  var Logger= (function () {
    //private variable
    var loggerName = "AppLogger";

    //private method
    var formatMessage = function (message) {
      return message + " logged at: " + new Date();
    }

    //private method
    var logMessage= function (message){
      console.log(formatMessage(message));
    }

    //private method
    var showAlert = function(message){
      alert(formatMessage(message));
    }

    return {

      //public methods and variable
      logConsoleMessage: logMessage,
      showAlertMessage: showAlert,
      loggerName: loggerName
    };

  }) ();
```

```
    Logger.logConsoleMessage("Hello World");
    Logger.showAlertMessage("Hello World");
    console.log(Logger.loggerName);
</script>
```

In the preceding code, `logMessage()` and `showAlert()` will be accessible through `logConsoleMessage()` and `showAlertMessage()` methods.

Modularizing JavaScript code through RequireJS

Modules in RequireJS are an extension of the module pattern with the benefit of not needing globals to refer to other modules. RequireJS is a JavaScript API to define modules and load them asynchronously when they are required. It downloads the JavaScript files asynchronously and reduces the time to load the whole page.

Creating modules using the RequireJS API

A module in RequireJS can be created using the `define()` method and loaded using the `require()` method. RequireJS provides two syntax styles to define modules that are as follows:

- **Defining module in CommonJS style**: Here is the code snippet to define the module in the CommonJS style:

```
define(function (require, exports, module) {
  //require to use any existing module
  var utility = require('utility');

  //exports to export values
  exports.example ="Common JS";

  //module to export values
  module.exports.name = "Large scale applications";

  module.exports.showMessage = function (message) {
    alert(utility.formatMessage(message));
  }
});
```

The preceding CommonJS style syntax uses the `define()` method of RequireJS API that takes a function. This function takes three parameters: `require`, `exports`, and `module`. The last two parameters, `exports` and `module`, are optional. However, they have to be defined in the same sequence. If you are not using `require`, and only wanted to export some functionality using the `exports` object, the `require` parameter needs to be provided. The `require` parameter is used to import modules that were exported using `exports` or `module.exports` in other modules. In the preceding code, we have added the dependency of the `utility` module by specifying the path of the `utility.js` file in calling the `require` method. When adding any dependency, we just need to specify the path followed with the filename of the JavaScript file and not the `.js` file extension. The file is automatically picked by the RequireJS API. Exporting any function or variable that we need to be used by other modules can be done through `exports` or `module.exports` appropriately.

- **Defining module in AMD style**: Here is the code snippet to define the module in an AMD-style syntax:

```
define(['utility'], function (utility) {
  return {
    example: "AMD",
    name: "Large scale applications",
    showMessage: function () {
      alert(utility.formatMessage(message));
    }
  }

});
```

The AMD-style syntax takes the dependencies array as the first parameter. To load the module dependencies in an AMD-style syntax you have to define them in an array. The second parameter takes the `function` parameter, taking the module name that maps to the module defined in the dependencies array so that it can be used in the function body. To export the variables or methods, we can export them through the object literal syntax.

Bootstrapping RequireJS

Let's go through a simple example to understand the concepts of using RequireJS in an ASP.NET application. To use the RequireJS API in the ASP.NET Core application, you have to download and place the `Require.js` file in the `wwwroot/js` folder. In the following example, we will write a `logging` module that contains a few methods such as writing to console, showing an alert, and writing on the server.

Let's create the `Logging.js` file in the `wwwroot/js/common` folder and write the following code:

```
define(function () {
  return {
    showMessage: function (message) {
      alert(message);
    },
    writeToConsole: function (message) {
      console.log(message);
    },
    writeToServer: function (message) {
      //write to server by doing some Ajax request
      var xhr = new XMLHttpRequest();
      xhttp.open("POST",
        "http://localhost:8081/Logging?message="+message, true);
      xhttp.send();
    }
  }
});
```

The following is the code for the `Index.cshtml` page that displays an alert message when the page is loaded:

```
<script src="~/js/require.js"></script>
<script>
  (function () {
    require(["js/common/logging"], function(logging){
      logging.showMessage("demo");
    });
  })();
</script>
```

We can also wrap the preceding function in the `main.js` file and bootstrap it through the scripting `<script>` tag. There is one special attribute known as `data-main`, which is used by RequireJS as the entry point of the application.

The following is the code for `main.js` that resides under the `wwwroot/JS` folder. As `main.js` resides under the `wwwroot/js` folder, the path will be `common/logging`:

```
//Main.js
require(["common/logging"], function(logging){
  logging.showMessage("demo");
});
```

Finally, we can bootstrap `main.js` using scripting tag, as shown in the following code:

```
<script data-main="~/js/main.js" src="~/js/require.js"></script>
```

The following is the sample project structure containing the `Common` folder to have common JavaScript files; whereas, `FI` and `HR` folders for module-specific JavaScript files:

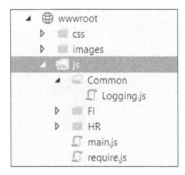

Suppose we want to modify the preceding example and pass the message from an input control on a button's `click` event. This can be done by developing a `view` module for a particular page and injecting the `logging` module inside it.

The following is the HTML markup containing `input` and `button` elements:

```
<div id="myCarousel" class="carousel slide" data-ride="carousel"
  data-interval="6000">
  <input type="text" id="txtMessage" />
  <button id="btnSendMessage" >Send Message</button>
</div>
```

The following is the `view.js` file that takes the `logging` module and call its `sendMessage()` method by reading the `txtMessage` element value:

```
define(['common/logging'], function(logging) {
  $('#btnSendMessage').on('click', function(e) {
    sendMessage();
    e.preventDefault();
```

```
      });
      function sendMessage(){
        var message= document.getElementById('txtMessage').value;
        logging.showMessage(message);
      }
      return {
        sendMessage: sendMessage
      };
    });
```

When the button is clicked, an alert message will be displayed.

Event-driven messaging

In the preceding section, we enabled the modularization support for JavaScript files and converted them into modules. In large applications, we cannot just rely on injecting the modules in other modules, we may need some flexibility to invoke events of certain modules through some the Pub/Sub pattern. We have already seen the Pub/Sub pattern in *Chapter 7, JavaScript Design Patterns*, which maintains a centralized list to register events that point to some callback functions and are invoked through a publisher object. This pattern is very useful when enabling event-driven messaging between modules, but there is another better pattern known as a mediator pattern, which is a superset of the Pub/Sub pattern. The mediator pattern is better as it allows publishers or mediators to access other events/methods of the subscribed object and allows the mediator to decide the method or event that is needed to be called.

Implementing mediator pattern for communication between modules

Mediator encapsulates objects in a centralized list and uses them by invoking their methods. This list keeps all the objects (or modules) at central location, thus allowing improved communication between them.

Let's go through a practical example of implementing the mediator pattern. The mediator acts as a centralized controlling object where modules can subscribe or unsubscribe. It provides abstract methods that can be invoked by any of the source subscriber module to communicate with the target subscriber module. The mediator holds a centralized dictionary object to hold subscriber objects based on some key, or mostly name, and invokes target module method based on the module name passed by the subscriber. In the following example, we have MediatorCore (mediator), EmployeeRepository (subscriber), and HRModule (subscriber) objects. We will use the RequireJS API to convert JavaScript files into modules.

The following is the `MediatorCore` JavaScript file:

```
//MediatorCore.js
define(function () {
  return {

    mediator: function () {
      this.modules = [];

      //To subscribe module
      this.subscribe = function (module) {
        //Check if module exist or initialize array
        this.modules[module.moduleName] =
          this.modules[module.moduleName] || [];

        //Add the module object based on its module name
        this.modules[module.moduleName].push(module);
        module.mediator = this;
      },

      this.unsubscribe = function (module) {
        //Loop through the array and remove the module
        if (this.modules[module.moduleName]) {
          for (i = 0; i < this.modules[module.moduleName].length;
            i++) {
            if (this.modules[module.moduleName][i] === module) {
              this.modules[module.moduleName].splice(i, 1);
              break;
            }
          }
        }
      },

      /* To call the getRecords method of specific module based on
         module name */
      this.getRecords = function (moduleName) {
        if (this.modules[moduleName]) {
          //get the module based on module name
          var fromModule = this.modules[moduleName][0];
          return fromModule.getRecords();
        }
      },

      /* To call the insertRecord method of specific module based
         on module name */
      this.insertRecord = function (record, moduleName) {
        if (this.modules[moduleName]) {
```

```
            //get the module based on module name
            var fromModule = this.modules[moduleName][0];
            fromModule.insertRecord(record);
        }
    },

    /* To call the deleteRecord method of specific module based
       on module name */
    this.deleteRecord = function (record, moduleName) {
        if (this.modules[moduleName]) {
            //get the module based on module name
            var fromModule = this.modules[moduleName][0];
            fromModule.deleteRecord(record);

        }
    },

    /* To call the updateRecord method of specific module based
       on module name */
    this.updateRecord = function (record, moduleName) {
        if (this.modules[moduleName]) {
            //get the module based on module name
            var fromModule = this.modules[moduleName][0];
            fromModule.updateRecord(record);

        }
    }


    }
   }
});
```

This mediator exposes four methods to perform CRUD operations. This example showcases a simple HR module that uses certain repositories to do certain operations. For example, the HR module can have the `EmployeeRepository` module to save record in employee-specific tables, `DepartmentRepository` to do operations specific to department, and so on.

Here is the code snippet for `EmployeeRepository` that contains the concrete implementation of the abstract methods defined in the mediator:

```
//EmployeeRepository.js
define(function () {
    return {

        //Concrete Implementation of Mediator Interface
        EmployeeRepository: function (uniqueName) {
```

```
    this.moduleName = uniqueName;
    //this reference will be used just in case to call some
      other module methods
    this.mediator = null;

    //Concrete Implementation of getRecords method
    this.getRecords = function () {
      //Call some service to get records

      //Sample text to return data when getRecords method will
        be invoked
      return "This are test records";

    },
    //Concrete Implementation of insertRecord method
    this.insertRecord = function (record) {
      console.log("saving record");
      //Call some service to save record.
    },

    //Concrete Implementation of deleteRecord method
    this.deleteRecord = function (record) {
      console.log("deleting record");
      //Call some service to delete record
    }

    //Concrete Implementation of updateRecord method
    this.updateRecord = function (record) {
      console.log("updating record");
      //Call some service to delete record
    }

  }
 }
});
```

EmployeeRepository takes a name parameter at initialization and defines the
mediator variable that can be set when it is registered at mediator. This is provided
in case EmployeeRepository wants to call some other module or repository
of a subscriber module. We can create multiple repositories, for example,
RecruitmentRepository and AppraisalRepository for HRModule and use them
when needed.

Here is the code for `HRModule` that calls `EmployeeRepository` through a mediator:

```
//HRModule.js
define(function () {
  return {
    HRModule: function (uniqueName) {
      this.moduleName = uniqueName;
      this.mediator = null;
      this.repository = "EmployeeRepository";

      this.getRecords = function () {
        return this.mediator.getRecords(this.repository);
      },

      this.insertRecord = function (record) {
        this.mediator.insertRecord(record, this.repository);
      },

      this.deleteRecord = function (record) {
        this.mediator.deleteRecord(record, this.repository);
      }

      this.updateRecord = function (record) {
        this.mediator.updateRecord(record, this.repository);
      }

    }
  }
});
```

Now, we will register `HRModule` and `EmployeeRepository` with the mediator and call the `HRModule` methods to perform CRUD operations.

The following is the code for `HRView.js` that is used to capture the button's `click` event on the form and calls the `getRecords()` method when the button is clicked:

```
//HRView.js
define(['hr/mediatorcore','hr/employeerepository','hr/hrmodule'],
  function (mediatorCore, employeeRepository, hrModule) {
    $('#btnGetRecords').on('click', function (e) {
      getRecords();
      e.preventDefault();
    });
    function getRecords() {
```

```
    var mediator = new mediatorCore.mediator();
    var empModule = new hrModule.HRModule("EmployeeModule");
    mediator.subscribe(empModule);

    var empRepo = new
      employeeRepository.EmployeeRepository("EmployeeRepository");
    mediator.subscribe(empRepo);

    alert("Records: "+ empModule.getRecords());
  }
  return {
    getRecords: getRecords
  };
});
```

The following is the `main.js` file that is used to bootstraps the `HRView.js` file
through the RequireJS API:

```
//main.js
require(["./hrview"], function(hr){
});
```

Finally, we can use the preceding `Main.js` module on the `Index.cshtml` page in
ASP.NET, as follows:

```
//Index.cshtml

@{
  ViewData["Title"] = "Home Page";
}
<script data-main="js/main.js"  src="~/js/require.js"></script>

<div id="myCarousel" class="carousel slide" data-ride="carousel"
  data-interval="6000">
  <input type="text" id="txtMessage" />
  <button id="btnGetRecords" >Send Message</button>
</div>
```

The following is the logical diagram that shows how the modules communicate with each other:

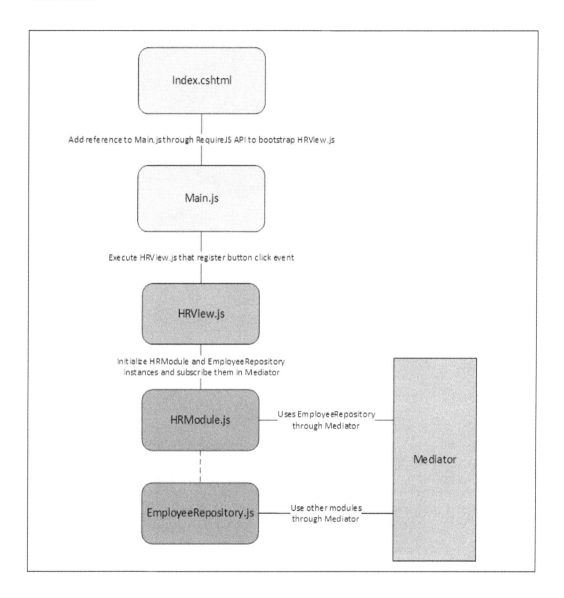

Encapsulating complex code

Another core principle of developing highly scalable and maintainable application is to use wrappers and encapsulate complex code into a simpler interface. This can be achieved by implementing a Facade pattern.

The Facade pattern is used to simplify the complex code by exposing a method and hiding all the complex code inside the Facade object. For example, there are many ways and APIs available to perform Ajaxified operations. Ajax requests can be made using a plain `XmlHttpRequest` object, or with jQuery, it is quite easy to use `$.post()` and `$.get()` methods. In AngularJS, it can be achieved using its own `http` object to invoke services and so on. These type of operations can be encapsulated and benefited in scenarios when the internal API is modified, or when you decided to use some other better API; modification needs to be done, which is far lesser than changing it at all the places where it has been used. With the Facade pattern, you can only modify it in the Facade object and save time on updating it everywhere where it has been used.

Another advantage of using Facade is that it reduces the development effort by encapsulating a bunch of code to a simple method and make it easy for the consumer to use. Facade reduces the development effort by minimizing the lines of code required to call a certain functionality. To learn more about Facade, refer to *Chapter 7, JavaScript Design Patterns*.

Generating documentation

Proper documentation increases the maintainability of your application and makes it easier for developers to reference it when needed or customizing applications. There are many documentation generators available in the market. JSDoc and YUIDoc are very popular JavaScript documentation generators, but in this section, we will use JSDoc3 that not only generates documentation, but also enables intellisense for your custom JavaScript modules to facilitate during development.

JSDoc is an API similar to JavaDoc and PHPDoc. Comments can be added directly to the JavaScript code. It also provides a JSDoc tool through which the documentation website can be created.

Installing JSDoc3 in ASP.NET Core

JSDoc3 can be added as a Node package and we can use it with the Gulp task runner to generate documents. To add JSDoc3 to your ASP.NET Core project, you can start by adding an entry to the `package.json` file used by Node. This entry has to be done in the development dependencies:

```
{
    "name": "ASP.NET",
    "version": "0.0.0",
    "devDependencies": {
        "gulp": "3.8.11",
        "gulp-jsdoc3": "0.3.0"
    }
}
```

The first development dependency defined in the previous screenshot is Gulp which is required to create tasks, and gulp-jsdoc3 is the actual documentation generator that generates the HTML website when you run that task.

The task can be defined as follows:

```
/// <binding Clean='clean' />
"use strict";

var gulp = require("gulp"),
jsdoc = require("gulp-jsdoc3");

var paths = {
  webroot: "./wwwroot/"
};

paths.appJs = paths.webroot + "app/**/*.js";

gulp.task("generatedoc", function (cb) {
  gulp.src(['Readme.md', paths.appJs], { read: false })
  .pipe(jsdoc(cb));
});
```

In the preceding code snippet, we have one task named generatedoc, in which we are reading the files placed at wwwroot/app/**/*.js and generating documentation. The jsdoc object takes the configuration defaults to generate documentation. To pass the default configuration attributes, we can just specify the cb parameter injected in the function level by Gulp. When you run this generatedoc task from the task runner in Visual Studio, it will add a docs folder at the root path of your web application project. As in ASP.NET Core, we already know that all static content should reside in the wwwroot folder, and to access it from browser, simply drag and drop this folder in the wwwroot folder and access it by running your website.

Adding comments

To generate documentation, we need to annotate our code with comments. The more the comments are provided, the better the documentation will be generated. Comments can be added through /** as the starting tag and */ as the ending tag:

```
/** This method is used to send HTTP Get Request **/
function GetData(path) {
  $.get(path, function (data) {
    return data;
  })
}
```

If the function is a constructor, you can specify `@constructor` in the comments to give more meaning to the readers:

```
/** This method is used to send HTTP Get Request
    @constructor
*/
function GetData(path) {
  $.get(path, function (data) {
    return data;
  })
}
```

A function takes parameters as well, and this can be indicated by using `@param` in your comments. Here is the same function that takes the actual path of some service as a parameter to retrieve records:

```
/** This method is used to send HTTP Get Request
    @constructor
    @param path - Specify URI of the resource that returns data
*/
function GetData(path) {
  $.get(path, function (data) {
    return data;
  })
}
```

When you run your application, it will show the documentation as follows:

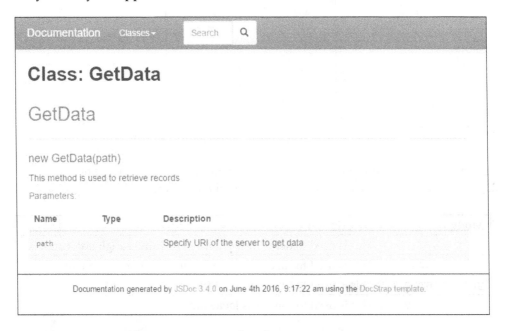

We have seen how easy it is with JSDoc3 to generate documentation. This not only helps to understand the code, but also helps the developer during development by providing intellisense. To learn more about JSDoc3, refer to `http://usejsdoc.org/`.

Deployment optimization

Large-scale application consists of large number of JavaScript files. When the page is downloaded, it is parsed and it downloads all the JavaScript files defined with the `<script>` tag. Once the JavaScript files are downloaded, they are parsed and executed. So, it depends on the number of JavaScript files you have referenced on the page, followed by the lines of code each JavaScript file contains. To optimize the page-loading cycle, it is recommended to compress them through a minification process. This makes the JavaScript file smaller in size and the page-loading cycle becomes faster.

In ASP.NET, we can compress the JavaScript files using Grunt and Gulp modules. These are Node modules and are highly integrated with ASP.NET Core. In ASP.NET Core, we can add these modules by adding a Node package reference in the `package.json` file, and each module has its separate configuration file known as `GulpFile.js` or `GruntFile.js`.

In this example, we will use the Gulp module to minify and compress our JavaScript files. In ASP.NET Core, we can enable Gulp by adding the Gulp module to the `package.json` file:

```
{
  "name": "ASP.NET",
  "version": "0.0.0",
  "devDependencies": {
    "gulp": "3.8.11",
    "gulp-concat": "2.5.2",
    "gulp-cssmin": "0.1.7",
    "gulp-uglify": "1.2.0"
  }
}
```

The preceding code snippet uses `gulp`, `gulp-concat`, `gulp-cssmin`, and `gulp-uglify`. The following is the description of each module:

Module	Description
Gulp	This is used to define tasks that can be run through task runners
gulp-concat	This is used to concatenate JavaScript files into a single file
gulp-cssmin	This is used to compress CSS files
gulp-uglify	This is used to compress JavaScript files

The following is the sample `gulpfile.js` that can be used to compress JavaScript and CSS files:

```
/// <binding Clean='clean' />
"use strict";

//Adding references of gulp modules
var gulp = require("gulp"),
rimraf = require("rimraf"),
concat = require("gulp-concat"),
cssmin = require("gulp-cssmin"),
uglify = require("gulp-uglify");

//define root path where all JavaScript and CSS files reside
var paths = {
  webroot: "./wwwroot/"
};

/* Path where all the non-minified JavaScript file resides. JS is
   the folder and ** is used to handle for sub folders */
paths.js = paths.webroot + "js/**/*.js";

/* Path where all the minified JavaScript file resides. JS is the
   folder and ** is used to handle for sub folders */
paths.minJs = paths.webroot + "js/**/*.min.js";

/* Path where all the non-minified CSS file resides. Css is the
   main folder and ** is used to handle for sub folder */
paths.css = paths.webroot + "css/**/*.css";

/* Path where all the minified CSS file resides. Css is the main
   folder and ** is used to handle for sub folder */
paths.minCss = paths.webroot + "css/**/*.min.css";

/* New JavaScript file site.min.js that contains all the
   compressed and merged JavaScript files*/
paths.concatJsDest = paths.webroot + "js/site.min.js";

/* New CSS file site.min.css that will contain all the compressed
   and merged CSS files */
paths.concatCssDest = paths.webroot + "css/site.min.css";

//to delete site.min.js file
gulp.task("clean:js", function (cb) {
```

```
    rimraf(paths.concatJsDest, cb);
});

//to delete site.min.css file
gulp.task("clean:css", function (cb) {
  rimraf(paths.concatCssDest, cb);
});

/* To merge, compress and place the JavaScript files into one single
file site.min.js */
gulp.task("min:js", function () {
  return gulp.src([paths.js, "!" + paths.minJs], { base: "." })
  .pipe(concat(paths.concatJsDest))
  .pipe(uglify())
  .pipe(gulp.dest("."));
});

/* to merge, compress and place the CSS files into one single file
  site.min.css */
gulp.task("min:css", function () {
  return gulp.src([paths.css, "!" + paths.minCss])
  .pipe(concat(paths.concatCssDest))
  .pipe(cssmin())
  .pipe(gulp.dest("."));
});
```

In the preceding code snippet, there are four tasks and the following is their description:

- clean:js: This removes the site.min.js file
- clean:css: This removes the site.min.css file
- min:js: This merges all the files specified in paths.js and paths.minJs, minifies them using uglify(), and finally creates the site.main.js file
- min:css: This merges all the files specified in paths.css and paths.minCss, minifies them using cssmin(), and finally creates the site.main.css file

In Visual Studio 2015, you can run these tasks using **Task Runner Explorer**, and also bind them with the `build` events:

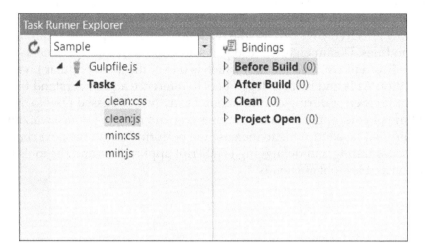

The following are the options that you can have to associate them with specific `build` events:

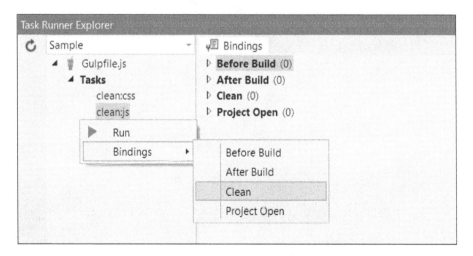

The preceding screenshot shows the steps to bind the `clean:js` task with a **Clean** build event. So, whenever your clean your project, it will run `clean:js` and remove the `site.min.js` file.

Summary

In this chapter, we discussed a few concepts of structuring JavaScript-based projects and splitting them into modules to increase the scalability and maintainability. We also saw how effectively we can use the mediator pattern to provide communication between modules. Documentation also plays an important role and increases the maintainability, and we used JSDoc3, which is one of the most popular JavaScript documentation APIs and helped developers to reference and understand the functions of JavaScript during development. Lastly, we discussed how to optimize the load time of your application by compressing and merging your JavaScript files into one minified JavaScript file to increase the performance. In the next chapter, we will discuss testing and debugging JavaScript applications and the tools that are available to troubleshoot efficiently.

10
Testing and Debugging JavaScript

In every software life cycle, testing and debugging play an important role. Thorough testing makes software flawless and good debugging techniques makes it easy to not only troubleshoot problems, but also helps to identify and fix any problems by reaching out to the exact point.

Testing is the core essence of creating any robust application. However, there are different practices and frameworks used by the application to serve particular objective, and the architecture varies as per the nature of the application. Therefore, sometimes it becomes difficult for a developer to test client-side code, for example, if an application contains some JavaScript code on a page itself, such as inline event handlers, make it tightly coupled with the page. On the other hand, even when modularizing the JavaScript code into different modules bring some test suite limitations and become harder to execute the testing process of an application.

Debugging is the process of finding and fixing errors in an application. It is one of the most important and core skillset in software development. If developers have a solid grasp on the debugging tools and know the ins and outs of debugging, they can quickly identify the root cause and start fixing the errors. Debugging is a basic process in any software development life cycle. Whether application is a complex one or a simple one, to trace and rectify errors debugging plays an important role. It helps the developer to break the program execution through breakpoints and identify the program flow by stepping into the chain of program execution. Moreover, there is other useful information almost all debugging tools provide, such as watching the current state of the variables or objects being used within the program and watching them on every stage of the debugging life cycle.

Testing the JavaScript code

Normally, web applications go through different types of testing, such as **user interface** (UI) testing, which checks the functionality of the UI by making certain inputs to the form and verifies the behavior of an application. This type of testing is mostly done manually or through automated testing tools. The other type of testing is **load testing**, which is used mostly to check the performance of an application and by putting up some load on the application. In simple terms, it can be an example of signing in to an application with many number of users or doing some operations through automated routines to test how the application behaves. There are a few more testing types, but the most essential type of testing that ensures the functionality of the application and certifies whether the application complies with the requirements is unit testing. In this section, we will discuss about unit testing JavaScript code using Jasmine (a popular JavaScript unit test framework) and use it with Karma and Grunt to execute test cases in an ASP.NET application using Visual Studio 2015 IDE.

Unit testing

Unit testing is a method to test individual units of modules together with associated data and procedures to verify the application's functionality compliance to the requirements. Unit testing is done by developers, and it allows developers to test each use case of the application to guarantee that it meets the requirement and works as expected.

The basic advantage of unit testing is that it separates each part of the application into a smaller unit and helps developers to focus and identify the bug initially during the development cycle. Unit testing is the first testing any application endures and allow testers and developers to release the application for **user acceptance testing** (UAT).

Writing unit tests

To test JavaScript code, there are many testing suites available. The most popular ones are Jasmine, Mocha, and QUnit. In this chapter, we will use Jasmine with Karma and Grunt.

Jasmine

Jasmine is a behavior-driven development framework for testing JavaScript code. This provides certain functions such as `it()`, `describe()`, `expect()`, and so on to write test scripts for the JavaScript code. The basic advantage of this framework is that it is very easy to understand and helps to write the test JavaScript code with very simple lines of code.

For example, consider the following JavaScript code that sums up two numbers passed as parameters:

```
(function () {
  var addTwoNumbers = function (x, y) {
    return x+y;
  };


}) ();
```

The test case for the preceding function will look similar to the following:

```
describe('Calculator', function () {
  it('Results will be 20 for 10 + 10', function () {
    expect(addTwoNumbers(10,10)).toBe(20);
  });
});
```

Karma

Karma is a test runner for JavaScript that can be integrated with other testing frameworks such as Jasmine, Mocha, and so on. It executes test cases defined through Jasmine or other test frameworks by providing a mock test environment and load browsers that executes the test JavaScript code according to the configuration. The Karma configuration file is known as `Karma.config.js`. Once the tests are executed, the results are displayed in the console window.

Grunt

Grunt is equivalent to Gulp. It is used to execute tasks such as minification of CSS file or JavaScript files, concatenation and merging of multiple JavaScript file, and so on. Grunt has hundreds of plugins that can be used to automate specific tasks. Unlike the previous chapters, where we used Gulp, we will use Grunt and see what it provides with Karma (test runner) and Jasmine (testing suite). Grunt and Gulp are both renowned task runners for development. The reason for using Grunt here is to get an understanding of another task runner of JavaScript that is equally renowned and supported by Visual Studio 2015 and discuss the packages that it provides to perform testing using Karma and Jasmine.

Developing unit test using Jasmine, Karma, and Grunt

In this section, we will develop a simple unit test to show how unit testing can be done in an ASP.NET Core application using Jasmine, Karma, and Grunt frameworks. To start with, create an ASP.NET Core application from Visual Studio 2015.

Adding packages

Open the `package.json` file in your ASP.NET Core application and add packages such as `grunt`, `grunt-karma`, `karma`, `karma-phantomjs-launcher`, `karma-jasmine`, `karma-spec-reporter`, and `karma-cli`, as shown in the following:

```
{
  "name": "ASP.NET",
  "version": "0.0.0",
  "devDependencies": {
    "grunt": "1.0.1",
    "grunt-karma": "2.0.0",
    "karma": "0.13.22",
    "karma-phantomjs-launcher": "1.0.0",
    "karma-jasmine": "1.0.2",
    "karma-spec-reporter": "0.0.26",
    "karma-cli": "1.0.0"
  }
}
```

The following table shows the description of each package:

Package Name	Description
`grunt`	This configures and runs tasks
`grunt-karma`	This is the Grunt plugin for the Karma test runner
`karma`	This is the test runner for JavaScript
`karma-phantomjs-launcher`	This is the Karma plugin to launch the PhantomJS browser
`karma-jasmine`	This is the Karma plugin for the Jasmine test suite
`karma-spec-reporter`	This is the Karma plugin to report test results to the console
`karma-cli`	This is the Karma command-line interface

Adding the Grunt file

Add `Gruntfile.js` in your ASP.NET application to define Grunt tasks. `Gruntfile.js` is the main file where all the tasks are configured. Configured tasks can be seen in Visual Studio from the **Task Runner Explorer** window.

Adding Karma specifications

The `Gruntfile.js` file provides the main `initConfig()` method that is called when the Grunt is loaded. This is the starting point where we define the Karma specifications.

The following is the Karma specifications defined within the `initConfig()` method:

```
grunt.initConfig({
  karma: {
    unit: {
      options: {
        frameworks: ['jasmine'],
        singleRun: true,
        browsers: ['PhantomJS'],
        files: [
          './wwwroot/js/**/*.js',
          './wwwroot/tests/**/*.test.js'


        ]
      }
    }
  }
});
```

In the preceding script, we first started by specifying the target platform for Karma. Inside `karma`, we will specify the unit that is used to run unit tests. Inside `unit`, we can define certain configuration attributes such as `frameworks`, `singleRun`, `browsers`, and `files`:

- `frameworks`: This is an array of test frameworks that we want to use. In this exercise, we used Jasmine. However, other frameworks such as Mocha and QUnit can also be used.

> Please note that when using any framework in Karma, an additional plugin/library of that framework has to be separately installed using **Node Package Manager** (**NPM**).

- `singleRun`: If this is set to `true`, Karma start capturing the configured browser(s) and executes tests on them. Once the tests are completed, it exits smoothly.

- `browsers`: This is an array to define multiple browsers in a comma-separated value. We have used PhantomJS in our example, which is a headless browser and runs the test in background. Karma supports other browsers such as Chrome, Firefox, IE, and Safari, and these can be configured through this property.

- `files`: This contains all the test files, source files, and dependencies. For example, if we are using jQuery in our test scripts, or original source code, we can add the path to this library as well. In the preceding configuration, we used wildcard characters to load all the source files defined under the `js` folder, and tests files under the `tests` folder with a `test.js` suffix.

There are many more attributes that can be used in the Karma configuration and it can be referred here:

`http://karma-runner.github.io/0.13/config/configuration-file.html`

Load npm task

To load the Karma test runner tool, we need to specify it in `Gruntfile.js` after the Karma configuration, as shown in the following:

```
grunt.loadNpmTasks('grunt-karma');
```

Register task

Finally, we will add the Grunt task to register tasks. The first parameter is the task name, which will be available in the **Task Runner Explorer** in Visual Studio, and the second parameter takes an array to execute multiple tasks:

```
grunt.registerTask('test', ['karma']);
```

Source JavaScript file

In this example, we have a `product.js` file that contains a `saveProduct()` method, which will be invoked on the **Save** button's click event.

Add this file to the `wwwroot/js` folder path:

```
window.product = window.product || {};

(function () {
  var saveProduct = function () {
    var prodCode = document.getElementById('txtProdCode').value;
    var prodUnitPrice = document.getElementById(
      'txtProdUnitPrice').value;
    var prodExpiry = document.getElementById(
      'txtProdExpiry').value;
    var prodQuantity = document.getElementById(
      'txtProdQuantity').value;
    var totalPrice = prodUnitPrice * prodQuantity;
    document.getElementById('totalAmount').innerHTML = totalPrice;
  };
```

```
    window.product.init = function () {
      document.getElementById('save').addEventListener('click',
        saveProduct);
    };

})();
```

In the preceding code snippet, we have a saveProduct() method that reads the HTML elements and calculates the total price based on the quantity and unit price entered. On the page initialization, we will register the **Save** button's click event handler that calls the saveProduct() method and calculate the total price.

 It is a recommended approach to keep your JavaScript code separate from your HTML markup.

Adding unit test script file

Here, we will add another JavaScript file under the wwwroot/tests folder and named it product.test.js. When writing tests, you can add the *.test.js suffix to make it uniquely identified, and separates it from the source JavaScript files.

Here is the code for product.test.js:

```
describe('Product', function () {

  // inject the HTML fixture for the tests
  beforeEach(function () {
    var fixture = '<div id="fixture">'+
      '<input id="txtProdCode" type="text">' +
      '<input id="txtProdExpiry" type="text">' +
      '<input id="txtProdUnitPrice" type="text">' +
      '<input id="txtProdQuantity" type="text">' +
      '<input id="save" type="button" value="Save">' +
      'Total Amount: <span id="totalAmount" /></div>';

    document.body.insertAdjacentHTML(
      'afterbegin',
      fixture);
  });

  // remove the html fixture from the DOM
  afterEach(function () {
    document.body.removeChild(document.getElementById('fixture'));
```

```
  });

  // call the init function of calculator to register DOM elements
  beforeEach(function () {
    window.product.init();
  });

  it('Expected result should be 0 if the Unit price is not valid',
    function () {
      document.getElementById('txtProdUnitPrice').value = 'a';
      document.getElementById('txtProdQuantity').value = 2;
      document.getElementById('save').click();
      expect(document.getElementById(
        'totalAmount').innerHTML).toBe('0');
  });

  it('Expected result should be 0 if the Product Quantity is not
    valid', function () {
      document.getElementById('txtProdUnitPrice').value = 30;
      document.getElementById('txtProdQuantity').value = 'zero';
      document.getElementById('save').click();
      expect(document.getElementById(
        'totalAmount').innerHTML).toBe('0');
  });

});
```

The Jasmine framework provides certain keywords to define specific blocks that run on specific conditions, which are as follows:

- describe(): This is a global Jasmine function that contains two parameters: a string and a function. The string is the name of the functionality that is going to be tested. The function contains the code that actually implements the Jasmine suite and contains logic of unit tests.

- it(): Here, specs are defined by calling the global Jasmine function it(). This also takes the string and function, where it contains the actual unit test name and the function block contains the actual logic of the code to be executed followed with the expected results.

- expect(): The expected results can be specified by using the expect() function that takes some value defined within the it() function. This is also chained with a matcher function, such as toBe() or not.toBe(), to match or unmatch the expected value.

In .NET, it is equivalent to the **Arrange**, **Act**, and **Assert** pattern. Here, Arrange is used to initialize objects and set values of the data that is passed to the method under test. The Act pattern actually invokes the method under test, and Assert verifies that the method under test behaves as expected.

Running test task

Running these tasks is straightforward, it can simply be run through the **Task Runner Explorer** window in Visual Studio 2015. Here is the screenshot of the **Task Runner Explorer** window that shows the tasks defined in `Gruntfile.js`:

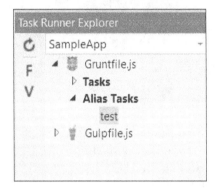

When we run the test task, it will show something similar to the following output:

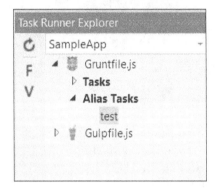

In our `product.test.js` test script, we have two tasks. One is to check whether passing the string values to one of the two elements such as `txtProdUnitPrice` and `txtProdQuantity` will return `0`. As our `product.js` file does not handle this condition, it will give an error.

To fix this, we will modify our `product.js` and add these two lines to handle this logic to check whether the value is a number or not:

```
prodUnitPrice = isNaN(prodUnitPrice) ? 0 : prodUnitPrice;
prodQuantity = isNaN(prodQuantity) ? 0 : prodQuantity;
```

Now, when we run our test again, we will get the following output:

```
Bindings    test ×
> cmd.exe /c grunt -b "C:\Sessions\ASP.NET Core 1.0\WebApplication7\src\WebApplication7" --gruntfile "C:\Sessions\ASP.NET Core 1.
Running "karma:unit" (karma) task
11 06 2016 15:04:55.083:INFO [karma]: Karma v0.13.22 server started at http://localhost:9876/
11 06 2016 15:04:55.112:INFO [launcher]: Starting browser PhantomJS
11 06 2016 15:04:59.391:INFO [PhantomJS 2.1.1 (Windows 8 0.0.0)]: Connected on socket /#Ipuw-bsN7Jlo0yfsAAAA with id 24075618
PhantomJS 2.1.1 (Windows 8 0.0.0): Executed 0 of 2 SUCCESS (0 secs / 0 secs)
PhantomJS 2.1.1 (Windows 8 0.0.0): Executed 1 of 2 SUCCESS (0 secs / 0.018 secs)
PhantomJS 2.1.1 (Windows 8 0.0.0): Executed 2 of 2 SUCCESS (0 secs / 0.02 secs)
PhantomJS 2.1.1 (Windows 8 0.0.0): Executed 2 of 2 SUCCESS (0 secs / 0.02 secs)
Done.
Process terminated with code 0.
```

In the preceding example, we defined the HTML markup within the `beforeEach()` function in the `product.test.js` file. With simple applications, this may not be a cumbersome process to redefine the HTML markup as fixtures and use them to execute tests. However, most web applications are using some client-side frameworks such as Knockout, AngularJS, and so on, that separates the binding of controls specified in an HTML view to a ViewModel, and this ViewModel is responsible to read or write control values.

In the following example, we will use the Knockout JavaScript library that implements an Model-View-ViewModel pattern and see how unit tests can be written in this way.

Implementing Model-View-ViewModel using Knockout and Run test

Model-View-ViewModel (MVVM) is a design pattern for building user interfaces. It is divided into three parts, as show in the following diagram:

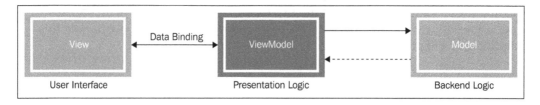

These three parts are described as follows:

- **Model**: This contains the backend logic to invoke backend services and save or retireve data by communicating with the persistant storage.

- **ViewModel**: This contains the view-specific operations and data. It represents the model of the view to which the view elements binds to. For example, a form that contains some HTML elements will have a ViewModel, which is an object containing some properties to bind these controls with the data.

- **View**: This is the user interface to which the user interacts. It displays information from the ViewModel, raises events at the ViewModel, and updates it when the ViewModel changes.

Let's implement the MVVM pattern using the **Knockout** JavaScript library using the following steps.

Adding the Knockout package

To start with, let's add Knockout.js in your ASP.NET Core application through `bower.json`. It can be added by making an entry in the dependencies section of the `bower.json` file, and Visual Studio automatically downloads the package and places it in the `wwwroot/lib/knockout` folder.

The following statement can be added in the `bower.json` file:

```
"knockout": "3.4.0",
```

Adding ProductViewModel

`ProductViewModel` contains properties such as the product code, unit price, quantity, expiry, and total amount. Here is the code snippet of `ProductViewModel.js`:

```
var ProductViewModel = function () {

    this.prodCode = ko.observable('');
    this.prodUnitPrice = ko.observable(0);
    this.prodQuantity = ko.observable(0);
    this.prodExpiry = ko.observable('');
    this.prodTotalAmount =0;

    ko.applyBindings(this);

    this.saveProduct=function(){
      var unitPrice = this.prodUnitPrice();
      var quantity = this.prodQuantity();
      var total = unitPrice * quantity;
```

```
    this.prodTotalAmount = total;

    //call some service to save product
  }

};
```

In the preceding code snippet, we have a `ProductViewModel` class that contains a few properties, each property is assigned to `ko.observable()`.

`ko` is basically the Knockout object that provides a complimentary way of linking an object model to the View, where `ko.observable()` is a Knockout function that makes the Model properties observable and sync with the View data. This means that when the ViewModel property's value changes, View is updated; and when the control value is modified, the ViewModel property is updated.

Values are also pre-populated as shown in the following code snippet. Passing `0` in the following statement will set the control value `0` when the control binding is done:

```
    this.prodUnitPrice = ko.observable(0)
```

`ko.applyBindings()` actually activates Knockout to perform the binding of the Model properties with the View elements.

Add the Product view

Knockout provides a very decent way of binding ViewModel properties to the control elements. Binding consist of two items, name and value, separated by a colon. To bind the ViewModel with the input elements, we can use the data-bind attribute and specify the value name followed with : and ViewModel's property name. Each control has a specific set of properties and it can be used to bind elements accordingly.

For example, the span element can bind to the view model property using the text name as shown in the following:

```
    Product code is: <span data-bind="text: prodCode"></span>
```

Here is the modified version of the Product view:

```
    <body>
      <div>
        <label> Product Code: </label>
        <input type="text" data-bind="value: prodCode" />
      </div>
      <div>
        <label> Product Unit Price: </label>
        <input type="text" data-bind="value: prodUnitPrice" />
      </div>
```

```
<div>
  <label> Product Expiry: </label>
  <input type="text" data-bind="value: prodExpiry" />
</div>
<div>
  <label> Product Quantity: </label>
  <input type="text" data-bind="value: prodQuantity" />
</div>
<div>
  <input id="btnSaveProduct" type="button" value=
    "Save Product" />
</div>
<script src="lib/knockout/dist/knockout.js"></script>
<script src="Js/ProductViewModel.js"></script>
<script>
  (function () {
    var prod = new ProductViewModel();
    document.getElementById("btnSaveProduct").onclick = function
      () { prod.saveProduct(); };
  })();
</script>
</body>
```

This is all what we need to configure Knockout in the Product view. When the btnSaveProduct button is clicked, it will calculate the total amount and call the product service to save the record.

Modifying test configuration

Here is the modified version of Gruntfile.js created earlier. We added the ProductViewModel.js and the Knockout dependency in the files array:

```
/*
This file in the main entry point for defining grunt tasks and
  using grunt plugins.
*/
module.exports = function (grunt) {
  grunt.initConfig({
    karma: {
      unit: {
        options: {
          frameworks: ['jasmine'],
          singleRun: true,
          browsers: ['PhantomJS'],
          files: [
            './wwwroot/lib/knockout/dist/knockout.js',
            './wwwroot/js/ProductViewModel.js',
            './wwwroot/test/**/product.test.js'
```

```
        ]
      }
    }
  }
});

grunt.loadNpmTasks('grunt-karma');
grunt.registerTask('test', ['karma']);
};
```

Modifying the product-testing script

As we are not dependent on the HTML view directly, we can test our unit test cases through the Product view model. Here is the modified version of `product.test.js` that does not have any of the fixtures defined:

```
describe('Product', function () {

  it('Expected Total Amount should be 600', function () {
    var product = new ProductViewModel();
    product.prodQuantity(3);
    product.prodUnitPrice(200);
    product.saveProduct();
    expect(product.prodTotalAmount).toBe(600);
  });
});
```

The following output will be generated when the test is run:

Debugging JavaScript

JavaScript runs on client browsers, and almost all browsers, such as Internet Explorer, Microsoft Edge, Chrome, and Firefox, provide the integrated JavaScript debugger and **Developer Tools** window. With Visual Studio, we can also debug the JavaScript code by setting Internet Explorer as the default browser. Chrome is not supported out of the box, but with certain steps, its can be achieved.

Debugging options in Visual Studio 2015

Visual Studio provides certain decent features to debug JavaScript and troubleshoot errors. JavaScript debugging in Visual Studio only works with Internet Explorer. Debugging can be started by starting the application in a debug mode and then placing some breakpoints in the JavaScript code. When the breakpoint is hit, we can use all sorts of debugging options in Visual Studio that we already know of and used in debugging the C# and VB.NET code. Options such as Step into (*F11*), Step over (*F10*), Step out (*Shift + F11*), conditional breakpoints, and watches, all work with the JavaScript code.

Debugging from Visual Studio with Internet Explorer

The default browser in Visual Studio for a particular web application project can be set from the **Web Browser (Internet Explorer)** | **Internet Explorer** option, as shown in the following screenshot:

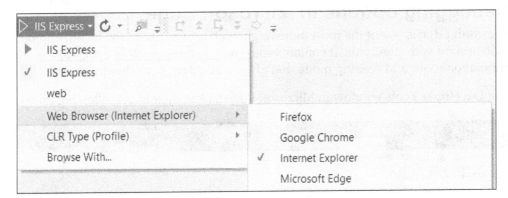

Debugging from Visual Studio with Google Chrome

Visual Studio 2015 does not provide out-of-the-box support to debug JavaScript applications, except with Internet Explorer. Alternatively, with Node.js, debugging works perfectly fine in Visual Studio, and as technically, both Node.js and Google Chrome are based on the V8 engine, there is no drawback.

To start debugging with Chrome in Visual Studio, we have to run the Google `chrome.exe` file with a remote-debugger argument. The following command runs Google Chrome with remote debugging, and from Visual Studio, it can be attached by pointing to the same Chrome instance:

```
chrome.exe - remote-debugging-port=9222
```

`9222` is the default port where Visual Studio connects on attaching to its process.

From the Visual Studio, you can attach the process by hitting *Ctrl + Alt + P*, or by going to **Debug** | **Attach to Process** in menu bar and selecting the Chrome instance.

Developer Tools

Almost all the browsers support built-in developer tools that helps to debug and troubleshoot JavaScript errors. These tools are commonly known as *F12 tools* and opens up the **Developer Tools** window by hitting the *F12* key.

Debugging options in Microsoft Edge

Microsoft Edge is one of the most lightweight web browser with the layout engine built around web standards. It contains some new features such as Cortana, annotation tools, and reading mode that gives it an edge over other browsers.

The **Developer Tools** window in Microsoft Edge look similar to the following image:

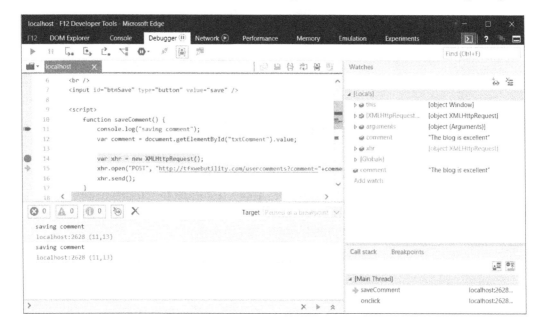

The first pane in the top left-hand corner is the **Script** pane that shows the content of the JavaScript containing the page.

The second pane in the the top right-hand corner is a **Watches** pane where the variable values are displayed.

The third pane in the the bottom left-hand corner is the console window where messages are displayed, all the messages logged using `console.log()`; calls are printed on the console window. Microsoft Edge provides errors, warnings, and messages in three different tabs that give a glimpse at the errors, warnings, and messages, and it also helps the developer to directly jump into the exact code snippet by clicking on the error line link.

The fourth pane is the **Call stack** and **Breakpoints**. Call stack shows the chain of function calls that are executed and it is helpful to understand the code-execution flow. For example, if an `A()` method calls a `B()` method, and the `B()` method calls a `C()` method, it shows the complete flow of execution from the `A()` method to the `C()` method.

The **Breakpoints** tab shows the list of all the breakpoints being used in the script, and the users can manage these breakpoints by enabling or disabling and deleting or adding new events:

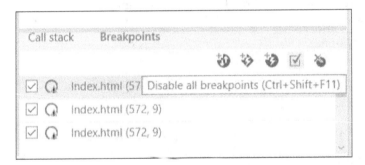

Debugging can only start if the **F12 Developers Tools** window is opened and this can be opened through the **...** | **F12 Developer Tools** window option from menu bar or by hitting the *F12* key. Once the window is opened, you can set breakpoints on the JavaScript code and take specific actions on the page.

The following table shows some important options available in the debugger toolbar:

Icon	Option	Shortcut Key	Description
▶	Continue	F5 or F8	This releases the break mode and continues till the next breakpoint.
‖	Break	*Ctrl + Shift + B*	This breaks on the next statement.
↳•	Step Into	*F11*	This steps into the function being called or the next statement.
↳→	Step Over	*F10*	This steps over the function being called or the next statement.
↱•	Step Out	*Shift + F11*	This steps out of the current function and into the calling function.
⇥‖	Break on new worker	*Ctrl + Shift + W*	This breaks on the creation of a new web worker.
⓪ ▾	Exception Control	*Ctrl + Shift + E*	This can be used to break on all exceptions or unhandled exceptions. By default, it is set to ignore exceptions.
✕	Disconnect Debugger		This disconnects the debugger and no breakpoints run.
{👤}	Debug just my code	*Ctrl + J*	This ignores the third-party libraries from debugging.
(¶)	Pretty print	*Ctrl + Shift + P*	This searches the minified version of the JavaScript block and makes it readible.
abc↵	Word wrap	*Alt + W*	This wraps the sentence to adjust it as per the content pane size.

Microsoft Edge provides the following five types of breakpoints:

- Standard
- Conditional
- Tracepoints
- XHR
- Events

Standard breakpoints

These breakpoints can be set by simply selecting the statement from the script code:

```
19          (function () {
20              debugger;
21              console.log("adding event");
22              document.getElementById("btnSave").onclick = function () {
23                  saveComment();
24              };
25          })();
```

Conditional breakpoints

These type of breakpoints are hit when specific conditions are met or when the value of the variable reaches a specific state. For example, we can use this with a statement inside a loop and break the execution when the counter reaches a value of 10.

It can be set by clicking on the existing breakpoint and selecting **Condition...** from the **context** menu:

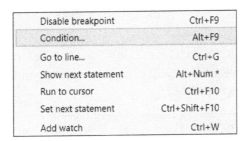

This option opens up the **Conditional breakpoint** window and the condition can be set as shown in the following screenshot:

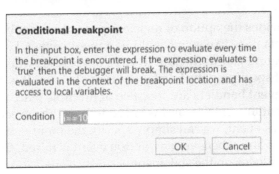

Once the condition is set, the icon changes to

Tracepoints

Tracepoints are used to write the message on the console when it passed through the statement where the tracepoint is configured. It can be set by clicking on the **Insert tracepoint** option from the **context** menu shown in the gutter by right-clicking:

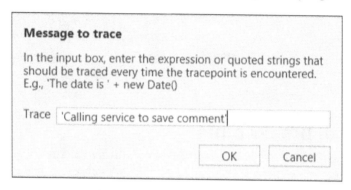

Once the tracepoint is set, the icon changes, as follows:

```
14          var xhr = new XMLHttpRequest();
15          xhr.open("POST", "http://tfxwebutility.com/usercomments?comment="+comment, true);
16          xhr.send();
17      }
```

When the statement is executed, it will print the message on a console window as shown in the following screenshot:

```
Calling service to save comment
localhost:2628 (14,13)
```

Event

Microsoft Edge provides the option of registering event tracepoints and breakpoints from the **Breakpoints** pane. An event could be a mouse event, keyboard event, or timer event. This feature is heavily used in large or complex web applications where the exact location of specifying the breakpoint is not known. It is also more useful in cases where the event handlers are specified at multiple places. For example, if a page contains five button controls, and we need to break the execution whenever any button raises the click event, we can simply specify the mouse-click event through the breakpoint event; and whenever any button event is raised, the breakpoint will be executed and will focus on the statement.

Add event tracepoint

A user can add event tracepoints with the help of the following option:

The following window shows the registration of an event tracepoint when the mouse is clicked:

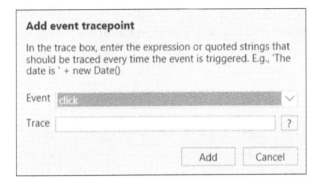

Add event breakpoints

User can add event breakpoints with the help of the following option:

The following window shows the registration of an event breakpoint when the mouse is clicked:

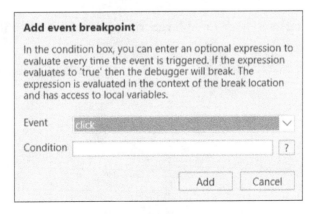

XHR

Just like events, XHR events can also be registered from the **Breakpoint** pane of browser. These events are invoked when any of the Ajax request is being made from the JavaScript code. A user can register the XHR event from the icon shown in the following screenshot:

Once we click on this event, it will be added in the **Breakpoints** window, as shown in the following screenshot:

Debugging TypeScript

In *Chapter 5, Developing an ASP.NET Application Using Angular 2 and Web API*, we already discussed TypeScript and how it transpiles into the JavaScript code that eventually runs on the browser. The developers write code in TypeScript, but on the browser, a generated JavaScript file is run. When the TypeScript file is transpiled to a JavaScript file, a mapping file is generated with a *.map.js extension. This file contains the information about the actual TypeScript file and the generated JavaScript file. Not only this, but the generated JavaScript file also contains one entry about the mapping file that actually tells the browsers to load the corresponding source TypeScript file by reading the mapping file.

Here is the entry that every generated JavaScript file contains when it is transpiled from TypeScript:

```
//# sourceMappingURL=http://localhost:12144/todosapp/apps/
    createTodo.component.js.map
```

This can be configured from the TSConfig.json file through the sourceMap property. If the sourceMap property is true, it generates the mapping file and makes an entry in the generated JavaScript file. Also, when working in an ASP.NET Core application, all the static files have to be in the wwwroot folder. So, to debug the typescripts, all the corresponding typescript (.ts) files have to be moved to any folder under the wwwroot folder so that it can be accessible from the browser.

Here is the debugger window, showing the list of TypeScript files on the left-hand side and the icon in the upper-right corner to toggle between the source file and compiled JavaScript version:

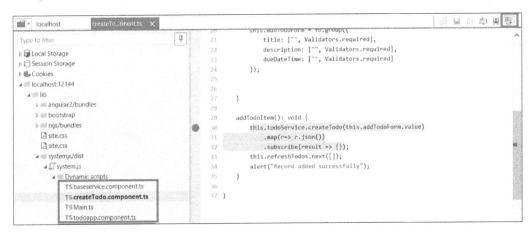

Debugger keyword supported by all browsers

We can also explicitly force to break the control at some point through the debugger keyword. If the breakpoint is not set, but the debugger keyword is specified, the debugging will be enabled and break the execution. It can be set from code as shown in the following screenshot:

```
(function () {
    debugger;
    document.getElementById("btnSave").onclick = function () {
        saveComment();
    };
})();
</script>
```

Summary

In this chapter, we discussed how JavaScript applications can be tested and debugged. For testing JavaScript applications, we discussed the Jasmine testing suite that can be easily plugged in with Karma, which is a test runner and can be used with Grunt to be executed from Visual Studio **Task Runner Explorer** window. We also discussed the basics of the MVVM pattern and how to implement it using the Knockout JavaScript library. We then modified the test case to work with the View model. For debugging, we discussed some tips and techniques of debugging JavaScript with Visual Studio and what Microsoft Edge offers through the **Developer Tools** window to make debugging easy. In the end, we also learned about the basic topics such as how Microsoft Edge enables debugging for TypeScript files and what configurations are required to achieve it.

Index

empty() 103
insertAfter() 102
insertBefore() 102
prepend() 102
remove() 103
removeAttr() 103
removeClass() 103
removeProp() 103

E

EJS view engine 288-292
elements, of JavaScript
  about 15
  case sensitivity 16
  character set 16
  comments 15
  constants 15
entity-relationship model (ERD) 58
environment
  setting up 4
event-driven messaging
  about 318
  complex code, encapsulating 324, 325
  mediator pattern, implementing 318-324
event, Microsoft Edge
  event breakpoints, adding 353
  event tracepoint, adding 353
events
  about 47, 48, 219
  binding, on and off used 108-111
  blur() 105
  change() 105
  click() 105
  dblclick() 105
  focus() 105
  handling, in jQuery 105
  hover events, using 111, 112
  keydown() 105
  keyup() 105
  mousedown() 105
  mouseenter() 105
  mouseleave() 105
  mouseup() 105
  registering, in jQuery 105-107
  URL 106

exception handling, OOP
  about 68
  Error 69
  RangeError 69
  ReferenceError 69
  TypeError 69
  URIError 69
Express framework, for web applications
  Express view engines 287
  simple Node.js, extending 286, 287
  using 285
expressions
  about 16
  class expression 21
  class statement 21
  function expression 20
  function statement 20
  grouping operator 22
  new keyword 22
  sequence, of code execution 19
  super keyword 22
  this keyword 17-19
Express view engines
  about 287
  EJS view engine 287-292
  Jade view engine 292-295
  routing, in Express application 296

F

façade pattern 255
factory pattern 244, 245
function arguments 49

G

get functions
  jQuery.getJSON(), using 131, 132
  jQuery.getScript(), using 132
  jQuery.get(), using 131
  used, for data loading 130
global events, Ajax
  ajaxComplete 134
  ajaxError 134
  ajaxSend 134
  ajaxStart 134
  ajaxSuccess 134